COOKING PROVENCE

COOKING PROVENCE

Four Generations of Recipes and Traditions

ANTOINE BOUTERIN

AND JOAN SCHWARTZ

MACMILLAN · USA

MACMILLAN
A Prentice Hall Macmillan Company
15 Columbus Circle
New York, NY 10023

Copyright © 1994 by Antoine Bouterin

Color photographs copyright © 1994 by Michael Mundy

Library of Congress Cataloging-in-Publication Data
Bouterin, Antoine.
Cooking Provence : four generations of recipes and traditions /
Antoine Bouterin and Joan Schwartz.
p.   cm.
Includes index.
ISBN 0-02-513955-X
1. Cookery, French—Provençal style. 2. Cookery—France—
Provence. I. Schwartz, Joan, 1938–   . II. Title.
TX719.2.P75B68   1994
641.59449—dc20   94-7743   CIP

Manufactured in the United States of America

10 9 8 7 6 5 4 3 2 1

To my mother, Marie Thérèse,
and to my ancestors

Contents

Acknowledgments

❧❧❧

My thanks to my coauthor, Joan Schwartz, who made writing this book so enjoyable. She heard my voice and translated it perfectly, and in the process I think she became almost Provençal herself.

I am grateful to Fifi Oscard and Pam Hoenig who gave me the chance to do this book and to Peter Sawyer and Justin Schwartz, who helped me over all the hurdles.

Warmest thanks to Kathy Burke, a wonderful friend, who was the first to support my projects when I came to this country; and to Igor Segotta, an ambassador of Mediterranean cuisine and a valued friend.

I am grateful to my "family" at Le Périgord, especially George and Marie Thérèse Brigaud, Eric LeDily, and Turgo Jeune—and all the hard-working, good-humored kitchen staff.

And finally, *merci* to my customers and friends who appreciate the spirit of Provence in my cuisine and encouraged me to write about my heritage.

COOKING PROVENCE

$\mathcal{I}$ntroduction

You never forget the place where you were born, and I can think of no better place for a chef to be born than on a farm in Provence. On our farm in Saint-Rémy-de-Provence, my family lived close to the earth, planning our lives according to the seasons and our meals according to the harvests. We appreciated the earth and its gifts in ways that other people are now just beginning to understand. Our diet was healthful, based on vegetables, herbs, olive oil, and, of course, garlic in hefty amounts. (The woman from Arles who celebrated her one-hundred-nineteenth birthday in 1994 attributed her longevity to garlic.)

This book isn't about a year, or a month, or a meal in Provence, as charming as those may be. It is about traditions that stretch back over centuries, and a life—my life—that has been Provençal through and through. Provence is beautiful beyond comparison and rich in history and folklore. Situated between Italy and France, it was the bridge between them and suffered many invasions: Greek, Roman, Arab, Moorish, and Spanish. In Roman times, Julius Caesar was so taken with the South of France that he wanted to move his quarters to Nîmes. (If he had done that, Provence would be in Italy today, and that would have changed my story!) In the Middle Ages it was an independent region with its own language, living happily under the rule of the Comte de Provence and keeping its Catholic religion separate from the French Church. Nostradamus, the Renaissance astrologer who was born in Saint-Rémy-de-Provence in 1503, believed the region to be the center of the world and its people to be closest to the earth's mystical vibrations.

Nearer to our time, Van Gogh said that the only true color in the world is in Provence. If you have seen the surrealistic fields of lavender, the incendiary sunflowers (the artist wasn't exaggerating), the blazing trees and herbs, and the fantastic sky, you must agree—Provence is full of the aggressive color and the fire that illumine Van Gogh's canvases. And the smells of Provence, the lavender, rosemary, and thyme perfuming the air you breathe every moment, are intoxicating. Growing up on the farm, I was aware of a power in my heritage that has been transmitted for generations.

Mas Antoine was my grandfather Antoine's enchanting little farmhouse in Saint-Rémy, in the heart of Provence. You approached it by walking through a grove of cypress and pine trees and up a long path bordered with wild herbs and white flowers. Deep green shutters framed the white-bordered windows, and earthenware pots of bright pink and red blossoms stood before the front door. I have always felt a special love for that house because I was born in it and later, when my sister, Marguerite, was ill, I lived there for a while with my maternal grandparents. I still remember my grandmother Marguerite bustling around the kitchen early each morning in her long, dark cotton skirt and polka-dotted blouse, her gray hair done up in

a bun. It seemed she always was happy, and I was happy following her around, tasting and smelling the delicious things she cooked. From her, I received my earliest introduction to cooking, and I believe that my career began in this kitchen. I loved to hear my grandparents and my parents speak in the lilting Provençal dialect that is more like music than speech. (When my mother was in school, children were punished if they didn't speak formal French, but France has since become more accepting of its traditional languages.)

Long before, Marguerite had owned a little restaurant in Saint-Rémy. It was in a large farm-

Grandmother Marguerite and Grandfather Antoine in front of the barn with Loulou, the dog, and Vivi, the cat—all taking some sun.

house, and was really a grocery, a bar, and a restaurant combined—with a barber-shop next door. Grandfather tended the bar, while she ran the grocery and cooked. They were friendly people, their restaurant was quite popular, and the pot-au-feu was famous. This is where my mother was born, on New Year's Eve, a lucky birthdate.

I was very close to my grandfather Antoine, a wise and loving man. My grand-father knew all the secrets of the mountains near our home. Sometimes, at night, he would see a red line in the sky and tell me that tomorrow there would be a lot of wind. He knew when it was going to rain and when the first white asparagus and morels would be ripe. Whenever he had some free time, he went for a solitary walk in the hills, among the pine trees.

I used to feed his big angora cat, whom he called Indivividouga, and while the cat was eating, Grandfather would pull his tail and a coin would drop onto the floor. I couldn't believe my eyes—the cat was laying money the way chickens laid eggs! This was a very interesting cat, I concluded, and I followed him around the house and pulled his tail whenever I got the chance. Strangely, he never laid money for me the way he had for Grandfather.

My father's parents, Joseph and Marie, whom we called Mamé and Papé, were another story: they were remote and demanding—I thought of them as the king and queen. Mamé was an authoritarian, not mean, but never happy. She must have been embittered by losing her father and mother all in one week as a young woman, and a few years later, by her sister dying in childbirth. She had sharp blue eyes like marbles under scowling eyebrows, and lips pursed like she wanted to put her smile in prison forever. But she had earned fame as a healer, using herbal remedies and mystical invocations in the old Provençal language, and sometimes conversing with spirits. I was more than a little afraid of her.

My father's grandmother, whom I called Mamïe, was special to me. She had many great-grandchildren, but she loved me so much and treated me like a little god. Her face was wrinkled like a dried apple and she had deep green, wise eyes. She was an extraordinary woman, who had acted as mayor of the town of Saint-Étienne-du-Gres during the First World War and had raised her seventeen children alone, after her husband died in battle. In her long black dress, faded from many washings, with a fringed black shawl, a white apron embroidered with lace, and a lace cap in the Arlesian style, she was beautiful to me. I remember her sitting in an old rocking chair by the fireplace, rocking just a little bit, very slowly. When I hugged her, I was enveloped in her scent of dried lavender.

I spent the greater part of my childhood with my parents in Mas de Capon,

Grandmother Marie and Grandfather Joseph in front of their farmhouse, Mas de Capon.

where my father was born. This sturdy farmhouse was built in the sixteenth century and was restored in 1724 and again in 1945, after the war. Ivy climbed its stone walls, huge plane trees, older than the house itself, shaded the doorway, and in the front yard stood a massive antique plow and a big stone sink filled with flowers. My father's family had been farmers for centuries, raising flowers that they sold for their seeds and *primeurs,* the delicate first vegetables of each season.

On beautiful spring and summer mornings, I would wake up in my simple bedroom, under a doleful portrait of Pope Pius X, and run to the window to see the dew sparkling like crystal on the trees and flowers. All around me were the smells of thyme, rosemary, sage, and wild lavender. The *montagnette* behind our house was covered with wild herbs and red and yellow flowers, and my sister and I would play hide-and-seek in a big field of *belles-de-nuit* (colorful lady-of-the-night flowers that bloom only after dark) or play in front of the house, under a plane tree.

My parents worked hard all day and I was free to roam around the countryside. My favorite walk was to a mansion called Bagatelle, owned by a nobleman from Paris. It had beautiful herb gardens and lots of beehives—the herbs were planted around the hives and the bees drank their nectar and produced fragrant thyme and rosemary honey. I always wanted to see what was inside the hives, but I knew it would be dangerous to look. The house had a formal garden, too, and a guard who tried to scare away curious children. But I was too smart for him—I would sneak up to the house and gaze through the shining windows at the luxurious rooms and furnishings, so different from our farm.

One autumn day I walked to the Mas à Chaber, an old, abandoned farm surrounded by pine and cypress trees. Under an ancient tree, I saw a glint of gold, lightly covered by pine needles. I pushed away the needles and, to my amazement, there was a bed of treasured yellow morels, the sublime wild mushrooms that grow in the woods of Provence. I was so proud that I had discovered them! I ran home for a basket and filled it with morels and my mother made a wonderful omelette for the family.

My cousin Jean, my sister, Marguerite, and I used to visit our neighbor Leontine, a very old woman who lived in a ramshackle, but still beautiful, ivy-covered farmhouse. To the ticktock of her big Provençal clock, she taught us children's dances and songs, such as "Where Are You Going, Basile?" Leontine told our fortunes and always gave us a little sweet before we left.

Because Saint-Rémy was the site of an ancient Roman city, sometimes a farmer, turning the earth with his plow, would bump up against a buried piece of a sarcophagus or a piece of ancient pottery. Our neighbor stumbled upon the entrance to an underground passage, perhaps a tomb, in his field one day. Jean and I climbed down the opening and followed the damp, silent passage as far as we dared before scurrying back up into the sunlight. Then it was sealed off by our neighbor, as these finds always were, to keep out the government meddlers, who would have torn apart the fields in the name of history. We were happy to live beside (or just above) our Roman ancestors, in peace.

Every summer, when the season was going well for my father, he would drive us all to Saintes-Maries-de-la-Mer, the Mediterranean beach town. The road led us

through the Camargue, that beautiful wild area where the earth is white and salty, full of little rivers and swamps with tall reeds and pink flamingoes. There was always a breeze moving the reeds slowly and bringing us the smell of salty sea air. We passed the wild white horses and black bulls who lived in the fields, and the white cottages with cane roofs that belonged to the guardians, the cowboys of the Camargue. In the middle of our trip, we would stop the car so Mamé could get out and communicate silently with the spirit of the Midi. She also liked to pick an herb called *cansoude,* which she dried at home, and used for scouring pots.

We usually stopped along the way at Méjane, an animal preserve, to see a bullfight, which my grandfather and father loved, but I found boring, with all those men running around and bothering the poor bull. Then it was time for a pastis at a nearby café, with lemonade for the children, and a lot of animated conversation about how the day had gone so far. This was when I would wander off to ride the small train that circled the marshy area and offered a wonderful view of the animals and birds. When I returned and we finally finished our drive to Saintes-Maries-de-la-Mer, it was lunchtime, so our first stop was the restaurant. I usually ordered sea snails, a really delicious dish, but my grandfather insisted that I taste his lunch, some kind of bull ragout, which never failed to make me sick.

Everyone felt relaxed and jolly after our meal, and we walked around the town, a bustling, colorful place that the gypsies of Provence considered their capital. Their legends tell of Mary, Joseph, and Mary Magdalene leaving the Holy Land after the crucifixion and arriving at the port in a small boat. Mary Magdalene jumped into the sea and walked through the waves, pulling the boat ashore at this very spot, which the gypsies later consecrated to her. We never actually went into the sea, because it was too treacherous to swim in, but we found more than enough to do on this outing, the high point of our summer.

In Provence everyone venerates the seasons, especially the spring, when the earth is reborn. On April 25, at the fair of Saint Mark, we admired the four couples who were costumed to represent the saints, and we always bought a big bouquet of cypress and olive branches that had been blessed, to bring a good harvest. Later each year I could barely contain my excitement as I awaited our village's grand parade of horses and carts decorated with fruit and vegetables—*carreto ramado*—that symbolized a prosperous season. Young people dressed like the characters in Frédéric Mistral's poetic story of Vincent and Mireille (our Romeo and Juliet) danced the *farandolle* to the music of fifes and tambours. Fifty or sixty beautifully decorated horses, with their riders costumed as Arlesians, marched down the street. In still another summer parade, *abrivado,* one hundred white horses from the Camargue were set free to run in the street.

After that, exciting games were held either in our ancient Roman arena or in our newer arena, that was about one hundred years old. Bulls with streamers tied to their horns were pursued by *razorteurs,* brave men who tried to cut off the colorful decorations. Whenever one succeeded, he would bow and wave the streamer in front of the cheering, applauding crowd.

In August, to celebrate Pentecost, the shepherds came down from the surrounding mountains and gathered in Saint-Rémy, and we had an event similar to the running of the bulls in Spain. A majestic old cannon was fired three times and at the third shot, twenty or thirty wild black bulls

My father, Etienne, my mother, Marie Thérèse, my sister, Margo, and me at a festival in Saint-Rémy, around 1958.

were set free to charge down the street—it was dangerous, but people loved it.

Even winter had its beauty and mystery. We knew that the bitterly cold mistral would come roaring down upon Provence every year, strong enough to keep people huddled in their houses—even strong enough to move cars. But it would come just to this place. We believed it was the powerful spirit of the Midi.

The winter brought everyone closer. One frozen night in January, my father and I walked to the stable to check on the animals. There, in the straw, our mule Qui-Qui lay on his side and snuggled against his warm belly were our dog Sultan and five little cats, all keeping each other warm and safe in the frosty air. This was the way of nature, my father explained to me.

Each year, when the time came to prepare for the coming winter, the family would work together. We would set up a large table outside the house and my mother, my two grandmothers, and the children would help to peel and squeeze tomatoes for preserves. My grandmother cooked the tomatoes (as well as green beans and other vegetables, in their turn) in an enormous cauldron she used just for preserving. She did a lot of jam, too, and she made *vin de noix*—a wine made with green walnuts. In the cold months of January and February the farm slept, but we had plenty to eat for the winter.

But all year round, food meant much more than sustenance to families in Provence: it played a part in confirming our everyday faith and, of course, in celebrating the religious holidays. A bottle of red wine appeared on our table for every lunch and dinner, even if it was not drunk, because wine symbolized the blood of Christ. Because we believed that certain traditional dishes would bring good luck, for the feast of Saint Mark we ate a special anise bread; for Good Friday, a savory omelette with pork breast; for Christmas, thirteen desserts; and for Epiphany, *la galette des Rois,* my mother's fruit-studded brioche.

I come from a family where the men were farmers, not chefs, but when I decided on my profession, it was as though I had known all along that this was to be my life. When I was twelve years old, my teacher, Mr. Allemagne, asked every boy in my class what he would like to be when he grew up. They all answered "doctor" or "lawyer," the most prestigious professions, but I said, "I would like to be a cook." Everyone laughed, but the teacher announced, "I think Antoine is the most honest because he chose the most humble job."

My mother always encouraged me to do what I wanted. She told a friend from church, Mrs. Tallet, about my choice, and Mr. Tallet, who was a chef, came to see me on the farm. "So you want to be a cook," he said, kindly. "Do you know that it is a very tough job?" I answered, "It's what I want to do," and from that moment, he became a kind of godfather to me. He arranged my apprenticeship in Les-Baux-de-Provence at a two-star restaurant, Riboto de Taven.

When I think of that apprenticeship now, I consider it slavery, but at that time it was the best thing that could have happened in my life. I was a country boy from a very modest family, and this was like another world! I was fourteen years old and I had never seen cream or smoked salmon before I started to work at Riboto de Taven. I began a three-year apprenticeship at a salary of five dollars a month plus room and board—just enough so they could say they were paying me. And I was lucky, because many boys had to pay a restaurant to be admitted into the kitchen. I worked twelve hours a day, seven days a week, preparing vegetables, cleaning fish, and scrubbing floors, and the chef was not always in a good mood. I slept in a bare attic and I had no energy to go out at night or have friends. It was a lonely and difficult time, made even worse by my father's death and my knowledge that I had no money to help my mother. That was the system when I was a young boy—now it has changed, fortunately.

After three and a half years I moved to L'Escale, a restaurant in the little seaport town of Carry-le-Rouet, near Marseille, and worked under the renowned chef Charles Berot. What a beautiful place that was: you felt you were dining in a ship, with a spectacular view of the bay. After a few more jobs, including a pastry apprenticeship with a chef who had worked for the queen of England, off I went to Paris. Despite my youth, I was chef at the fashionable Quai d'Orsay restaurant during the exciting birth of nouvelle cuisine. I blossomed in that creative climate, and my next move was to New York and Le Périgord.

If you ask me what Provençal cooking—my cooking—is all about, I would say, simplicity, respect for the natural taste of foods, staying in tune with the seasons and the earth's rhythms, and being creative. We rarely use butter or cream in Provence, and most of our meals, relying on vegetables, fish, poultry, garlic, and herbs, are healthful and naturally low in cholesterol. I am happiest when I cook these foods. I love the simple, farm-style dishes I learned from my grandmother and my mother, which I present in this book. But I have allowed myself some flights of fancy, a soupçon of the exotic. When you work with nature's bounty, as we did on the farm, you are inspired to be creative. I urge you to feel free when you cook my recipes and to create your own delicious dishes in the Provençal style.

In Provence, our meals are served in small consecutive courses (as opposed to fish or meat, a couple of vegetables, and potatoes all on one plate). We like to keep flavors distinct and to enjoy each food for itself. My mother prepared a typical farm meal for my coauthor, Joan Schwartz, and her husband, Allen, when they visited her in Provence. She served each course separately, several in sequence on the same plates. This was the menu:

Lentil broth with tiny pasta
Cooked lentils with oil and garlic
Cooked green beans with oil and garlic
Eggplant Marie-Thérèse
Farm-style tomatoes
Codfish baked with potatoes
Assorted cheeses
Baguettes

Fougasse
Caramel custard
Tiny bow-tied pastries
Red wine

I suggest you try serving a meal Provençal style. It will give you a new appreciation of the foods you prepare. The portions I suggest after each recipe are American-size; you can increase the number of servings by about half when you serve this way. This style also lends itself very well to all vegetarian menus. With course after course of interesting vegetables, you won't notice that no meat appears on the table.

But the best reason for eating Provençal style is that it provides an experience to share. A talking, laughing group seated around a table grows closer together as a beautiful meal unfolds course by course—dining imitates life.

CHAPTER 1

The Provençal Kitchen

My grandmother Marguerite's large, warm kitchen, perfumed with sweet spices and herbs, was a magical place to me. Its walls were white, but faded to ivory by the passage of time. Drying thyme, rosemary, sage, and bay leaves hung from pegs, pungent cloves spilled out of their terra-cotta bowl, and jars of ginger, peppercorns, and cumin filled the shelves. The smell of herbs was all around, mingling with the aromas of citrus peels, garlic, onions, and olives.

At the far end of the room, like a piece of art, stood a cast-iron, wood-burning stove paved in sculpted green tiles. Bundles of orange and lemon peels were hung from the tall iron stovepipe, drying, so they could be added to Grandmother's stews. A large fireplace stood nearby, where food simmered in old-fashioned clay pots that were strong and weathered, but too fragile for the intense heat of the stove.

At one side of the room was Grandmother's big oak worktable, holding many little pots of spices, a big pot of sea salt, her kitchen tools, and a large, green kerosene lamp. At night, when the big stove glowed, it would shine on the lamp, making it look like a huge emerald. (Because of that lamp, green has always been my favorite color.) On the wall behind the table hung a shelf crowded with jars of preserves and Grandmother's well-used copper pots and pans. Near them, portraits of my great-grandparents watched benevolently over this happy place.

Against the opposite wall stood a grand, eighteenth-century Provençal *petrain* (buffet) made of walnut. Resting on top was a *panetière,* a deep, square cabinet, sculpted on the surface and lined with brightly printed cotton. As its name implies, it was a storage box for freshly baked bread. When it was opened, the smell of wood mingled with the smell of warm bread—a very good combination.

The floor was paved in old burgundy-colored tiles, worn down over time by many footsteps. Windows framed in red Provençal fabric let in the glorious southern light and allowed us to watch for Grandfather's return from the fields at dinnertime. In a warm corner beside the fireplace, Grandfather's eighteenth-century chair, made of dark, heavy wood with a woven rush seat, awaited him. The bright, gathered curtains always gave me the feeling of being in a specially decorated place, a kind of theater, that somehow inspired me. I know now that this is where my love of cooking was born.

The long dining table in the middle of the room was covered by a cheerful red-and-yellow cloth printed in a Provençal pattern, and Grandmother always placed a big bowl of colorful flowers in the center. The rush-seated chairs surrounding it made me think of the chairs awaiting the seven dwarfs—so pretty and so perfect. This was a place I always wanted to be, with its fragrance of spices, herbs, and wonderful food simmering.

On this same table, Grandmother kept her records in a red, paper-covered notebook, which eventually became our source for all the family's domestic lore. In delicate "fly's feet" script—*écriture pattes de mouche*—she wrote recipes for medicines, teas, and cleaning products, as well as information on seeds and the best seasons for planting. She couldn't buy the variety of household products that we can today, but she knew how to use natural ingredients for cleaning and healing, and they worked. She even had a method for banishing evil spirits, and that seemed to work, too.

For Grandmother's curative teas, as well as her recipes for food, my sister and I were sent to gather herbs on the *montagnette,* the little hill in back of the house. Thyme, rosemary, sage, lavender, and bay grew wild and their fragrance wafted around us in the gentle breezes—no one who has breathed these herbal scents can ever forget them.

Here are some *trucs* (tricks) I have translated from Grandmother's notebook.

- For colic and digestive trouble, brew a tea with sprigs of fresh thyme or rosemary and drink it a few times a day.
- Also for digestive trouble, drink garlic water three or four times a day. To make it, combine 6 cups water with 8 cloves garlic and boil a short time. Add a few leaves of fresh sage and let it infuse. Plain sage tea also is good for the stomach.

- Thyme tea is good for colds and also cures insomnia. (Before we went to sleep my mother always gave us a cup.)
- To make a brush for basting meat, fish, or poultry on the grill, take 2 branches of sage, 1 of rosemary, 2 or 3 of fresh thyme, and a few sprigs of oregano. Tie them all together with raffia into a little brush. If the herbs have flowers, even better. To make a marinade, mix together in a small terra-cotta bowl 1 cup olive oil, 1 teaspoon sea salt, 1 turn of the peppermill. When you cook meat or fish, just put the brush in the marinade and brush the food.
- To make a lavender potpourri for the closet or armoire, in a bowl mix 2 cups dried lavender flowers (it is very important that they have been dried in the sun). Add 2 tablespoons lavender essence, 3 or 4 cloves, 2 tablespoons orange-flower water, and 2 tablespoons dry rice, to absorb the moisture. Tie this in a scarf or a square of fabric, or put it in a flannel bag.
- To keep evil spirits away, sprinkle sea salt on the floor around the area where you suspect they are lurking. Then sweep it up with a broom, put it into a bag, and burn it.
- For red ink to label clothes and linens (as young women did when preparing their trousseaus), combine 1 egg white and 3 tablespoons cold water. Beat well with a fork until emulsified. In the center of a square of cloth, put 1 teaspoon ground vermilion (cinnabar). Dip the cloth into the egg mixture and red color will drip down, coloring it. Use this as ink to write your monogram or name on a piece of clothing or linen; then iron with a very hot iron. The egg white makes the ink coagulate and it will stay forever. In my grandmother's closet, everything was marked with this ink, which had turned red-purple over time. After years of ironing, the monograms on her trousseau looked like part of the fabric.
- To clean silver, pour some whiting powder (calcium carbonate) into a bowl and dilute it with pure alcohol to form a smooth paste. Apply to the silver and let it dry and brush it away with a very soft brush. Then polish with a cloth.
- To clean a gilt picture frame, mix 3 tablespoons chlorine bleach with 3 egg whites and beat very well into an emulsion. Apply with a soft fabric and rinse.
- To clean kerosene lamps, heat whitewash to warm, put it in the lamp and shake very strongly. When you pour it out, all the caked dust and soot will go with it.

- To keep silk soft and shiny, wash with natural white soap (such as *savon de Marseille*) and rinse with pure water. Fill a pot with water, bring to a boil, and put in a handful of wheat germ for each garment you are washing. When the water has cooled to warm, put in the silk and swish it around. Rinse again with pure water and iron with a warm iron. Then hang the garment to dry.
- To make shampoo, combine 1 egg yolk with about 3 tablespoons cologne and a few drops of vinegar, making a lotion. Massage it into the scalp generously, rinse with warm water, and let your hair dry naturally. Your hair will be shiny and healthy.
- To remove the smells of cauliflower, cabbage, and other strong vegetables when cooking, put a heel of very dry bread in the pot.

My other grandmother, Marie, had her own household recipes. She wasn't a skilled cook like Grandmother Marguerite, but she was known for her medical ability. She cured eye diseases and could compose an infusion that created a metabolic balance, so that you never got fat, no matter what you ate (I think it contained hare's ear). She kept a cocoon in her pocket to protect herself from toothaches.

When she treated someone with one of her medicines, Grandmother would chant a sentence or two from the ancient, magical Provençal language. These strange incantations made me a little afraid of her, but I gradually came to accept the fact that my family was somewhat out of the ordinary, even for mystical Provence. (I'm happy to say that we are more quiet today.)

Other towns in Provence had healing women and their own medicinal recipes. "In the next town it's different," she would say, when talking about her medicines. But Grandmother's cures came down to her in a straight line from her female ancestors (never through males). Unlike Grandmother Marguerite, she never wrote down any recipes or incantations, intending to pass them on only to my sister, Margo. When she unexpectedly went into a coma and died, all her mystical lore died with her.

STOCKING YOUR PROVENÇAL KITCHEN

Like Provence itself, Provençal cooking is a glorious medley of herbs, flavors, and light. The south of France has one of the most healthful cuisines in the world, relying on herbs, olive oil, garlic, and fresh vegetables. To us, these foods are more than wholesome, they are almost mystical in their power to connect us to the earth.

The vegetables I remember from the farm market at Saint-Étienne-du-Gres were close to perfection, but American vegetables are excellent, too, and they work very well in Provençal recipes. When someone tells me that the vegetables in America aren't as good as the ones in France, I say, "They are exactly the same, they just don't speak the same language." And when you get an inferior tomato (which happens in France, too), there will always be another ingredient to give you the authentic feeling of a dish. If the tomatoes are not strong, the garlic is there to remind you of Provence.

This chapter describes the ingredients that will help you to cook Provençal style. They are the notes on the scale and with them you will be ready to create music. But if you follow the recipes letter for letter, that is not good cooking—play with the recipe a bit. Inspiration and creativity are important ingredients in Provençal cuisine.

Even when you add your own inspiration, follow the steps in the recipe and respect its organization and order. Don't start at the end instead of the beginning. In cooking that is so important! First, read the recipe to see what ingredients and utensils you need, and have them at hand. Clean up your work area and utensils after each step, and, most important, wash your hands after working with each ingredient. If you touch garlic and don't wash your hands, everything else you touch will have that smell. Cooking times in each recipe are approximate, not precise, because all stoves are different and even two onions of the same size can differ in

how long they must be cooked. Cooking is not about timing, it is about results. The same is true for refrigerator and freezer storage: I will offer approximate times, but you must still rely on your own judgment. Just bear in mind that color and freshness are central to Provençal cuisine—if you keep some things, like fresh sauces, even a few days, they will deteriorate.

I often tell you to keep something warm while you proceed with the recipe. In our farm kitchen, we would just put the skillet on a warm corner of the stove; you can place it near your stove and cover it with a lid, a plate, or a sheet of aluminum foil—use your imagination.

Here are the most common Provençal ingredients.

Oil. Olive oil is the elixir of Provence, the magic potion, the blood that makes our hearts beat strongly. It is rich in vitamins, and Provençal mothers are rumored to put some in their babies' bottles. We use it to flavor salads and cooked foods, as well as for baking, and it even can be used to moisturize the skin. In the old days, olives were smashed by a huge millstone to release their oil. (A few of the old mills still exist in Provence, but most have been turned into elegant private homes.) On the farm, we got our oil from my grandfather's brother, Oncle de la Tour, who grew olive trees and pressed an oil that was very pure and almost black.

Extra virgin olive oil has a strong fragrance and deep color. To preserve its flavor and aroma, I like to use it pure and cold or at room temperature, and to add it at the end of a recipe. For high-temperature cooking, use an unflavored vegetable oil such as corn or peanut.

A word about oil for cooking: when you heat a little of it to a high temperature and sauté food, a tasty, golden crust is formed, sealing in flavor and juices. Then pour off the excess or drain the food well in a strainer. Your food is cooked fast and well, and it is not greasy! Plus it has an appetizing color—you can't brown an onion in water.

Vinegar. You will need red and white wine vinegars and verjus vinegar, made from unripened grapes and imported from France.

Rice, beans, and nuts. Have long- or short-grain rice, red lentils, and dried white beans. Your pantry should also stock almonds, walnuts, hazelnuts, and pignoli.

Fresh vegetables. I consider vegetables kitchen staples, even though you can't store them for very long. Provençal cooking relies on tomatoes, onions, shallots, fennel, zucchini, eggplant, red and green peppers, turnips, carrots, mushrooms, cabbage, and potatoes. Salad greens may be romaine, dandelions, or mâche.

Cheese. Goat cheese is the cheese we eat the most in the south, because we have so many goats. We also use sheep's milk cheese, like Roquefort.

Swiss cheese is grated into many dishes and often used for gratins.

For baking. You will need orange flower water, usually imported from France and available in specialty food stores, and vanilla, anise, and almond extracts. Provençal lavender honey will add wonderful flavor to your desserts.

I find frozen puff pastry indispensable for baking, even though it is a shortcut my grandmother would not have approved of. Simply follow package directions to defrost and roll out, and you will have a perfectly fine crust for tarts. Ready-made pie crusts are also acceptable, in a pinch.

I bake some cakes, pastry, and cookies with butter, although this is not traditional in Provence. When my recipe calls for butter, do not substitute oil.

Herbs and spices. Herbs are abundant in the summer (several are available all year round) and it is easy to dry them for the winter. Simply put up a wooden tie rack in a warm spot in your kitchen—over the stove, if possible—and hang herb bouquets from the pegs. Hang strips of orange and lemon peel, tied in little cheesecloth bags.

I like to buy spices where they are sold in bulk, because they are freshest there and usually cheaper. I always use sea salt in cooking and I advise you to buy it, both for its flavor and its magical properties. (In Provence, it is believed to banish evil spirits.)

Before I list the herbs and spices you will need to prepare the recipes in this book, I would like to tell you something about their history. Herbs have been used since ancient times in medicines, cosmetics, and foods. In ancient times, they were used in sorcerers' potions; before refrigeration, they masked spoiled food; and more recently, they have been adopted by people who want light, natural flavorings for their foods.

The ancient Egyptians imported many spices from Arabia and the Orient and from there sent them throughout the Mediterranean area. Later, the Romans imported large quantities of spices and exported them to Italy and France. Provence was the bridge between France and Italy, and I am sure the Roman invasion marked the entrance of herbs and spices into Provençal cooking.

Our ancestors wrote about herbs and spices in *herbiers,* or herbals. Chen-Nong, an emperor of China, wrote one of the first five thousand years ago; the Sumerians produced one, written on a stone tablet, in 3200 B.C.; and the Egyptians wrote herbals on papyrus in about 2800 B.C. These spoke of the value of herbs for medicine, science, and beauty and some even promised that herbs held the secret of eternal life. Somewhat later, in the first century A.D., Dioscorides, a Greek doctor who lived in Rome, wrote his *herbier,* which was later illustrated and republished, and used for over sixteen hundred years. *L'Herbarium d'Apulée* was published in Italy in 1481 and the beautifully illustrated *L'Herbarium Vivae Eicones* was written by Otto Bunfels in Strasbourg in 1530.

Today, there are many *herbiers* in print. I would like to add my description of Provençal herbs to the list.

A PROVENÇAL HERBIER

These are the major herbs and spices called for in this book, many of which have been used in Provençal cooking for centuries.

Allspice, bois d'anes. Allspice tastes like a combination of cinnamon, cloves, and nutmeg. It was discovered by Columbus in the fifteenth century, but not used as a spice until the seventeenth century.

Although allspice is not used much in Provençal cooking, I love it and make it my personal touch in soups, fish dishes, and stews.

Basil, basilic. Basil has a pungent, peppery taste, more or less the same in all its varieties, such as purple and pepper basil. First cultivated in India and Asia, it was brought to Italy and spread throughout Europe by the Romans.

In Provence, basil flavors salads, stews, vegetables, fish, meat, and poultry, often rolled and cut into ribbons called *chiffonade.* It is available here all year long at greengrocers. A good way to preserve it is in olive oil or vinegar.

Basil is a good digestive stimulant and its oil can calm headaches. A pot of basil in your window will repel flies.

Bay leaves, feuillede laurier. Bay has a beautiful sweet and bitter smell and a pungent taste. The bay tree, also known as laurel, was consecrated to Apollo, the Greek god of music and poetry, and Greek heroes and Roman emperors alike wore crowns of laurel. According to superstition, bay trees protect against thunderstorms, the anger of the gods, bad spirits, and witches.

Bay is used a lot in Provençal cooking because it grows locally. The trees never lose their leaves in the winter, so if you are lucky enough to have a tree, you can pick them all year long. We had a row of bay trees in front of my house and my mother used them both fresh and dry (she liked to have a bouquet of bay leaves drying somewhere in the kitchen). I loved the smell of the fresh leaves when I crushed them in my hand.

Bay leaves are used in stews, court bouillon, and soups and with fish, poultry, and meat. They are usually sold dried in the United States and all the recipes in this book call for dried leaves.

Clove, girofle. Cloves have a powerful warm and spicy flavor. Their origin probably was China.

When you add cloves to stew or court bouillon, stick them in an onion; in making orange wine, add an orange stuck with cloves. Use them with discretion, because of their robustness, and use them whole, not powdered, for greater control over the flavor of the finished dish.

Cloves are used to calm tooth pain.

Cumin. Cumin has a spicy, exotic flavor. Originally from Egypt, it is common in India and the Arab countries.

I prefer to use it finely ground, although it also is available in seeds. It gives a lot of body to dishes.

Curry, cari. A blend of spices, curry powder originated in India and is sensual and powerful. Use it with discretion because too much can dominate your dishes. In Provençal cooking it isn't used much, but I like its exotic touch.

I prefer Madras curry, which is rich in cumin.

Dill, aneth. Dill has a pungent, peppery taste. It originated in southern Europe and is used a lot in Scandinavia and Russia. It is mentioned in an old Egyptian papyrus. Dill seeds are believed to quiet hunger pangs.

Use dill feathers to season fish, seafood, meat, and vegetables. Dill is easy to find in the market all year round, fresh and dried.

Fennel, fenouil. Fennel seeds have a licorice flavor. The fennel plant, a member of the parsley family, is a native of the Mediterranean coast. It is said that Charlemagne grew fennel in his garden.

Use the seeds in court bouillon, sauces, stews, meat, fish, and seafood and sometimes in breads and desserts.

Lavender, lavande. Lavender, which is a member of the mint family, is the queen of our flowers and a symbol of Provence. It grows wild on the hills and among the rocks in the Mediterranean countries.

In Provence, we use the dried flowers in desserts and other dishes, to make tea, and to perfume our closets. Lavender essence is used to treat headaches.

Mint, menthe. Mint has a cool, fresh, and spicy flavor. There are many kinds of mint, which grow everywhere in the world and are used in a variety of dishes, especially in the Middle East. In Provence, we use it for desserts, tea, and garnishes.

Mint is available fresh all year round in the United States, so don't bother to use the dried leaves. Crushed mint leaves can be used as an antiseptic and an ant repellent. Mariners used dried mint leaves to purify their water during long voyages.

Nutmeg, noix de muscade. With its sophisticated flavor and silky sweetness, nutmeg is the most elegant spice in your rack. It resembles a peppercorn and grows on trees in a tropical climate.

I put a little freshly grated nutmeg in many meat dishes and in some desserts.

Parsley, persil. Parsley has a light, sweet flavor. It originated east of the Mediterranean Sea and has been harvested for thousands of years. The original is flatleaf or Italian parsley; curlyleaf parsley is a later hybrid.

Parsley is indispensable in cooking, especially in bouquet garni, and in stews, poultry, meat, fish, seafood, and vegetable dishes. You can find it all year long in the markets, so there is no reason to use dried.

In Provence, we chew parsley to sweeten the breath, especially after eating garlic, and that is the reason we often use garlic and parsley together. Parsley juice can relieve insect bites.

Pepper, poivre. Pepper comes from the Indian Archipelago and also from Asia. Its hot, sharp flavor is essential in cooking almost everything.

A pepper mill is one of the indispensable instruments in the kitchen; always use pepper freshly ground.

Rosemary, romarin. Rosemary has a pronounced strong, warm, and bitter flavor. It was the symbol of friendship and fidelity, and an ancient *herbier* said that just the smell can keep you young. The herb grows wild in the Mediterranean area, especially on hills and among rocks, favoring poor soil; in rich soil, it grows like a tree and is not flavorful.

Rosemary can be used to flavor game, fish, meat, seafood, and vegetables, but use discretion because too much can ruin a dish. It is found in most markets and is better fresh than dried.

Family members during a winter parsley harvest.

An infusion of rosemary can calm nerves and aid digestion.

Saffron, safran. Saffron has a golden color and a heavenly aroma. It is the most expensive spice in the world, since many thousands of the crocuslike plants are needed to produce one pound of the spice. Originally from the Middle East, it was introduced into Spain by the Arabs.

In Provence, saffron is indispensable in fish soup and bouillabaisse. I love to use it with sauces, fish, seafood, and some desserts. Because of its expense, use it in small quantities and use only the threads, not packaged powdered saffron.

Sage, sauge. This aromatic herb grows wild around the Mediterranean coast. It is used to flavor charcuterie and other meats, along with poultry, fish, vegetables, and cheese. I like to use sprigs of sage as a brush to baste barbecue. Sage is good dried, but you can buy it fresh all year.

Sage facilitates digestion, calms fevers, and purifies the blood. A sage infusion can be used as a mouthwash and to heal bleeding gums.

Tarragon, estragon. Tarragon is native to southern Europe and the Mediterranean coast. It has a warm and strong taste and a sweet perfume.

Use tarragon with fish, seafood, meat, poultry, eggs, and vegetables. You can find it in the market almost all year round and can preserve it in vinegar or dry it.

Thyme, thym. Thyme has a robust and spicy flavor and aroma, and grows wild in the south of France. There are many varieties, such as lemon, pepper, and silver thyme. In the days of the crusades, thyme was a symbol of bravery and courage.

Thyme is indispensable to Provençal and southern European cuisine and is always part of a bouquet garni. It goes well with garlic, tomatoes, and olives. Use it with meat, poultry, fish, stews, vegetables, and eggs. It is found fresh all year round in the market.

If you smash some thyme on your skin, it will calm insect bites. An infusion of 1 cup hot water and 2 branches of thyme is good for coughs, colds, and indigestion.

The following are vegetables that we use in Provence for flavoring, much like herbs.

Bell pepper, poivron. Originally from South America, the pepper is available in green, red, yellow, orange, and purple varieties. It has a warm, sweet, and bitter taste.

We eat peppers raw in salad, peeled and grilled in oil, in a colorful stew (*poivronade*), and in many other dishes. During warm seasons, it is easy to find beautiful peppers in the market.

Garlic, ail. Originally from Central Asia, and one of the oldest cultivated plants in history, garlic's powerful taste has been important in many cuisines. Aristophanes said that athletes ate garlic for courage and strength in the stadium. In ancient Egypt, the pyramid builders consumed the cloves, and in the Middle Ages, garlic was believed to rout bad spirits and vampires.

In Provence you always see a rosary of garlic in the kitchen. It is eaten raw in salads and on bread, roasted, candied in syrup, and added to just about everything. I often smash a garlic clove with the flat side of a knife and then mince it. Old people carry a clove of garlic in their pockets to protect them from any kind of sickness. It is an antiseptic, helps blood circulation, and is an antidote to snakebites. Most important, we believe garlic is the secret of longevity.

Garlic is the number-one ingredient in the south of France. It is the root of health—we knew that before the doctors said so. Use it fresh. To smash a clove of garlic and enjoy its aroma and flavor is to be blessed by God.

Olive. The olive tree originated in Asia and has been important in Mediterranean countries since antiquity. In Jerusalem some olive trees are said to date back to the lifetime of Christ. The olive tree is highly symbolic in Provence, its mystic form full of religious and spiritual meaning and its wood expensive and highly prized.

There are many varieties of olives, but the difference between green and black is simply the time of harvesting. In Provence the people are gourmands of olives, using them in countless recipes. On every table, there is a bowl of *tapenade,* replacing butter as a spread for country bread.

Onion, oignon. Originally from Asia, the onion has been known for more than four thousand years. It was highly esteemed in antiquity.

Onions give spirit to almost every kind of dish, and I use onions in most of my recipes. There are many varieties, such as yellow, white, purple, and the sweet Bermuda.

In Provence, the old people say that when the onion has many skins, the winter is going to be rigorous and cold.

Like its cousin garlic, use it only fresh.

Scallion, ciboule. Aromatic scallions originated in Asia and were introduced into Europe in the Middle Ages. In antiquity they were considered precious and were used as money.

I like to use scallions in many kinds of dishes. They can be found fresh all year round.

Shallot, échalote. Shallots taste a little sweeter and milder than onions and they are easier to digest. In Provence they say the shallot is the bride of the onion.

When you have a subtle dish and want a subdued flavor, it is sometimes better to use shallots than the more robust onion.

Shallots should be used fresh and can be found all year round in the market.

BOUQUETS GARNIS AND SPICE MIXTURES

A bouquet garni is a mixture of fresh and dried herbs that is tied together with string or enclosed in a small cheesecloth bag and placed in the pot to cook with soups or stews. The basic bouquet garni contains thyme, parsley, and bay leaves, but there are no rules, and you can add anything you have on hand, like a piece of carrot, leek, or basil. Use your imagination to make the bouquet interesting. Always use the best part of the plant: parsley stems have more taste than the leaves, so use the leaves for something else (or include them, if you prefer). Add a fennel branch for fish; add a strip of dried orange peel for beef stew.

Make your own spice mixtures to give aroma to stews, stocks, cooking dishes, court bouillon, sauces, and desserts. Replace the spices in your rack after a year with small quantities from shops that sell them in large quantities, so they are always fresh. These mixtures smell so good, you can use the leftovers as potpourri.

Herbes de Provence is a potpourri of dried Provençal herbs that is available in many markets. An easy recipe to do at home would include 4 tablespoons thyme, 2 tablespoons rosemary, 1 tablespoon lavender, 1 tablespoon fennel seeds, and 3 bay leaves. Many mixtures also include dried basil, sage, chervil, and savory. There really are no rules and you can use your imagination. Use *herbes de Provence* on just about anything—meat, fish, or vegetables.

Quatre épices is a mixture of ground spices that usually includes four of the following: bay leaves, thyme, rosemary, white pepper, cumin, cloves, ginger, and nutmeg. It is used mainly for pâté and is available at many markets.

Spice Mixture for Fish and Seafood

½ teaspoon fennel seeds
1 teaspoon dried thyme
¼ teaspoon ground cumin
⅛ teaspoon smashed allspice berries
¼ teaspoon chopped dried lemon peel
¼ teaspoon dried rosemary
Pinch saffron threads
Pinch crushed bay leaf
Pinch unsprayed dried lavender flowers (available in specialty food stores)
Pinch salt
¼ teaspoon freshly ground black pepper

Mix well and store covered at room temperature for up to 1 month. Add to recipes toward the end of cooking.

MAKES ABOUT 1 TABLESPOON

Spice Mixture for Vegetables

½ teaspoon dried thyme
¼ teaspoon dried rosemary
½ teaspoon dried parsley
½ teaspoon dried minced scallion
⅛ teaspoon curry powder
⅛ teaspoon minced dried lemon peel
Pinch unsprayed dried lavender flowers (available in specialty food stores)
Pinch saffron threads
Pinch crushed bay leaf
Small pinch garlic powder
Pinch salt
¼ teaspoon freshly ground black pepper

Mix well and store covered at room temperature for up to 1 month. Add to recipes toward the end of cooking.

MAKES ABOUT 2½ TEASPOONS

Barbecue Spice Mixture for Meat and Fish

½ teaspoon ground cumin
1 tablespoon dried thyme
½ teaspoon dried rosemary
1 teaspoon unsprayed dried lavender flowers (available in specialty food stores)
¼ teaspoon chopped dried orange zest
½ teaspoon dried sage
Pinch salt
½ teaspoon freshly ground black pepper

Mix well and store covered at room temperature for up to 1 month. Use toward the end of cooking.

WINE

Late September, when the grape harvest ended and the beautiful days of fall began, was the time our family made wine. My father grew grapes, and pressed the wine himself with a special machine, a *pressoir*. He had a large *cuve*—a big wooden barrel with a faucet—which is still on the farm. New wine was poured into the *cuve* and then, all year long, we could go there, turn on the faucet, and take our wine. Many of our neighbors had vineyards and made their own wine, too, and everyone had a *cuve*. When my father died, we sold our wine-making license, but my cousin still presses wine on his farm in the old-fashioned way.

It was a very festive time for the whole family, with laughing and singing, and children and pets running all over the place. The only problem was the mosquitoes! Attracted by the humidity of late summer, the sweet fragrance of the ripe grapes, and the grape skins that littered the ground, they buzzed around us and attacked mercilessly.

When my father pressed the wine, he also made a strong drink called *piquet* from the discarded grape skins mixed with water. You had to drink it right away, because it didn't keep. To me, it tasted like vinegar! He made something much better with the white grape skins, sugar, and water, which was called *carthagène*. It was very strong, too, and it could make you very drunk, but it was delicious.

My grandmother made green walnut, violet, and orange wines at home, for apéritifs. When she served them, it was like a little ceremony, where the family sat under the trees and raised their glasses together. In the south, everything is tradition and ceremony. There was always wine on our table, whether or not anyone drank it, to symbolize the blood of Christ. At Christmas, we blessed wine and sprinkled it over a blazing log, and for the Feast of Epiphany, everyone went house to house, neighbor to neighbor, to share a bottle of sweet wine.

In Provence today, wine-making is still a family or village enterprise. Commonly, farmers band together in cooperatives to make wine for their own consumption from the grapes they have grown. Wine producing is natural and old-fashioned, not high-tech. The different kinds of soil in each area, along with the blazing summers, short, cold winters, and salty sea winds all contribute flavor to the grapes. In modern vineyards in France and the United States, vines are watered automatically by a sprinkler system and the water is carefully measured—in Provence the sky gives the water. Small cooperatives can't afford to buy a lot of the technical equipment that big vineyards in other places have, but they don't need it. Provençal farmers produce wine the same way they live, taking their time and enjoying the gifts of nature.

What we are known for particularly in Provence is rosé wine, although all the vineyards also produce white wines, which are usually light, and reds, which are rich, fruity, and generous. (When you produce a rosé, the grape skins are kept with the juice for the least possible time, usually just a few hours. If you keep the skins longer, you get red wine.) Our rosé is a simple wine, but more interesting and with more character than the reds and whites. Dry, fragrant, and spicy, it matches the spicy food of Provence and goes with everything we eat. The wine can be drunk almost immediately after it is finished, and should be kept no more than two or three years. When it is fresh, it is so good and full of character!

The ancient Greeks planted the first vineyards in Provence, in the Bellet region, and the Romans who succeeded them planted many more, all over the territory. Some of the Roman vineyards still produce grapes, but, of course, with new vines (vines have a lifetime of about seventy-five years). Provence has seven wine-producing areas, all of which provide rosés, reds, and whites: Bandol, on the Mediterranean coast; Bellet, near Nice; Cassis further west on the coast; Coteaux d'Aix-en-Provence, near that town; Côtes de Provence, in the center of the region; Côtes du Lubéron, to the north; and Palette, just east of Aix-en-Provence. All of these areas differ from one another in their soil or weather or altitude, so that the wines each produces are distinct.

Thirteen types of grapes can be used for rosé in Provence, including the Mourvèdre, an old variety, which gives body to the wine. Each area uses a different grape—some varieties grow well in Bellet, some in Aix-en-Provence, some do better in a vineyard by the sea, and some thrive on a mountaintop. Most of the wines produced from these grapes never leave the south of France. They simply don't travel well and they don't keep well, either. But enthusiastic local markets exist for them, and among individual families and restaurants, all the wines are consumed. Two vineyards that regularly export their products are Domaine Tempier, in Bandol, and Domaines Ott, in Bandol and Côte de Provence. You may be able to find their wines in shops and restaurants in the United States, but for the fresh, local rosés that sing of Provence, you must come to the source.

Orange Wine

Vin d'Orange

My grandmother made this spicy orange wine as a summer refreshment.

4 medium-size navel oranges, washed well, 2 left whole and 2 halved,
  seeded, and thinly sliced
20 cloves stuck into the oranges
1 vanilla bean, halved lengthwise
12 cups dry white wine
1 cup sugar

Combine all the ingredients in a nonreactive bowl and marinate 6 hours or overnight at room temperature.

In a large, nonreactive pot over high heat, bring the mixture to a boil. Reduce the heat to medium-high and boil gently until reduced by about one third, about 15 minutes.

Place the clove-studded whole oranges in two jars and strain the wine into them. Serve cold.

MAKES ABOUT 1 QUART

EQUIPMENT FOR THE PROVENÇAL KITCHEN

You don't need a lot of expensive equipment to cook Provençal style. Like the foods themselves, your pots and pans should be simple and of good quality. Since many dishes begin with a quick sauté of onions and garlic, frying pans are essential in large, medium, and small sizes. An 8- to 9-inch nonstick frying pan is good for making *tarte tatin,* and a nonstick crêpe pan is nice to have. You will use, as well, large, medium, and small saucepans. A sturdy stockpot is important, as is a large, heavy saucepot.

For roasting, you will use large and medium roasting pans. A gratin dish is useful, as are 8- and 10-inch tart pans with removable bottoms, a 5-cup kugelhopf pan, and ¾-cup individual soufflé molds. Sometimes I use 4-inch individual savarin molds and a 9- to 10-inch savarin mold. I like to bake loaves of country bread in pans that measure about 6 by 2½ inches (mine come attached, in a loaf plaque). If this size is hard to find, just use small loaf pans.

A heavy mortar and pestle for pulverizing nuts, garlic, and spices stood on the shelf of my grandmother's kitchen, and have a place in my own.

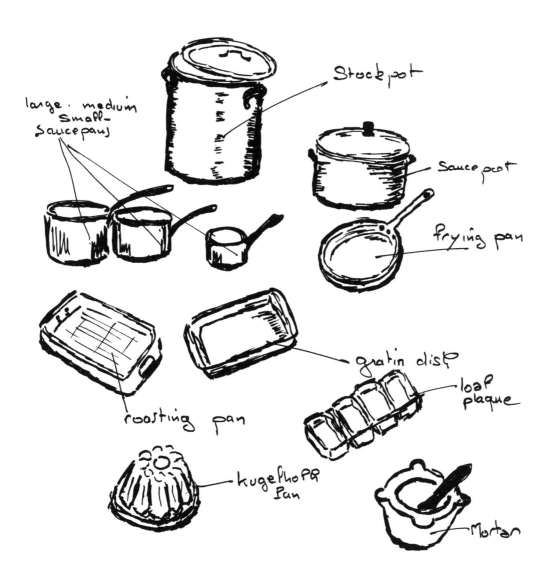

CHAPTER 2

Le Goûter: Small Meals

At many meals, in my mother's words, "The men eat with a fork and the women eat with a cup." For my father and grandfather, breakfast on the farm usually meant several kinds of local cheese, warm chunks of rough-textured country bread pulled from a crusty loaf, spicy home-cured sausage, and an omelette with wild mushrooms or sweet onions. My mother and grandmother, however, were content with cups of steaming coffee and perhaps a slice of bread.

In addition to the breakfast omelettes, we used our plentiful supply of eggs for soufflés, custards, and cakes. Gathering the freshly laid eggs was the chore assigned to me and my sister and it became one of my happiest memories of my childhood on the farm. Our hens roamed free during the day and laid their eggs all over the place, so we had to wait until after dark, when they were returned to their pen. Then Marguerite and I would go off with a flashlight and a basket and search the entire farm for eggs, and sometimes we could find sixty on a single excursion. For breakfast the next day, the fresh eggs were unbelievably good.

We ate breakfast early, lunch at noon, and dinner close to nine at night. To make a little bridge between lunch and dinner, there was a *goûter*, like the English afternoon tea, around 4:00 (I don't know who stole the idea from whom). We had many of the same things we had eaten at breakfast, along with a simple fruit or nut cake and coffee, soft drinks, and lemonade.

On late summer afternoons, the cool farmhouse was an oasis from the sun-baked fields. My grandfathers, Antoine and Joseph, my father, the field hands, and assorted friends came to *le goûter* directly from work, in their overalls. My grand-mothers, Marguerite and Marie, along with me and my sister, joined them around my mother's wide kitchen table. Assorted neighbors always felt free to drop in and eat a small meal with us before returning to the fields.

My father's cousin Marius was always there, because Papa, who was an only child, loved him like the brother he never had. Marius was an old bachelor, with yellow teeth and a purple nose, always in need of a shave, and dressed as though there were no mirrors in his house. We called Marius "the picador" because he was a water thief—no small sin in Provence, where water is as precious as diamonds. He was known to turn the irrigation water toward his own fields and away from his neighbors'. He also was a gossip, who found out everything that happened in town and didn't hesitate to spread each story. And he exaggerated even the smallest event, filling our ears with fantastic stories. But Marius had a lot of company. In Provence, we say: *On ne ment pas, on enjolive.* (We don't lie, we just make things beautiful.)

In the south of France, people say things like "I grew a zucchini that is as big as this table." When a Provençal fisherman says he caught a giant fish, it's probably a sardine. Our reputation for tall tales was recorded by Alphonse Daudet, the famous Provençal writer. In his tale, *Tartarin and Tarascon,* Tartarin bragged that he was hunting elephants, when actually he was after rabbits.

At our table, everyone gossiped loudly, joked, and told tall stories. Gathered together in our kitchen, the men talked spiritedly about the war and their military service—the only time they had ever left Saint-Rémy. Among the women, death was a popular topic: "You won't believe who died! The daughter of the aunt of the brother!"

My father would joke loudly about the latest family expedition to the seacoast. For that annual trip, my parents, Marguerite and I (fighting for my mother's lap), a cousin or two, my grandmother, and my parents all piled into our old Torpedo sedan. But inevitably, after half an hour on the road, Grandmother would gasp, "I didn't turn off the stove!" and my father would have to turn the car around and go back home. He would shout at his mother and she at him (we make a lot of noise in Provence), and, of course, the gas had been off all the time.

Whenever this story was repeated, the men around the table loudly agreed with my father and the women clucked sympathetically at my grandmother. I ignored the boisterous talk, waiting for my special treat: my mother would spread a thick slice of warm bread with butter and melt a layer of dark chocolate on top. With a little bowl of light coffee, it made me the happiest boy in the world.

We eat a lot of pasta in Provence, probably because of our closeness to Italy and our history of being her colony. The pasta dishes in this section follow the simple methods we used on the farm, where pasta was often a quickly prepared appetizer or light meal in itself. Not all the recipes come from my home, but they are inspired by my mother's and grandmother's style. The same is true of the appetizers I include here, which offered me a chance to use farm ingredients or methods in dishes that are a bit more elegant than rustic.

Almond Milk

Lait aux Amandes comme Grand-mère Marie

My grandmother Marie made this healthful drink for me from very fresh almonds that she crushed in a mortar. She promised that it would help me to grow up strong, but it was so delicious, I didn't need that incentive to drink it.

½ cup ground blanched almonds
½ cup sliced blanched almonds
½ cup sugar
¼ teaspoon orange flower water (available in specialty food stores)
½ teaspoon pure almond extract
2 cups whole or low-fat milk

In a small mixing bowl, whisk together all the ingredients and refrigerate covered 2 to 3 hours. Strain through a fine strainer and serve.

MAKES 2 SERVINGS

Light Eggs Benedict Antoine's Way

Oeufs Façon Bénédictine

I always prefer to eat eggs along with a vegetable—that way everything is in a good balance. Here the bright red tomato sauce and the flavorful steamed spinach add a little Provençal touch. The result is a dish with the feeling of Eggs Benedict, but one that is far lighter in fat and cholesterol. It makes a colorful, delicious brunch entrée.

For the eggs

2 tablespoons white wine vinegar
1 tablespoon sea salt
4 large eggs

For the sauce

1 tablespoon unsalted butter
1 tablespoon all-purpose flour
Salt and freshly ground black pepper to taste
1½ cups cold regular or low-fat milk
A few gratings of nutmeg
8 leaves spinach, tough stems discarded and leaves steamed 1 minute over
    boiling water
¼ cup Provençal Touch Light Tomato Sauce (page 105), heated
2 tablespoons minced fresh parsley for garnish

In a medium-size saucepan over high heat, bring half a pan of water to a gentle boil with the vinegar and salt. Carefully break each egg into a bowl so that the yolk remains intact and add, one by one, to the boiling water. When the eggs rise to the top, turn with a spoon just once and cook another 30 seconds for a medium egg. With the spoon, gently break off any ragged edges of the white. Lift the eggs out of the water with the spoon, draining off the water as you do so. Set aside, covered, in a warm spot on or near the stove.

To prepare the sauce, in a large saucepan over high heat, melt the butter and quickly add the flour, salt, and pepper, whisking to incorporate the flour. Add the cold milk slowly and bring it to a boil, whisking the sauce constantly for 2 minutes. Add the nutmeg, whisk again, and reduce the heat to medium. Cook 8 to 10 minutes to remove the raw flour taste.

On each serving plate, arrange two leaves of spinach and top with 1 tablespoon of the tomato sauce. Place 1 egg over the sauce, nap with 2 tablespoons of the sauce, and garnish with the chopped parsley.

MAKES 4 SERVINGS

Crispy Eggs

Oeufs Croustillants

You may make the crêpes ahead of time and refrigerate them, but this may make them stiff. Just warm them in a 350°F oven for about 1 minute to soften.

4 buckwheat crêpes (page 354)
4 large eggs
Salt and freshly ground black pepper to taste
1 tablespoon corn or peanut oil
2 thin lemon wedges for garnish

For each serving, place a crêpe on a plate and break an egg onto it. Season with salt and pepper and bring all four sides of the crêpe up over the egg, wrapping it securely.

In a small frying pan over medium-high heat, heat the oil and add the crêpes, folded sides up. Cook 1 minute on each side, for soft eggs. Serve each egg garnished with a lemon wedge.

MAKES 4 SERVINGS

Baked Eggs with Lettuce

Oeufs aux Laitues

Steaming the lettuce leaves with olive oil gives them an appetizing shine.

2 heads Boston lettuce or 4 heads Bibb lettuce, leaves separated
Salt and freshly ground black pepper to taste
3 tablespoons plus 1 teaspoon extra virgin olive oil
4 large eggs
Pinch freshly grated nutmeg
Toast as an accompaniment

Preheat the oven to 350°F. Reserve 12 large outer leaves of the lettuce. Season the remaining leaves lightly with salt, pepper, and 1 teaspoon of the olive oil. In a steamer set over boiling water, steam the seasoned lettuce until softened, 6 to 8 minutes. Pat the lettuce dry with paper towels, place in a food processor with 2 tablespoons of the olive oil, and process till smooth.

Season the reserved leaves with salt, pepper, and 1 teaspoon of the olive oil and steam for 10 seconds. Rinse with cold water and dry with paper towels.

With 1 teaspoon of the olive oil, grease four individual soufflé molds. Line the bottom and sides of each mold with two lettuce leaves, leaving an overlap all around. Add half of the pureed lettuce, top with 1 egg, and season with nutmeg, salt, and pepper. Cover with a third leaf and bring up the overlapping leaves, smoothing the top. Dot with the remaining 1 teaspoon of olive oil.

Place the molds in a high-sided ovenproof pan and pour boiling water two thirds of the way up their sides. Bake 10 to 15 minutes for very soft eggs and longer for firmer eggs. Serve with toast.

MAKES 4 SERVINGS

Thin Omelette Marie-Thérèse

Omelette Fine Marie-Thérèse

My mother made this thin omelette for me when I was little and I loved to eat it cold, especially for picnics. Even now, when she comes to New York to visit me, I ask her to make it, because she has a special touch. Since the omelette is served cold, it should be cooked through, but should not be too dry.

2 tablespoons peanut or corn oil
1 large onion, cut in half and very thinly sliced
1 large tomato, peeled, seeded, and chopped into small dice
3 to 4 cloves garlic, thinly sliced
½ teaspoon minced fresh thyme
1 tablespoon minced fresh parsley
Salt and freshly ground black pepper to taste
4 large eggs, lightly beaten

In a large skillet over high heat, heat the oil, then add the onion and sauté until it turns quite brown, about 10 minutes. Add the tomato and garlic and stir well. Add the thyme, parsley, salt, and pepper and sauté another 5 minutes, just to soften the tomato.

Whisk the eggs with salt and pepper, then spread the onion mixture out over the bottom of the skillet and pour the eggs over it. Shake the pan to distribute the eggs. Cook the omelette 5 minutes, loosen it around the circumference, and invert it over a pan or dish. Wipe out the skillet, add a little more oil, and heat it to very hot. Return the omelette to the skillet uncooked side down and cook until well set, another 5 minutes. (If the omelette breaks, it doesn't matter. This is a country dish, not gastronomy.) Refrigerate and serve cold.

MAKES 4 SERVINGS

Fluffy Vegetable Omelette

La Pipérade

When you make a fragrant ratatouille, put a little aside. Combine it with creamy scrambled eggs and you have a favorite supper dish of my childhood.

    1 teaspoon peanut oil
    2 large eggs, lightly beaten
    Salt and freshly ground black pepper to taste
    2 to 3 tablespoons Ratatouille (page 142)

In a small frying pan over medium heat, heat the oil until very hot but not smoking.

Whisk the eggs with the salt and pepper, add them to the pan, and cook, stirring, until just set. Mix in the ratatouille and serve immediately, or refrigerate and serve cold.

MAKES 1 SERVING

White Swiss Chard Omelette Marie-Thérèse

Omelette de Blette Marie-Thérèse

Separate the white stems from the green leaves and use only the stems of the Swiss chard for this omelette. (Use the leaves for Green Swiss Chard Tart on page 171.) Because you boil the stems briefly before sautéing, they are tender and sweet. This is a fantastic dish for brunch or a light lunch.

If you are watching your cholesterol, substitute egg whites for the whole eggs.

4 packed-down cups 2-inch lengths Swiss chard stems, about 1 pound (you
    don't have to peel young chard, but you may have to peel mature
    stems)
1 tablespoon sea salt
2 tablespoons corn or peanut oil
2 to 3 large eggs, lightly beaten
3 tablespoons minced fresh parsley
Salt and freshly ground black pepper to taste

In a large saucepan over medium-high heat, combine the Swiss chard with water to cover and the salt and bring to a boil. Boil 10 minutes and pour into a strainer to drain. Gently squeeze out as much water as possible.

In a large skillet over medium heat, heat the oil until very hot but not smoking. In a large bowl, combine the drained chard, eggs, and parsley and stir to combine well. Pour into the skillet and spread into a thin pancake. Season with salt and pepper. Cook until brown and crisp, about 3 minutes, then flip or invert the omelette. Cook until brown and crisp on the other side, about 2 minutes.

MAKES 4 SERVINGS

Dr. Bressler's Cholesterol-Free Omelette

Omelette sans Cholesterol à la Dr. Bressler

This beautiful, elegant omelette, created for a longtime customer's special diet, is as thin as a crêpe and speckled with green herbs. You may use any fresh herb you like, or add a little onion for even more flavor. Serve it with a tomato or vegetable salad.

    2 large egg whites
    Salt and freshly ground black pepper to taste
    1 clove garlic, thinly sliced
    1 tablespoon minced fresh herbs, such as thyme, basil, tarragon, or rose-
        mary, or any combination
    1 tablespoon peanut or corn oil

Whisk together the egg whites, salt, pepper, garlic, and herbs.

In a small, heavy skillet over high heat, heat the oil to very hot but not smoking. Add the egg mixture and cook 4 minutes without turning. Remove the pan from the heat, roll the omelette from either end into the middle, like a scroll, and place on a plate.

MAKES 1 SERVING

Egg White Omelettes with Fiddlehead Ferns

Omelettes de Blanc d'Oeufs aux Coeurs de Fougères

Serve these light, cholesterol-free omelettes with Uncooked Tomato Sauce (page 106). The golden eggs are dotted with chunks of beautiful green ferns and herbs. Fiddleheads are available in the spring and summer at the greengrocer's.

3 to 4 tablespoons sea salt
1 pound fresh fiddlehead ferns, stem tips cut off and rinsed
¼ cup corn or peanut oil
1 tablespoon minced shallots
4 large egg whites
Salt and freshly ground black pepper to taste
2 tablespoons minced fresh parsley
1 tablespoon minced scallions, white and tender green parts
1 teaspoon minced fresh thyme or basil

Over high heat, bring to a boil a large saucepan of water with the sea salt. Add the fiddlehead ferns and boil until tender but still firm and green, 30 to 60 seconds. Drain and rinse in cold running water.

In a large omelette pan over medium-high heat, heat 2 tablespoons of the oil until hot but not smoking and sauté the fiddleheads and shallots together for 30 seconds. Season with salt and pepper. Remove half the vegetable mixture and reserve.

Beat the egg whites until thick and fluffy. Add the salt, pepper, parsley, scallions, and thyme. Over medium-high heat, stir the vegetables in the pan and pour half the egg whites over them. Cook just until brown around the rim, about 2 minutes, then invert the omelette and cook another 2 minutes. Remove to a serving plate. Repeat with the remaining vegetables and egg whites.

MAKES 2 OMELETTES; 4 SERVINGS

Eggless Omelette

Omelette à la Fleur de Lait

You will be fooled by this dish, which looks and tastes exactly like eggs. Always use a heavy, nonstick pan or a well-seasoned frying pan to cook it, or the *fleur de lait* will stick to the bottom. If you do not get a perfect-looking omelette, just serve this dish as you would scrambled eggs. It will still be delicious.

  2 quarts whole milk
  Juice of 2 lemons
  ¼ teaspoon ground turmeric
  ½ cup grated Swiss cheese
  Salt and freshly ground black pepper to taste
  1 generous tablespoon butter or margarine
  Sautéed onions or tomatoes or fresh herbs to taste (optional)

In a large saucepan over high heat, bring the milk to a rolling, full boil. Then pour in the lemon juice. The curds—*fleur de lait,* the flower of the milk—will begin to separate from the whey. Continue boiling until the curds are completely separate, then pour into a strainer and discard the whey.

Mix the turmeric, cheese, salt, and pepper with the curds. In a large skillet over high heat, melt the butter, then pour in the curds and stir in the onions. Cook until the bottom is crisp, 5 to 10 minutes, and invert onto a serving platter.

MAKES 4 SERVINGS

Zucchini Cake

Petit Pot aux Courgettes

With a fork, mash or chop the poached zucchini to a coarse, chunky consistency. Don't use a food processor or blender—that will kill the feeling and texture of the dish.

This should be a little soupy. Serve it in the mold and eat it with a spoon, along with a nice slice of toasted country bread, the way we did in my mother's kitchen.

3 cups water
1 tablespoon sea or coarse salt
2 small zucchini, cut into ½-inch dice
Freshly ground black pepper to taste
Paprika to taste
1 teaspoon extra virgin olive oil
4 large eggs
2 teaspoons chopped fresh parsley for garnish

In a large pot over high heat, bring the water to a boil with the sea salt, then add the zucchini and cook until tender, about 10 minutes. Drain and place in a mixing bowl. Preheat the oven to 400°F.

With a fork, mash the zucchini coarsely with the pepper, paprika, and olive oil. Butter four medium-size custard cups and divide the mashed zucchini among them. Break 1 egg on top of each pot and sprinkle with a little of the parsley. Place the pots in a baking pan half filled with hot water and bake to desired doneness, 10 to 15 minutes. Serve with a slice of country bread.

MAKES 4 SERVINGS

Grandmother Marguerite's Baked Macaroni

Gratin de Coquillettes comme Marguerite

When I visited my grandmother Marguerite's kitchen as a child, there was always a little gratin waiting for me. I loved to break up the crisp crust and eat a bit with every forkful of noodles. Although this dish tastes rich and creamy, it contains no cream—just fresh whole milk and nutty sweet Swiss cheese.

2 tablespoons unsalted butter
2 generous tablespoons all-purpose flour
2½ cups cold whole milk
Generous pinch salt
6 drops Tabasco sauce or pinch cayenne pepper
Pinch freshly grated nutmeg
1 pound elbow macaroni, slightly undercooked and drained (it will finish cooking in the oven)
½ cup grated Swiss cheese
2 to 3 tablespoons plain bread crumbs

Preheat the oven to 400°F. Butter a medium-size gratin dish.

In a large saucepan over medium-high heat, melt the butter. Sprinkle the flour over it and mix well with a spatula. (The mixture will be very thick.) Raise the heat to high, add the milk slowly, and cook, whisking thoroughly. Add the salt, Tabasco, and nutmeg and mix well. Lower the heat to medium and cook, stirring, about 3 minutes to get rid of any raw flour taste.

Put the macaroni in the gratin dish, pour the sauce over it, and mix well. Mix in the grated cheese and crumbs. Bake until brown and firm, about 40 minutes. If the top has not browned, put the dish under a broiler briefly until brown and crisp.

MAKES 4 SERVINGS

Pasta with Mushrooms

Pâtes aux Champignons

This recipe reminds me of the pasta I ate on the farm, which my mother cooked very simply. She made a meal like this for me in just a few minutes, because working in the fields, she didn't have a lot of time to cook. Whenever I eat this, I think of myself as a little boy, sitting at the great kitchen table with my mother and sister.

2 tablespoons corn or peanut oil
3 shallots, diced
12 medium-size mushroom caps, sliced ¼ inch thick
2 cloves garlic, minced
1 large tomato, coarsely chopped
2 teaspoons chopped scallions, white and tender green parts
2 teaspoons minced fresh parsley
Pinch each freshly ground black pepper and salt
1 pound pasta of your choice, such as linguine, cooked according to package instructions
4 to 6 pinches grated Swiss cheese for garnish
4 to 6 teaspoons extra virgin olive oil for drizzling

In a large skillet over medium-high heat, heat the oil, then add the shallots and cook until they soften but do not color, about 5 minutes. Add the mushrooms and sauté until they become soft and shiny, about 4 minutes. Add the garlic, tomato, scallions, pepper, and salt and sauté until the vegetables are softened, about 5 minutes.

Divide the pasta among four or six individual bowls and top each with the cooked vegetables. Top with a pinch of the cheese and drizzle with olive oil.

MAKES 6 APPETIZER OR 4 MAIN-COURSE SERVINGS

Pasta with Three Peppers

Pâtes aux Trois Poivrons

You can get fresh bell peppers all year round, and preparing them in this quick dish is a wonderful way to re-create the feeling of summer. With its fresh flavors and beautiful colors, it typifies southern French cooking.

2 tablespoons corn or peanut oil
1 medium-size onion, thinly sliced
1 large green bell pepper, quartered, seeded, and cut into julienne strips
1 large red bell pepper, quartered, seeded, and cut into julienne strips
1 large yellow bell pepper, quartered, seeded, and cut into julienne strips
2 cloves garlic, smashed and peeled
1 teaspoon chopped fresh or dried thyme
2 tablespoons chopped fresh parsley
4 to 6 leaves fresh basil, chopped
Pinch each freshly ground black pepper and salt
1 pound pasta of your choice, such as linguine, cooked according to package instructions
4 to 6 pinches grated Swiss cheese for garnish
4 to 6 teaspoons extra virgin olive oil for drizzling

In a large skillet over medium-high heat, heat the oil until very hot but not smoking, then add the onion and sauté until golden, about 5 minutes. Add the peppers and sauté until soft and colored, about 5 minutes. Add the garlic, herbs, salt, and pepper and sauté 2 minutes.

Divide the pasta among four bowls. Arrange the vegetable sauté on top of each, top with a pinch of the cheese, and drizzle with the olive oil.

MAKES 4 SERVINGS

Pasta with Endive

Pâtes aux Endives

With just a green salad, this pasta can be a complete lunch—you don't need anything else.

4 to 6 endives, washed, cored, and outer leaves removed
2 tablespoons peanut or corn oil
Salt and freshly ground black pepper to taste
Pinch freshly grated nutmeg
Pinch sugar
2 tablespoons extra virgin olive oil
Few drops fresh lemon juice
1 pound bow-tie pasta, cooked according to package instructions
4 to 6 teaspoons grated Swiss cheese for garnish

Cut each endive in half lengthwise, then cut it on the diagonal into ½-inch slices.

In a large skillet over high heat, heat the oil until very hot but not smoking, then add the endive, salt, pepper, nutmeg, and sugar. Add the olive oil and sauté the endive until it is a uniform light brown color. Add the lemon juice, reduce the heat to medium, and cook until softened and candied, 10 to 15 minutes.

Pour the endive into a strainer to drain. Arrange the pasta in individual bowls, top with the endive, and garnish with the cheese.

MAKES 6 APPETIZER OR 4 MAIN-COURSE SERVINGS

Pasta with Fresh Figs

Pâtes aux Figues Fraîches

Love of experimentation is a family trait of the Bouterins and it led me to create this unusual sweet-and-sour pasta. It combines the sweet, juicy taste of beautiful, fresh green figs—never substitute dried—with honey, red wine vinegar, and a generous seasoning of ground pepper. Serve it as an appetizer before a simple main course, such as grilled fish.

  2 tablespoons corn or peanut oil
  6 fresh figs, halved
  2 tablespoons red wine vinegar
  2 generous tablespoons honey
  1 whole clove
  Generous pinch freshly ground black pepper
  ¾ pound pasta of your choice, cooked according to package instructions
  1 teaspoon minced fresh peppermint leaves

In a large skillet over medium-high heat, heat the oil until very hot but not smoking, then add the figs skin side down. Cook until the skins brown, about 1 minute, then turn and brown the other side. Cook 5 minutes, turning and pressing down with a spatula, until cooked through.

Pour out the oil and add the vinegar, honey, clove, and pepper to the skillet. Lower the heat to medium and cook slowly until the sauce has reduced, 5 to 10 minutes (it will bubble and thicken).

Divide the pasta among four bowls. Arrange the figs and sauce over the pasta and sprinkle with the minced peppermint leaves.

MAKES 4 APPETIZER SERVINGS

Christmas Pasta with Cranberries

Pâtes de Noël aux Airelles

Making a cheerful red-and-green plate for Christmas, this pasta is so easy to prepare that children will enjoy presenting it to their parents.

    2 tablespoons peanut or corn oil
    1 cup fresh cranberries
    3 small zucchini, the green skin only, julienned (reserve the inside of the
        zucchini to prepare as a vegetable)
    Pinch sugar
    Salt and freshly ground black pepper to taste
    1 pound angel hair pasta, cooked according to package instructions
    1 teaspoon extra virgin olive oil
    1 teaspoon chopped fresh parsley

In a large skillet over medium-high heat, heat the oil until very hot but not smoking, then add the cranberries and sauté 1 minute. Add the zucchini peel strips and sauté 1 minute. Add the sugar, salt, and pepper.

Arrange the pasta in individual bowls and top with the berries and zucchini. Drizzle each bowl with the olive oil and sprinkle with the parsley.

MAKES 6 APPETIZER OR 4 MAIN-COURSE SERVINGS

Pasta Salad with Rose Petals

Pâtes aux Pétales de Rose

Because flowers remind me of our farm, I like to use them in this pasta. Rose petals are edible and fragrant, with a haunting, flowery taste.

¾ pound tricolor pasta of an interesting shape, such as radiatore, cooked according to package instructions and cooled

For the vinaigrette

1 teaspoon salt
Juice of 1 lemon
½ cup extra virgin olive oil
½ teaspoon grated lemon zest

For the garnish

24 to 36 small rose petals, well rinsed
16 to 24 leaves fresh mint

Combine the vinaigrette ingredients in a large bowl. Add the cooked pasta and mix well. Arrange the pasta in individual bowls and top with the rose petals and mint leaves.

MAKES 6 APPETIZER OR 4 MAIN-COURSE SERVINGS

Pasta with Goat Cheese and Basil

Pâtes au Basilic et Fromage de Chèvre

In Provence the farmers raise a lot of goats and consequently we eat excellent goat cheese. The combination of the pasta, goat cheese, fresh tomato, and basil is fresh and summery.

2 tablespoons corn or peanut oil
4 rounds (about 3½ ounces each) goat cheese
1 pound pasta of your choice, such as linguine, cooked according to package instructions
16 leaves fresh basil
1 large tomato, diced
4 teaspoons extra virgin olive oil for drizzling
Pinch freshly ground black pepper

In a large skillet over medium-high heat, heat the oil until very hot but not smoking and cook the rounds of cheese until slightly brown but not melted, about 30 seconds on each side.

Divide the pasta among four bowls. Arrange on top of each 1 round of cheese, halved, 4 leaves of basil, and one quarter of the diced tomato. Drizzle with the olive oil and sprinkle with pepper.

MAKES 4 SERVINGS

Phony Bologna Pasta Sauce with Ground Turkey

Amusante Bolognaise à la Chair de Dinde

People will never guess that this Bolognese sauce contains low-fat turkey, rather than the traditional beef. When you have winter tomatoes that are less than perfect, make the best use of them in this colorful preparation. Their flavor will come through, enhanced by the Provençal herbs and garlic.

1 tablespoon corn or peanut oil
1 large onion, cut into medium dice
1 pound ground turkey
Salt and freshly ground black pepper to taste
2 cloves garlic, smashed and peeled
1 teaspoon minced fresh sage
1 teaspoon minced fresh rosemary
1 teaspoon minced fresh thyme
1 large tomato, halved, juice and seeds gently squeezed out, and roughly
   diced
2 cups prepared tomato puree
1½ cups homemade (page 82) or canned low-salt chicken broth
1 pound pasta of your choice, cooked according to package instructions
½ cup grated Swiss cheese for garnish

In large, heavy saucepan over medium-high heat, heat the oil until very hot but not smoking, then add the onion and sauté until it begins to color, about 5 minutes. Add the turkey, stirring to break it up. Sprinkle with salt and pepper and cook, stirring, 5 minutes. Add the garlic and herbs and cook, stirring, another 5 minutes. Add the tomato, the tomato puree, and chicken broth and mix well. Reduce the heat to medium and cook 15 minutes. Serve over the pasta, sprinkled with the grated cheese

MAKES 4 SERVINGS

Pasta with Chicken Livers

Pâtes aux Foies de Volaille

There are no rules about which pasta to choose for any of my dishes. Any dried pasta, with the exception of lasagne noodles, works well with these recipes.

2 tablespoons peanut or corn oil
1 medium-size red onion, thinly sliced
1 pound chicken livers, cleaned and halved
1 teaspoon chopped fresh parsley
1 teaspoon thinly sliced scallions, white and tender green parts
Salt and freshly ground black pepper to taste
1 teaspoon chopped fresh basil
2 cloves garlic, thinly sliced
1 teaspoon red wine vinegar
¼ cup homemade (page 82) or canned low-salt chicken broth (optional)
4 to 6 teaspoons grated Swiss cheese for garnish

In a large skillet over medium-high heat, heat the oil until very hot but not smoking, then add the onion and sauté until golden, about 5 minutes. Add the livers and sauté 8 to 10 minutes. Add the parsley, scallions, salt, pepper, basil, and garlic. Reduce the heat to medium and cook slowly until the livers are cooked through, 10 to 15 minutes. Raise the heat to high, add the vinegar and broth, and reduce slightly.

Arrange the pasta in individual bowls and top with the livers. Garnish each bowl with 1 teaspoon of the grated cheese.

MAKES 6 APPETIZER OR 4 MAIN-COURSE SERVINGS

Pork Pâté

Pâté de Campagne

Marie-Thérèse Brigaud, of Le Périgord, got this recipe from her mother, Marie-Louise, who owned a charcuterie—a shop selling pork products—in Brittany. It is very similar to the pâtés I remember from my childhood in the south, and I have given the recipe Provençal flavor by adding garlic, bay leaf, and spices. It is an economical and impressive dish.

Fatback is an important ingredient, giving the pâté flavor and texture.

2 pounds boneless pork shoulder
1 pound pork liver
½ pound pork fat
1 pound unsalted fatback, boiled in water to cover until softened, about 45
    minutes, drained, 2 cups of the cooking liquid reserved, and allowed to
    cool to room temperature
2 medium-size onions, quartered lengthwise
7 cloves garlic, peeled
2½ teaspoons salt
2½ teaspoons freshly ground black pepper
2 bay leaves
1 teaspoon dried thyme
Pinch freshly grated nutmeg
3 whole cloves
Cornichons (gherkins) for accompaniment

Preheat the oven to 400°F. In a food grinder with a large-holed disk, grind together the pork shoulder, liver, fat, fatback, onions, and garlic. The mixture will be fatty and fibrous and you may have to unclog the disk midway through the process. Do not use a food processor, as it will make the mixture too smooth.

Add the fatback cooking water and mix thoroughly with your hands. Add the remaining ingredients, except the cornichons, and mix well with a spatula.

Taste for seasoning by thoroughly cooking 1 tablespoon of the mixture in a little hot oil in a small skillet over high heat. Correct the seasoning if necessary.

Pack the mixture lightly into two 5- to 6-cup oblong pâté or loaf pans, cover tightly with aluminum foil, and place on a baking sheet (to catch any spills). Bake for 1 hour. When the juices begin to bubble over onto the baking pan, reduce the heat to 350°F. After another hour, remove the aluminum foil and continue to bake until it shrinks from the sides of the pan and is brown and firm, about 1 more hour.

Remove from the oven and baste three or four times with the juices. Allow to cool to room temperature, then refrigerate for up to 2 weeks, covering the loaf tightly with plastic wrap. Serve with cornichons.

MAKES 12 APPETIZER SERVINGS

Spicy Olive Paste

Tapenade

Tapenade is the butter of Provence—we always have a little pot of this textured olive mixture on the table to spread on toasted country bread.

   3 cups black olives marinated in olive oil and herbs (from Provence,
      Greece, or Italy), pitted
   8 cloves garlic, peeled
   ¾ teaspoon freshly ground black pepper
   ¼ cup extra virgin olive oil
   4 to 5 oil-packed anchovy fillets
   1 tablespoon brine-packed capers, drained
   1 teaspoon chopped fresh basil
   ½ teaspoon fresh thyme or rosemary leaves

Place all the ingredients in a food processor or blender and process to a rough puree. The mixture should have some texture. It will keep up to 1 month in the refrigerator.

MAKES 1½ CUPS

Provençal Hummus

Purée de Pois Chiche

It is perfectly fine to use canned chick-peas—their quality is good, and they make things go a lot faster. Serve this puree in the center of your table to spread on thick slices of fresh country bread as another Provençal substitute for butter.

Two 19-ounce cans chick-peas, drained
⅓ cup extra virgin olive oil
Salt and freshly ground black pepper to taste
2 tablespoons minced fresh parsley
1 teaspoon minced fresh basil
3 cloves garlic, smashed and minced
Few drops Worcestershire sauce
Pinch freshly grated nutmeg
Pinch ground cumin

In a blender, puree the chick-peas and spoon into a large bowl. Add the remaining ingredients (be generous with the pepper) and combine well. Serve at room temperature.

MAKES ABOUT 2½ CUPS

Homemade Onion Relish

Condiment d'Oignons

Accompany pâté, fish, cold meat, or vegetables with this condiment. Keep it in a jar in your refrigerator and use it whenever you like. It will keep for up to 1 month.

1 tablespoon corn or peanut oil
½ medium-size onion, minced
1 stalk celery, quartered lengthwise and cut into ¼-inch dice
2 tablespoons golden raisins
1 large or 2 small cloves garlic, minced
3 tablespoons prepared tomato puree
1 tablespoon sugar
One 10-ounce jar pickled white cocktail onions, drained and 2 tablespoons
     of the pickling liquid reserved
Juice of 1 lemon
1 tablespoon extra virgin olive oil
1 sprig fresh dill
1 bay leaf
1 whole clove
2 allspice berries
Pinch dried thyme
Pinch cumin seeds
Pinch fennel seeds
½ teaspoon coriander seeds
1 tablespoon black peppercorns
Salt and a generous amount freshly ground black pepper

In a medium-size saucepan over medium-high heat, heat the corn oil until very hot but not smoking and sauté the onion until softened but not colored, about 4 minutes. Add the remaining ingredients and bring to a boil. Reduce the heat to low and cook until glazed, 10 to 15 minutes.

MAKES ABOUT 1½ CUPS

Onion Jam

Confiture d'Oignon

❧❦❧

Spread thickly over warm country bread, this makes a spectacular appetizer.

2 tablespoons corn or peanut oil
2 large onions, halved crosswise and thinly sliced
2 tablespoons sugar
1 large Rome Beauty or Golden Delicious apple, cored and cut into ½-inch dice.
2 tablespoons golden raisins
½ teaspoon grated lemon zest
Pinch freshly grated nutmeg
½ bay leaf

In a large skillet over medium-high heat, heat the oil until very hot but not smoking, then add the onions and sauté for 2 minutes. Reduce the heat to medium and cook 10 minutes. Sprinkle the sugar over the onions, mix well, and continue cooking until the onions are soft and caramelized, another 15 minutes.

Add the remaining ingredients, mix well, and cook until thick and syrupy, about 15 minutes. Serve warm.

MAKES 4 CUPS

Warm Asparagus with Orange Sauce

Asperges Tièdes Sauce Maltaise

On our farm, we never attempted to raise white asparagus, so popular in France but very difficult to grow. I am fond of American green asparagus, which lends itself to many accents, among them this orange-flavored sauce.

2 to 3 tablespoons sea salt
1 pound asparagus spears, tough bottom parts peeled (use a vegetable peeler and work from the bottom up)
6 tablespoons Hollandaise Sauce (page 103)
Pinch freshly grated nutmeg
Freshly ground black pepper to taste
Juice and grated zest of ½ orange
2 tablespoons minced fresh parsley

Over high heat, bring to a boil a large pot of water with the sea salt. Add the asparagus and boil 1 minute. Drain the asparagus and rinse in cold, running water.

In a mixing bowl, combine the remaining ingredients, mixing with a spoon. To serve, divide the asparagus among four plates and spoon a puddle of sauce alongside.

MAKES 4 APPETIZER SERVINGS

Napoleon of Asparagus

Asperges en Feuilleté

The napoleon pastry is crisp and light because you dry it in the oven after it has baked. Its vegetable filling is colorful and generous, spilling out over the pastry "sandwich" and making a delectable contrast with the fine-textured pastry.

Frozen puff pastry makes this recipe very easy to do.

1 sheet frozen puff pastry, thawed and cut into four 4- by 3-inch rectangles and sixteen 3- by ¼-inch julienne strips
Egg wash made with 1 large egg lightly beaten with 1 teaspoon water
2 to 3 tablespoons sea salt
12 medium-size asparagus spears, peeled (use a vegetable peeler and work from the bottom to the top of each stalk)
2 tablespoons corn or peanut oil
1 large onion, cut in half and thinly sliced
1 medium-size tomato, halved, juice and seeds gently squeezed out, and cut into 1-inch dice
2 cloves garlic, thinly sliced
1 tablespoon minced scallions, white and tender green parts
2 tablespoons minced fresh parsley
Salt and freshly ground black pepper to taste

Preheat the oven to 400°F. Place the puff pastry rectangles on a lightly buttered baking sheet and brush with the egg wash. Decorate the tops with the strips to form a lattice pattern and brush again. Bake 15 minutes.

Slice each rectangle horizontally into 3 layers and discard the center layer, which will be soft. Return the top and bottom layers to the oven until crisp and dry, about 5 minutes.

Over high heat, bring a large pot of water and the sea salt to a boil. Add the asparagus and boil 1 minute. Drain the asparagus and rinse in cold, running water. Cut on the bias into 2-inch slices and set aside.

In a large skillet over medium-high heat, heat the oil until very hot but not smoking, then sauté the onion until it begins to color, about 5 minutes. Add the asparagus, tomato, garlic, scallions, parsley, salt, and pepper and sauté 5 to 10 minutes. Drain well.

Arrange the 4 bottom pastry layers on individual plates. Spoon the sautéed vegetables generously over each, and cover with the top layer.

MAKES 4 APPETIZER SERVINGS

Asparagus Soufflés

Soufflés d'Asperges

You won't have to worry about lumps in a flour-based sauce if you remember to add cold milk to the hot roux (the flour-and-butter mixture). The opposite approach works, too: you won't have a lumpy sauce if you add hot milk to cold flour. The combination of cold and hot magically ensures smoothness.

You can prepare and refrigerate these soufflés, uncovered, up to 30 minutes ahead of time and put them in the oven when your guests sit down at the table.

2 to 3 tablespoons sea salt
12 thick or 24 thin asparagus spears, tough bottom parts peeled (use a vegetable peeler and work from the bottom up)
2 tablespoons unsalted butter
½ cup all-purpose flour
2 cups cold regular or low-fat milk
½ cup grated Swiss cheese
Salt and freshly ground black pepper to taste
Pinch freshly grated nutmeg
2 large egg yolks
6 large egg whites

Over high heat, bring to a boil a large pot of water and the sea salt. Add the asparagus and boil 1 minute. Drain the asparagus and rinse in cold, running water. Cut on the bias into ¼-inch slices and set aside.

Lightly grease and flour six 4-inch by 2-inch-high soufflé molds. Preheat the oven to 400°F.

In a large saucepan over medium-high heat, melt the butter. Add the flour and stir until combined. Add the milk slowly and cook, whisking, 3 minutes. Add the grated cheese and cook 2 minutes, whisking. Remove from the heat and season with salt, pepper, and nutmeg.

Off the heat, stir in the egg yolks and mix well. Set the pot aside in a cool place to cool the mixture. When the mixture has cooled to room temperature, remove it to a large bowl and add the asparagus pieces.

In the bowl of an electric mixer or with a hand-held mixer, beat the egg whites until stiff peaks form. Fold the egg whites into the asparagus mixture, combining well but taking care not to break down the beaten whites. Spoon into the prepared molds and run a finger around the inside rim, to a depth of about ¼ inch, so the mixture stands away from the mold at that point. Bake until risen, brown, and firm on top, 15 to 20 minutes.

MAKES 6 INDIVIDUAL SOUFFLÉS

Cheese Soufflé

Soufflé au Fromage

This is a classic dish, with a touch of thyme added to make it Provençal. Served with a simple salad of dandelion greens, it was a favorite in my mother's kitchen. The extra yolk added after the base has cooled ensures a perfect texture.

For the soufflé base

2½ tablespoons butter
½ cup all-purpose flour
1½ cups cold regular or low-fat milk

Salt and freshly ground white pepper
Pinch grated nutmeg
¼ teaspoon fresh thyme leaves
¾ cup coarsely grated Swiss cheese
½ cup coarsely grated Parmesan cheese
1 clove garlic, smashed and minced, optional
1 large egg plus 2 large yolks

To complete the soufflé

1 large egg yolk
8 large egg whites at room temperature

In a large saucepan over medium-high heat, melt the butter (don't let it brown) and whisk in the flour, forming a smooth paste. Add the cold milk and whisk 3 to 5 minutes both off and on heat (remove from the heat a few times as it cooks, continuing to whisk, and return to heat, still whisking) until the mixture is very thick and smooth with no taste of raw flour.

Remove from the heat and add pinches of salt, pepper, and nutmeg. Add the thyme and cheeses and whisk well. Add the optional garlic.

Whisk in the whole egg and 2 yolks. Place over medium-high heat and cook, whisking, 2 minutes, just to cook the eggs.

Put the mixture into a large mixing bowl and refrigerate until room temperature. When cooled, beat in the additional egg yolk.

Preheat the oven to 400°F. Butter and flour 4 individual (1-cup) soufflé molds.

In the bowl of an electric mixer or using a hand mixer, beat the egg whites until very stiff. Fold the beaten whites into the cooled egg-yolk mixture and pour into the prepared molds. Run a moistened finger around the inner rim of each mold, to the depth of about ¼-inch, making a space between the mixture and the mold. Bake until risen, firm, and golden, and still a bit creamy in the center, 15 to 20 minutes. Serve immediately.

MAKES 4 SOUFFLÉS, SERVING 4

Celery and Anchovy Canapés

Branche de Céleris, Sauce "Anchoïade"

At home we loved to spend warm Sunday afternoons sitting in the shade, the children drinking cool lemonade and the adults sipping pastis, and all of us nibbling on crisp celery dipped into tangy, smooth anchovy sauce. The anchovy sauce also is delicious spread on crunchy slices of warm toast.

> 4 stalks celery, leaves trimmed and strings removed, cut in half lengthwise
> and then into thick julienne sticks
> 2 tablespoons extra virgin olive oil
> 12 oil-packed anchovy fillets
> 1 large clove garlic, smashed and peeled
> ½ teaspoon minced fresh thyme

Arrange the celery standing up in a bowl of cracked ice.

In a small saucepan over medium-high heat, combine the oil, anchovies, and garlic and cook, stirring with a wooden spatula, until the anchovies have melted and the sauce is smooth. Do not allow to boil. Remove from the heat and mix until creamy (there will be a few small lumps). Pour into a serving bowl and mix in the thyme. Serve warm as a dip for the cold celery sticks.

MAKES 4 SERVINGS

Celery Root in Mustard Mayonnaise

Céleri-rave Rémoulade

Make sure you peel the roots carefully with a very sharp knife. It will be easier to slice them thin on the mandoline if you first cut them in half crosswise. This appetizer is best served cold.

2 medium-size celery roots, peeled and cut in half crosswise
3 medium-size lemons, cut in half
3 tablespoons Dijon mustard
Generous pinch freshly ground black pepper
Pinch salt
3 generous tablespoons mayonnaise

Thinly slice the halves of celery root on a mandoline, then cut them into ⅛-inch-wide julienne. Place the julienne strips in a nonreactive bowl and immediately squeeze the juice of 1 of the lemons over them.

In a small bowl, combine the mustard, the juice of the remaining lemons, the pepper, salt, and mayonnaise, mixing with a spoon or fork to make a soft, mayonnaiselike dressing. Pour the dressing over the celery root and mix well. Refrigerate until cold before serving.

MAKES 4 SERVINGS

Tartare of Cooked Potatoes

Tartare de Pommes de Terre

This all-vegetable tartare fools the eye and makes an interesting first course. I add 3 cloves of garlic, but you may use less if you prefer. The problem is, with less garlic, the taste will change and you will miss out on the secret of Provençal cooking.

12 medium-size red potatoes
1 tablespoon sea salt
3 large cloves garlic, smashed and minced
Salt and freshly ground black pepper to taste
2 tablespoons minced fresh parsley
1 teaspoon minced fresh basil
2 tablespoons minced scallions, white and tender green parts
1 shallot, minced
2 tablespoons extra virgin olive oil
3 or 4 oil-packed anchovy fillets
2 tablespoons brine-packed capers, drained and minced
Pinch curry powder
Pinch ground cumin
Pinch freshly grated nutmeg
2 teaspoons mayonnaise for garnish
Lettuce leaves for garnish

Place the potatoes, water to cover, and the sea salt in a large saucepan over medium-high heat and bring to a boil. Cook at a steady boil until tender, 30 to 40 minutes, then drain and peel.

In a large mixing bowl, combine the potatoes and garlic and mash coarsely with a fork. Season lightly with salt and generously with pepper. Add the remaining ingredients, except the garnishes, a few at a time and continue mashing until all the ingredients are combined. The mixture should be slightly chunky, like a beef or fish tartare.

To serve, place a 3-inch bottomless ring mold on a plate and fill with one quarter of the mixture. Remove, leaving the mixture in a round shape (or simply mound the mixture on the plate) and garnish the top with ½ teaspoon mayonnaise. Surround with lettuce leaves.

MAKES 4 SERVINGS

Smashed Potatoes

Brandade du Pommes de Terre

Brandade, which means "smashed," usually is a mixture of salt cod, cream, and milk. This delicious version, with its irresistible garlic aroma, is made instead with potatoes, garlic, herbs, and olive oil—no salt cod and no cream! The potatoes must be mashed with a fork to achieve the rough texture of a true brandade. Serve this as an appetizer, along with glasses of white or rosé wine.

For the brandade

12 small red potatoes, peeled and quartered
1 teaspoon sea salt
6 cloves garlic, smashed and minced
3 generous tablespoons minced fresh parsley
Generous pinch freshly ground black pepper
Pinch freshly grated nutmeg
1 tablespoon extra virgin olive oil

For the garnish

3 small red potatoes, peeled and cut into ¼-inch dice
Pinch sea salt
1 teaspoon extra virgin olive oil
2 tablespoons corn or peanut oil
2 slices or ends of a day-old loaf of country bread, cut into ½-inch dice

To prepare the brandade, in a large saucepan over medium-high heat, bring the potatoes, water to cover, and the sea salt to a boil and cook at a steady boil until tender, 20 to 30 minutes.

Drain the potatoes well, reserving about ½ cup of the cooking water, and place them in a large bowl. Add the garlic, parsley, pepper, nutmeg, and olive oil and mash with a fork until somewhat chunky, not pureed. Add the cooking water as needed, if the mixture is too thick. Season to taste with salt and pepper.

To prepare the garnish, in a small saucepan over medium-high heat, bring to a boil the diced potatoes with water to cover, the sea salt, and olive oil and cook at a steady boil until tender, about 5 minutes. Drain well and reserve.

Meanwhile, in a small frying pan over medium-high heat, heat the corn oil until it sizzles when a square of bread is immersed in it. Sauté the bread squares just until they brown, about 30 seconds, then drain well and set aside.

To serve, mound the brandade in a serving bowl and sprinkle the diced potatoes and croutons over it.

MAKES 4 SERVINGS

Spicy Sweet Potato Pie

Tarte de Pommes de Terre Douce

Herb-rich, spicy, earthy sweet potatoes go into a simple pie that makes a perfect appetizer or a fine light lunch. People are amazed at the range of flavors they find in a vegetarian dish like this one, but vegetables and herbs are our specialty in Provence.

Frozen puff pastry, available at supermarkets, makes preparation quick.

3 medium-size sweet potatoes, peeled, quartered lengthwise, and sliced 1 inch thick
1 tablespoon sea salt
1 tablespoon unsalted butter
1 large egg

Pinch salt
Pinch freshly ground black pepper
2 tablespoons minced scallions, white and tender green parts
2 tablespoons minced fresh parsley
1 teaspoon minced fresh thyme or rosemary
1 teaspoon minced fresh dill
Pinch freshly grated nutmeg
2 allspice berries, smashed
1 generous tablespoon sour cream
2 sheets frozen puff pastry, thawed
Egg wash made with 1 large egg yolk lightly beaten with 1 teaspoon water

In a large pot over medium-high heat, combine the potatoes, sea salt, and butter with water to cover and bring to a boil. Boil steadily until the potatoes are tender, about 45 minutes. Drain.

Place the potatoes in a food processor along with the salt, pepper, egg, scallions, parsley, thyme, dill, nutmeg, allspice berries, and sour cream and process to a thick puree.

Preheat the oven to 400°F. Fit 1 sheet of the puff pastry into an 8- or 9-inch tart tin with a removable bottom, prick the bottom all over with a fork, and crimp the edges. Spoon the sweet potato puree into the pastry crust. Roll out the second sheet of puff pastry to half its original thickness and cut it to the same diameter as the tart. Place the crust loosely over the puree and brush with the egg wash. If desired, cut the pastry scraps into ¼-inch-wide strips and form a decorative lattice pattern over the top crust and brush again with egg wash. Bake until firm and golden brown, 30 to 40 minutes.

MAKES 4 TO 6 SERVINGS

Spicy Sweet Potato Chips

Chips de Pomme de Terre Douce

These crisp, brown chips are marinated in spices before being fried in hot oil, so they don't need any seasoning afterward. Once you make your own potato chips, you will never again want those from the store.

2 medium-size sweet potatoes, peeled and very thinly sliced on a
    mandoline
Pinch salt
Pinch freshly ground black pepper
Pinch ground cumin
¼ teaspoon curry powder
4 cups corn or peanut oil

Place the sweet potato slices in a large bowl and sprinkle with the salt, pepper, cumin, and curry. Mix well and allow the potatoes to sit while the oil is heating.

In a large saucepan over medium-high heat, heat the oil to 375°F, or until a bit of potato sizzles when immersed in it. Add the potato slices to the oil a few at a time, keeping them separate. Fry, turning them, until brown and crisp. Using a skimmer, remove them from the oil and drain on paper towels. Repeat until all the potato chips are cooked and serve immediately.

MAKES 2 CUPS CHIPS

Antoine's Provençal Olive Tart

Paissaladiere a Ma Façon

¼ cup extra virgin olive oil
3 large red onions, halved and thinly sliced
8 cloves garlic, thinly sliced
Pinch sugar
2 large tomatoes, halved, juice and seeds squeezed out, and roughly chopped
1 tablespoon minced fresh thyme or rosemary
2 tablespoons coarsely chopped fresh parsley
3 tablespoons thinly sliced scallions, white and tender green parts
1 cup black olives marinated in olive oil and herbs (from Provence,
    Greece, or Italy), pitted but not cut up
1 tablespoon chopped oil-packed anchovy fillets
1 teaspoon brine-packed capers, drained
½ teaspoon grated lemon zest
Salt and freshly ground black pepper to taste
One 9- to 10-inch tart shell, baked until brown and crisp (use ½ recipe
    pâte brisée, page 345, or frozen puff pastry, thawed)
Minced fresh parsley for garnish

In a large skillet over medium-high heat, heat 2 tablespoons of the oil until very hot but not smoking. Add the onions and sauté until softened and colored, about 5 minutes. As they cook, separate them into rings with a spoon or fork. When they are almost done, add the remaining oil and mix well. Add the garlic and sugar and cook until the garlic is soft, about 2 minutes.

Add the tomatoes, thyme, parsley, and scallions and mix well. Add the olives, anchovies, capers, lemon zest, a little salt, and a generous amount of pepper. Mix well and cook 3 minutes.

Pile the vegetable mixture into the prepared crust and sprinkle with the minced parsley. Serve warm.

MAKES 6 APPETIZER OR 4 MAIN-COURSE SERVINGS

Smoked Salmon Tart

Tarte au Saumon Fumé

This dramatic appetizer is perfectly simple to prepare and it makes a sensational beginning for any meal. The prepared puff pastry sold in your supermarket freezer works beautifully as a base, just be sure to dry it thoroughly, so it will be crisp and grease-free. To do this, after you bake the rounds, halve them and then rebake the thin rounds.

You don't have to use the most expensive smoked salmon, because any rough edges to its flavor will be mellowed by the flavorful caramelized leeks.

I discovered smoked salmon when I began my apprenticeship at Riboto de Taven—we never had it on the farm.

Four 5-inch circles puff pastry, cut from prepared puff pastry that has been thawed and rolled ⅛ inch thick (use a demitasse saucer as a pattern)
2 tablespoons corn or peanut oil
4 large leeks, white and a little of the tender green part, well washed and very thinly sliced
Salt and freshly ground black pepper to taste
1 teaspoon sugar
1 tablespoon minced fresh thyme
1 clove garlic, smashed almost to a paste
1 tablespoon minced shallots
8 very thin slices smoked salmon
1 teaspoon chopped fresh basil
8 to 12 drops extra virgin olive oil
Mixed greens or mesclun, lightly dressed with vinaigrette, for garnish

Preheat the oven to 400°F. Place the puff pastry circles on a greased baking sheet and bake 25 minutes. Remove them from the oven and set aside until cool enough to handle, then cut each in half horizontally into two very thin circles. Return these pastry circles to the oven and bake until crisp, 10 to 15 minutes.

In a large skillet over medium-high heat, heat the oil until it is very hot but not smoking. Add the leeks, season lightly with salt and generously with pepper, and sauté 5 minutes. Add the sugar, thyme, garlic, and shallots, toss to mix, and sauté until caramelized, another 10 minutes.

Preheat the broiler. Heap the caramelized leeks generously on the pastry circles and arrange 2 slices of smoked salmon lightly over the leeks on each pastry circle, ruffling the salmon decoratively. Sprinkle generously with pepper and top each with ¼ teaspoon of the chopped basil and 2 to 3 drops of the olive oil. Place under the broiler for just a few seconds, until the salmon is slightly warmed but still remains pink in the center. Be careful that the salmon does not cook. To serve, arrange the greens lightly on each of four plates and place 2 puff pastry circles on top.

MAKES 4 SERVINGS

CHAPTER 3

Soups and Sauces

❧⸱❧

My mother's life, in many ways, has been typical of life in Provence in this century. When she was born, my grandparents owned the restaurant and grocery store that I described in the Introduction. Out in front, the men played petanque (a kind of bowling on the grass) and in back there was a ballroom for dancing and parties. The men from the countryside dropped in to read or play cards, women came to shop for groceries, and families gathered for dinner. Everyone came for enjoyment, and grandmother cooked her famous country dishes. This kind of thing still exists in some small villages, although it is rare today.

They left the café and moved to Mas Antoine when my mother was three years old and she had a happy childhood until the war. During the war years, there was very little food available, but because they lived on a farm, she never went hungry. My grandparents were luckier than the city people, who would come from Saint-Rémy and neighboring villages to exchange their ration coupons for dry beans or bread. But even in the country, it was hard to get sugar, oil, and flour, and when they were available, the quality was bad. Everything was rationed and everything went on the black market, even olive oil. There was no fertilizer, so crops suffered, and people couldn't raise their own pigs or chickens, because they had nothing to feed them.

Sometimes a shepherd would butcher a sheep or goat and sell meat to the neighbors at a reasonable price, or a farmer would clandestinely kill a cow and sell the meat on the black market. Meat was like a piece of gold. But after a while people became organized and little by little they learned how to feed themselves with what was available.

I think some of my mother's appreciation for good food comes from those times of hardship. She always set a bountiful table for her family. Lunch in her kitchen was a big meal, with a generous stew of carrots and eggplant, or ripe green beans, tomatoes, or zucchini from the farm. She served fish, eggs, bread, and cheese, as well. Dinner always began with a hearty soup, usually of fresh vegetables. My father liked soup, so she made a big pot every night, summer and winter. Then came plate after plate of vegetables, a salad, and all the leftovers from lunch.

Every Friday, when we ate fish, my mother made wonderful fish soups—she always put in a lot of salt and pepper and a lot of fish. In the south of France you can buy a packet of mixed fresh fish for soup, just as you can buy a little tube of saffron that is just enough for one pot of soup.

We didn't bake our own bread, but we got beautiful loaves, hot and fragrant from the oven, from either of two neighbors, Madame Novarra or Adelle. Madame Novarra had a little grocery store and bakery in one room of her home, and I would go there on my bike to get whatever my mother needed, as well as one of her crisp baguettes. When I entered, I passed through a hallway with the big bread mixer and an oven, manned by a baker she had hired from Italy. My father didn't like this bread—he said the crust was so hard it was like the skin of a donkey—but I liked it and my mother did, too. The grocery smelled deliciously of good things and I wanted to be around people making bread, so I always prolonged a very short errand. Sometimes I biked over to Adelle's bakery instead. She was a very old lady, dressed in traditional Provençal style, with a long black skirt, white apron, and lace cap. She lived on a big farm, where she operated a bakery just like Madame Novarra's, with a large mixer and oven right out in front. The bread smell was so good, I would stay and talk, answering all of Adelle's questions: "How are you? How is your sister? How is your mother? How is your father?" Things are much more relaxed in Provence, and it could take half an hour to buy a loaf of bread.

But back to the soup! I have been inspired by my mother's soups because, to me, they are the essence of farm cooking. When my mother stirred a steaming kettle, she was motivated by three things. One, she had a big family and not a lot of money, so she was trying to cook within a budget. Two, she lived in an area where it was natural to use the vegetables and the herbs that grew right outside her kitchen and the fresh fish from local waters. And three, she liked to cook simply. When she added these motivations to her natural creativity and her love of Provençal tradition, the results were fantastic. Her soups were so simple, very light, delicious, and low in fat. She flavored them with sweet garlic and onions, both unpeeled, a little virgin olive oil, fresh herbs, and sea salt. Often they were thickened with pasta.

Now, all around me, I see that people are enjoying and appreciating such natural soups again. Soup fell out of favor for a while (which I couldn't understand) but today it has regained its old popularity. It is a good appetizer that awakens your taste buds, as well as a nourishing light meal. If you are on a diet, it is the best thing you can have, especially if you cook it Provençal style, with no butter and plenty of vegetables. You won't gain weight eating soup, but you will feel satisfied.

In Provençal cooking, we prefer natural juices to classic stocks, but stocks have their place and often will make a dish more elegant. I use stock to deglaze a roasting pan or skillet: when the meat is done, remove it, pour a little stock into the pan, and stir over heat to loosen all the delicious particles stuck to the bottom.

Like my mother's creations, each of the country soups I include here consists of a colorful combination of vegetables and herbs that are thrown into a large pot, where they boil merrily on your stove for about an hour. Allow them to cook at a medium boil over medium heat; if the heat is too high, the vegetables will not be tender and the soup will evaporate too much. You can make most of the soups in this chapter with broth or stock (I give you several recipes) or water. And there are some good canned chicken broths available that may be substituted for your own, if necessary. When pureed, the vegetable soups make excellent low-fat sauces for grilled fish or chicken.

Veal Stock

Fond de Veau

Use this stock in Beef Shoulder with Carrots (page 239), Steak with Quick Green Peppercorn Sauce (page 245), and Rabbit Braised in Mustard (page 255).

2 tablespoons corn or peanut oil
3 to 4 pounds meaty veal bones from the leg and rib, split
1 large onion, roughly chopped
1 large carrot, roughly chopped
1 tablespoon tomato paste
1½ tablespoons all-purpose flour
1 cup dry white wine
Bouquet garni of 2 or 3 stalks each fresh basil and parsley and 1 scallion,
    tied together with kitchen string

Preheat the oven to 450°F. In a flameproof baking pan over medium-high heat, heat the oil until it is very hot but not smoking and cook the bones and vegetables until brown, turning with tongs, 5 to 10 minutes. Place the pan in the oven for 20 minutes. Add the tomato paste and flour and stir well with a wooden spoon. Return the pan to the oven and cook another 10 minutes.

Place the bones and vegetables in a large pot. Skim the fat from the juices in the pan, then place the pan over medium-high heat and deglaze with the wine, scraping to get up any browned deposits from the pan. Pour the wine into the pot and add the bouquet garni and water to cover.

Over medium-high heat, bring the contents of the pot to a boil and skim off the scum. Reduce the heat to medium-low and simmer 1 to 1½ hours. Strain it into a bowl and allow to cool at room temperature. The stock may be refrigerated up to 2 weeks (remove the fat that hardens on top) or frozen for up to 1 month.

MAKES ABOUT 4 CUPS

Lamb Stock

Fond d'Agneau

We use this stock a lot in Provençal cooking and you can substitute it for veal stock in many meat recipes.

2 tablespoons corn or peanut oil
2 pounds meaty lamb bones, separated
1 large onion, roughly chopped
1 large carrot, roughly chopped
4 cloves garlic, unpeeled
2 tablespoons all-purpose flour
1 tablespoon tomato paste
1 cup dry white wine
6 cups water
Bouquet garni made of 2 or 3 stalks each fresh basil and parsley and 1
    leek, tied together with kitchen string

In a large pot over medium-high heat, heat the oil until very hot but not smoking and sauté the lamb bones, onion, carrot, and garlic until brown, 5 to 8 minutes. Add the flour and tomato paste and mix until the ingredients hold together in clumps.

Add the wine, water, and bouquet garni. Mix well, scraping the bottom of the pot, and bring to a boil. Reduce the heat to medium-low and cook, skimming off any scum that comes to the surface, about 1 hour. Strain it into a bowl and allow to cool to room temperature. The stock may be refrigerated up to 1 week (remove the fat that hardens on top) or frozen up to 1 month.

MAKES ABOUT 4 CUPS

Chicken Broth

Fond de Volaille

You can build a lot of recipes around this little stock, as we do in Provence. It is always useful to have in your refrigerator (it keeps for up to 1 week) or freezer (for up to 1 month).

10 whole cloves
1 medium-size onion, halved
1 teaspoon corn or peanut oil
One 3½-pound chicken
Salt and freshly ground black pepper to taste
1 medium-size carrot, roughly chopped
1 medium-size turnip, peeled and roughly chopped
Bouquet garni of 3 stalks fresh parsley, basil, thyme, or rosemary or any
    combination, 1 scraped carrot, and 1 cleaned leek (the white and
    tender green part), tied together with kitchen string
1½ teaspoons sea salt
1 stalk celery, roughly chopped

Stick the cloves into the onion halves on the uncut sides. In a small pan over medium-high heat, heat the oil until very hot but not smoking, then quickly brown the cut sides of the onion.

Put the onion in a large pot with all the other ingredients and cover with water. Bring to a boil over high heat, reduce the heat to medium, and cook 45 minutes, skimming any scum that appears on the surface. At this point you can remove the breast meat and reserve it for other uses. Continue cooking the remaining chicken and broth for 15 minutes.

Strain the broth into a bowl. If you are serving it immediately, lightly run a paper towel over the top to absorb the fat. Or cool to room temperature, skim the fat from the top, and refrigerate or freeze.

MAKES ABOUT 4 CUPS

Brown Chicken Stock

Fond de Volaille Brun

This stock adds its deep flavor to chicken and game recipes.

3 tablespoons corn or peanut oil
1 large leek, white and tender green parts, well washed and roughly
     chopped
2 large onions, roughly chopped
1 large carrot, roughly chopped
2 chicken carcasses, roughly chopped
2 tablespoons all-purpose flour
1 tablespoon tomato paste
2 cups dry red or white wine
8 cups water
Bouquet garni of 2 or 3 sprigs each fresh basil and parsley and 1 scallion,
     tied together with kitchen string

In a large pot over medium-high heat, heat the oil until very hot but not smoking, then add the leek, onions, and carrot and sauté until browned, 5 to 10 minutes. Add the chicken carcasses and sauté until browned, another 5 to 10 minutes.

Add the flour and stir well with a wooden spoon. Add the tomato paste and stir. Add the wine, water, and bouquet garni. Stir, scraping the bottom of the pot to release any crust that has formed. Bring to a boil and skim the surface of any scum. Reduce the heat to medium-low and cook for 1 to 1½ hours.

Strain the stock into a bowl and allow to cool to room temperature. Skim the fat from the top or absorb it with paper towels and refrigerate for up to 1 week, or freeze for up to 1 month.

MAKES 4 TO 5 CUPS

Country Chicken Soup

Soupe de Poulet Campagnarde

In the winter, when it is very cold, it's a pleasure to have steaming chicken soup. And if you make it in the summer, you can eat cold chicken with mayonnaise and keep the broth to use in another recipe. Winter or summer, use both the broth and the chicken for Chicken with Sauce Poulette (page 287), a typical farm dish.

On the farm, we presented each portion of this soup beautifully, by heaping all the vegetables in a bowl and pouring the soup over them.

One 2½- to 3-pound chicken
1 medium-size white turnip, peeled and quartered
½ large onion or 1 small onion, cut in half and sliced lengthwise (for a
    deeper flavor, sauté the onion in 1 tablespoon oil over medium-high
    heat until brown)
1 stalk celery, cut in half crosswise
2 plum tomatoes, cut in half
1 large carrot, cut in half lengthwise and then into 2-inch crosswise
    sections
3 cloves garlic, smashed and peeled
1 leek, white and tender green parts, well washed and quartered lengthwise
1 teaspoon sea salt
2 whole cloves
3 allspice berries, crushed
1 bay leaf
2 chicken bouillon cubes (optional)
1 tablespoon extra virgin olive oil
Fresh thyme leaves for garnish

In a large saucepan over high heat, combine all the ingredients, except the garnish, with water to cover, cover, and bring to a boil. Uncover and reduce the heat to medium. Cook 1 hour from the time boiling begins.

Remove the vegetables and cut into bite-size pieces. Reserve the chicken for other uses. Skim the fat off the broth or lightly run paper towels over the surface of the broth to absorb the fat.

To serve, arrange a selection of vegetables in each bowl, pour the soup over, and sprinkle the thyme on top.

MAKES 4 TO 6 SERVINGS

Vegetable Stock

Fond de Légumes

Here is a good base for the many times you don't want to use a chicken broth or fish stock.

2 tablespoons corn or peanut oil
1 medium-size onion, roughly chopped
1 stalk celery, roughly chopped
1 medium-size carrot, roughly chopped
1 medium-size tomato, roughly chopped
½ medium-size zucchini, roughly chopped
4 lettuce leaves
2 cloves garlic, peeled
Bouquet garni of 3 sprigs fresh parsley, basil, thyme, or rosemary or any combination, 1 scraped carrot, and 1 cleaned leek, tied together with kitchen string
2 whole cloves
1 teaspoon black peppercorns
10 cups water

In a large saucepan over medium-high heat, heat the oil until very hot but not smoking, then add the onion and sauté until softened but not colored, about 4 minutes. Add the remaining ingredients, except the water, and cook 5 minutes. Add the water, bring to a boil, and reduce the heat to medium-low. Cook 30 minutes, then strain into a bowl. Cool the broth to room temperature and refrigerate up to 1 week, or freeze up to 1 month. The vegetables may be served as is or pureed in a food processor.

MAKES 5 TO 6 CUPS

Provençal Vegetable Soup

Soupe au Pistou

In the Provençal language, *pistou* means basil, and in general usage it has come to mean this soup as well. My grandmother made a wonderful pistou with summer vegetables from the farm, generously flavored with garlic. This recipe approximates hers.

2 tablespoons corn or peanut oil

1 large onion, roughly chopped

2 large carrots, cut into ½-inch dice

2 medium-size turnips, peeled and cut into ½-inch dice

8 cups water

4 cups homemade (page 82) or canned low-salt chicken broth

1 medium-size zucchini, cut into ½-inch dice

1 cup green beans, cut into ½-inch dice

2 large leeks, white and tender green parts, well washed and cut into ½-inch dice

4 medium-size potatoes, peeled and cut into ½-inch dice

1 cup canned flageolets, undrained (tiny kidney beans; these are available at specialty food stores or you may substitute cooked small lima beans)

1 cup broken pieces thin spaghetti

Salt and freshly ground black pepper to taste

3 large tomatoes, juice and seeds gently squeezed out and cut into ½-inch dice

6 cloves garlic, minced
2 tablespoons extra virgin olive oil
¼ cup minced fresh parsley
¼ cup shredded fresh basil

In a large pot over medium-high heat, heat the corn oil until very hot but not smoking, then add the onion and sauté until golden, about 5 minutes. Add the carrots and turnips and sauté 2 minutes. Add the water and broth and bring to a boil. Reduce the heat to medium and cook 10 minutes. Add the zucchini, green beans, leeks, and potatoes and simmer 30 minutes.

Add the flageolets and spaghetti and cook 15 minutes. Season with the salt and pepper.

In a small bowl, combine the tomatoes, garlic, olive oil, parsley, and basil and set aside. Just before serving the soup, add the tomato mixture and cook just until heated through. Serve the soup hot or at room temperature.

MAKES 6 TO 8 SERVINGS

NOTE: You can prepare the soup up to the point of adding the tomatoes and refrigerate up to 3 days. It will thicken in the refrigerator, so add a little water or broth as needed.

White Bean Soup

Soupe de Haricots Blancs

This delicate, creamy soup contains absolutely no cream or butter. Its rich flavor and texture come from vegetables and herbs. The soup should cook at an even boil—simmering won't do the job.

2 tablespoons corn or peanut oil
1 large onion, halved and thinly sliced
2 large potatoes, peeled and sliced ½ inch thick
4 cups cooked navy beans (drained canned or ½ pound dried navy beans, soaked overnight and cooked according to package instructions with 1 carrot, 1 onion, and 1 stalk celery, all quartered, added to the water)
2 cups reserved cooking water from the beans or plain water if using canned beans
4 cups homemade (page 82) or canned low-salt chicken broth
2 to 3 sprigs fresh thyme
2 or 3 leaves fresh sage
1 sprig fresh parsley
3 cloves garlic, smashed and peeled
2 to 4 drops Tabasco sauce (optional)
Salt to taste
1 cup regular or low-fat milk
Freshly grated nutmeg for garnish
Minced fresh parsley for garnish

In a large saucepan over medium-high heat, heat the oil until very hot but not smoking, then add the onion and sauté until lightly colored, about 5 minutes (don't let it brown, or it will color the soup, which should be white). Add the potatoes and stir well. Add the beans and stir well. Add the reserved cooking water and the broth. Add the thyme, sage, parsley, garlic, and Tabasco and season lightly with salt. Bring to a boil, then reduce the heat to medium and cook 30 to 45 minutes, uncovered, keeping the soup at a steady boil.

Add the milk and puree the soup using a hand-held blender. If you must use a stationary processor or blender, be very careful not to overprocess, which will give the soup a gluey texture. Pass the soup through a fine sieve to remove any bean skins and add a little water, if it is too thick. Return to medium-high heat to bring to serving temperature, and correct the seasoning. Garnish each serving with a soupçon of ground nutmeg and a little minced parsley.

MAKES 4 TO 6 SERVINGS

Lentil Soup

Soupe de Lentilles

When my mother made lentil soup, she strained out the lentils and served them as a separate course following the broth. I prefer to incorporate them, as in this recipe.

2 tablespoons corn or peanut oil
1 large onion, thinly sliced
4 cloves garlic, smashed and peeled
½ pound dried lentils, picked over and rinsed
2 large potatoes, peeled, quartered lengthwise, and cut into 1-inch slices
1 plum tomato, quartered
1 bay leaf
8 to 10 cups homemade (page 82) or canned low-salt chicken broth
Salt and freshly ground black pepper to taste

In a large pot over medium-high heat, heat the oil until very hot but not smoking, then add the onion and sauté until golden, about 5 minutes. Add the garlic and sauté 2 minutes. Add the remaining ingredients, bring to a boil, then reduce the heat to medium and cook at a medium boil until the lentils are tender, 40 minutes to 1 hour.

Using a hand-held blender, puree the soup and serve. If you use a stationary processor or blender, be very careful not to overprocess; the result will be a gluey texture.

MAKES 6 TO 8 SERVINGS

Tomato Soup

Soupe de Tomates Fraîches

This is a Provençal tomato soup, full of ripe vegetables and flavored strongly with fresh herbs and garlic. It can be served leaving the vegetables in chunks, for a glorious rustic look, or it can be pureed, for a more subtle presentation. Pureed, it also can be served cold in the summer. I include two kinds of tomatoes, because each has a slightly different taste and texture.

2 tablespoons corn or peanut oil
1 large onion, thinly sliced
6 to 8 cloves garlic, smashed and peeled
3 large ripe tomatoes, each cut into 8 wedges
4 plum tomatoes, quartered
½ large red or green bell pepper, seeded and cut into 1-inch dice
1 stalk celery, leaves removed and cut into 2-inch slices
2 large potatoes, peeled and cut into 1-inch dice
1 large leek, white and most of the green part, well washed and cut into 2-inch slices
3 scallions, white and tender green part, cut in halves or thirds crosswise
1 bay leaf
½ teaspoon minced fresh or dried thyme
4 sprigs fresh parsley, roughly chopped

1 to 2 sprigs fresh sage (about 12 leaves)
3 whole cloves
¼ teaspoon freshly grated nutmeg
½ teaspoon ground cumin
5 cups tomato juice
4 cups homemade (page 82) or canned low-salt chicken broth
Salt and freshly ground black pepper to taste

In a large pot over medium-high heat, heat the oil until very hot but not smoking, then add the onion and sauté until golden, about 5 minutes. Add the garlic and sauté 2 minutes. Add all the vegetables, herbs, and seasonings and mix well. Pour in the tomato juice and broth and bring to a boil. Reduce the heat to medium and cook at a medium boil until the vegetables are tender, 40 minutes to 1 hour.

Puree the soup with a hand-held blender and pass through a fine sieve if desired. If you use a stationary processor or blender, be very careful not to overprocess; the result will be a gluey texture. Or serve without pureeing, serving some broth and vegetables in each bowl.

MAKES 8 SERVINGS

Eggplant Soup

Soupe d'Aubergine

This soup doesn't need any thickeners because the eggplant gives it body. The finished soup has a sweet, vegetable flavor and, of course, lively garlic accents.

2 tablespoons corn or peanut oil
1 large onion, thinly sliced
8 cloves garlic, smashed and peeled
1 large or 2 small eggplant, about 2 pounds, peeled, quartered lengthwise, and cut into 2-inch dice
1 plum tomato, quartered
1 leek, white and most of the green part, well washed and cut into 1-inch slices
1 tablespoon thinly sliced scallion (white and tender green parts)
Leaves from 2 stalks celery
2 sprigs fresh parsley
2 bay leaves
Grated zest of ½ lemon
Juice of 1 lemon
1 teaspoon sugar
Salt and freshly ground black pepper to taste
4 cups water
4 cups homemade (page 82) or canned low-salt chicken broth
Generous pinch ground saffron

In a large saucepan over medium-high heat, heat the oil until very hot but not smoking, then add the onion and sauté until colored, about 5 minutes. Add the garlic and sauté 2 minutes. Add all the vegetables, herbs, lemon zest and juice, sugar, salt, and pepper and mix well. Pour in the water and broth and bring to a boil. Reduce the heat to medium and cook at a medium boil until the vegetables are tender, 40 minutes to 1 hour. Five minutes before the soup is finished, add the saffron and mix well.

Puree the soup with a hand-held blender and pass through a fine sieve if desired. If you use a stationary processor or blender, be very careful not to overprocess; the result will be a gluey texture.

Makes 8 servings

Velouté of Fresh Bell Peppers

Velouté de Poivrons

Wherever people eat a lot of garlic, there is happiness, life, and health—perhaps it is magic. Put twelve cloves of garlic in this soup, and even if it doesn't increase your lifespan, it will make you happy. The velouté has an intense fresh-vegetable flavor and is delicious hot or cold.

2 tablespoons corn or peanut oil
1 large onion, thinly sliced
12 cloves garlic, smashed and peeled
1 leek, white and tender green parts, well washed and cut into 1-inch slices
1 large tomato, cut into 8 wedges
2 large red bell peppers, seeded and cut into 2-inch dice
2 large green bell peppers, seeded and cut into 2-inch dice
2 large potatoes, peeled, quartered lengthwise, and cut into 2-inch dice
3 to 4 sprigs fresh parsley, roughly chopped
8 to 10 leaves fresh basil
2 to 3 tablespoons extra virgin olive oil
8 cups homemade (page 82) or canned low-salt chicken broth
1 bay leaf
4 allspice berries, crushed
3 whole cloves
Salt and freshly ground black pepper to taste

In a large saucepan over medium-high heat, heat the oil until very hot but not smoking, then add the onion and sauté until colored, about 5 minutes. Add the remaining ingredients and mix well. Bring to a boil, reduce the heat to medium, and cook at a medium boil until the vegetables are tender, 40 minutes to 1 hour.

Puree the soup with a hand-held blender and pass through a fine sieve. If you use a stationary processor or blender, be very careful not to overprocess; the result will be a gluey texture.

MAKES 8 SERVINGS

Fish Stock

Fumet de Poisson

Fumet de poisson is a good basic stock to use in deglazing the pan when you roast fish, and for thinning sauces.

1½ tablespoons corn or peanut oil
Bones from 2 sole or flounder, chopped into large pieces
1 medium-size onion, roughly chopped
⅓ medium-size carrot, roughly chopped
2 outer green leaves of 1 leek or 4 scallions, roughly chopped
Bouquet garni of 6 peeled shallots, 4 to 5 sprigs fresh parsley or basil, 2 bay leaves, and 1 to 2 sprigs fresh thyme or rosemary, wrapped in a square of cheesecloth and tied
2 cups dry white wine
4 cups water

In a large pot over medium-high heat, heat the oil until hot but not smoking, then add the bones, onion, carrot, and leek and sauté until the bones turn white, about 5 minutes. The onion should not brown. Add the bouquet garni, wine, and water and bring to a boil. Reduce the heat to medium and cook 5 minutes, skimming any scum that appears.

Strain through a cheesecloth-lined sieve, cool to room temperature, and refrigerate up to 1 week, or freeze for up to 1 month.

MAKES ABOUT 6 CUPS

Fish Bouillon

Bouillon de Poisson

Fish soups like the ones that follow have their genesis in Marseille, the major Mediterranean port and fishing center, where the fish are known for their wonderful flavor.

This fragrant bouillon is the base for a chunky *Cassolette du Pêcheur* (page 100), as well as for Light Fish Bouillon with Lettuce and Garlic (page 98).

3 pounds fish trimmings, including monkfish spine hacked into 5-inch sections and fish skin (your fish market will prepare the trimmings for you)
1 large onion, roughly chopped
1 large carrot, roughly chopped
1 head garlic, unpeeled, cut in half crosswise
1 stalk celery with leaves
1 plum tomato, quartered
6 sprigs fresh parsley
3 whole cloves
2 bay leaves
1 tablespoon sea salt
1 teaspoon black peppercorns
10 cups water
2 cups dry white wine
1 large live Dungeness crab

Combine all the ingredients except the crab in a large saucepan over high heat.

Bring to a boil, reduce the heat to medium-high, and boil steadily for 1 hour. Add the crab 20 minutes before the broth is done and boil with the broth. Strain the bouillon and discard the solids. Reserve the crab and 10 cups of bouillon for the *Cassolette du Pêcheur* and refrigerate the rest of the fish stock to use as needed for up to 1 week or freeze for up to 1 month.

MAKES ABOUT 4 QUARTS

Fish Soup Base

Soupe de Poisson

This fish stock is slightly heartier than the fish bouillon, with its mashed-up bones and trimmings offering the essence of the sea. It requires some muscle power to push the processed soup through a sieve and extract the last flavorful drops from the solids, but it is well worth the effort. The bouillon provides a richly flavored base for a simple fish soup, as well as for a light bouillabaisse that is every bit as magnificent as the traditional, more complicated version.

2 tablespoons corn or peanut oil
1 large onion, thinly sliced
4 pounds fish trimmings and frames, including heads, tails, and spines, from red snapper or bass
1 head garlic, unpeeled and halved crosswise
1 large carrot, halved lengthwise and cut into 1-inch slices
2 large tomatoes, cut into 8 wedges each
1 stalk celery with leaves, cut into 3-inch sections
2 leeks, white and green parts, well washed and cut into 3-inch lengths
1 zucchini, halved lengthwise and cut into 1-inch slices
6 sprigs fresh parsley
6 sprigs fresh thyme
8 leaves fresh basil
2 bay leaves

1 branch fresh fennel or 1 teaspoon fennel seeds
3 generous tablespoons tomato puree
3½ tablespoons all-purpose flour
3 cups dry white wine
6 cups homemade (page 82) or canned low-salt chicken broth
14 cups water, plus extra, if needed, to thin the soup

In a large saucepan over medium-high heat, heat the oil until very hot but not smoking, then add the onion and sauté until colored, about 5 minutes. Add the fish trimmings, stir well, and sauté 5 minutes. Add all the other vegetables and herbs, the tomato puree, and flour, stir well until everything sticks together in dry clumps, and cook another 5 minutes.

Add the liquids, raise the heat to high, and bring to a boil. Reduce the heat to medium-high and cook at a steady boil for 1 hour, skimming as needed.

Using a hand-held blender or in a food processor, process the soup to a rough puree (you will not be able to process all the bones and skins). Pass the soup through a fine sieve and discard the solids. Add a little water, if needed, to thin the soup to the desired consistency, and correct the seasonings. It will keep in the refrigerator for up to 1 week and in the freezer for up to 1 month.

MAKES 3 TO 3½ QUARTS

Light Fish Bouillon with Lettuce and Garlic

Bouillon Léger à l'Ail et Laitue

This light, natural bouillon is very nourishing and fresh tasting. It is a perfect appetizer soup and probably a perfect diet soup as well.

7 cups Fish Bouillon (page 95)
1 cup small elbow macaroni
5 cloves garlic, smashed and peeled
12 lettuce leaves, torn in half and spines discarded (outer leaves of Boston lettuce are good)
1 cup coarsely grated Swiss cheese for garnish

In a large saucepan over medium-high heat, bring the fish bouillon to a boil. Add the macaroni and cook until tender, about 8 minutes. Add the garlic and lettuce, stir, and cook 1 minute.

To serve, divide the grated cheese among four to six soup bowls and ladle the soup over it, including some lettuce and macaroni.

MAKES 4 TO 6 SERVINGS

Simple Fish Soup

Soupe de Poisson Facile

This soup could not be simpler or more delicious, with its haunting flavors of Marseille. Add the saffron at the very end, to preserve the intensity of its taste.

6 cups Fish Soup Base (page 96)
1 cup broken dry vermicelli or small elbow macaroni
1 teaspoon pastis or other anise-flavored liqueur
Generous pinch saffron threads
Freshly ground black pepper to taste

In a large saucepan over medium-high heat, bring the fish soup base to a gentle boil and cook the pasta until tender, 6 to 10 minutes, depending upon the type used.

Add the pastis, saffron, and a generous amount of pepper and serve immediately.

MAKES 4 TO 6 SERVINGS

Fisherman's Bowl

Cassolette du Pêcheur

This hearty fisherman's stew, with its magical variety of tastes and aromas, is a full meal in itself, requiring no more than a green salad afterward.

10 cups Fish Bouillon (page 95)
5 small red potatoes, sliced ½ inch thick
2 plum tomatoes, cut into thin wedges
3 tablespoons chopped shallots
2 pounds mussels, scrubbed, debearded, and well rinsed in 2 or 3 changes
    of water
Generous pinch freshly ground black pepper
1 pound monkfish fillet, well trimmed and cut on the diagonal into ¼-inch
    slices
1 large Dungeness crab, cooked (page 95) and cut into serving pieces
3 large leeks, white part only, well washed and cut ½ inch thick
2 tablespoons roughly chopped fresh parsley
2 tablespoons extra virgin olive oil
Salt and freshly ground black pepper to taste

For the garnish

3 to 4 slices day-old country bread, cut into quarters
1 clove garlic, cut in half
1 cup coarsely grated Swiss cheese
Reserved mussels in their shells

In a large soup pot over medium-high heat, bring to a boil 2 cups of the fish bouillon and add the potatoes, tomatoes, and shallots. Add the mussels and pepper. Cover and cook until the mussels have opened, 3 to 4 minutes, and discard any that do not open. Remove the mussels with a skimmer and shell them, reserving about 12 in their shells for garnish.

To the vegetables and bouillon in the pot, add the remaining 8 cups bouillon, the monkfish, crab, and leeks and continue cooking about 1 minute. Add the shelled mussels, parsley, and olive oil and stir well. Season with salt and pepper.

Rub the bread on both sides with the cut clove of garlic, divide among six soup bowls, and sprinkle with the cheese. Arrange some mussels in their shells around the bread. Ladle the soup over the bread, including vegetables, fish, and crab in each portion.

MAKES 6 SERVINGS

Marseille Fish Soup

La Bouillabaisse

The classic, original bouillabaisse is hard to do at home—even in Provence, where a large variety of Mediterranean fish is available. I will tell you a secret: in France, bouillabaisse is a very professional dish, most often enjoyed in seafood restaurants. But this fresh, briny version, based on an intense fish soup base you can prepare in your kitchen, comes amazingly close to the original.

The optional mayonnaise adds body to the soup, but add it off heat and don't let it cook. Remember, it is optional, not an obligation.

6 cups Fish Soup Base (page 96)
4 small red potatoes, sliced ¼ inch thick
2 plum tomatoes, sliced into thin wedges
12 to 16 mussels, scrubbed, debearded, and well rinsed in 2 or 3 changes
  of water
½ pound monkfish fillet, cut on an angle into 4 thin slices (or substitute
  red snapper)
4 cloves garlic, smashed and minced
Generous pinch saffron threads
1 teaspoon pastis or other anise-flavored liqueur
2 tablespoons mayonnaise (optional)
2 slices day-old country bread, cut into quarters
1 clove garlic, halved
Minced fresh parsley for garnish

In a large saucepan over medium-high heat, heat the fish soup base to a gentle boil, then add the potatoes and tomatoes and cook 8 minutes. Add the mussels, cover, and cook until opened, 3 to 4 minutes. Remove the mussels from their shells and set aside, discarding any that have not opened. Add the monkfish, minced garlic, saffron, and pastis to the soup and bring to a strong boil.

If you are adding the mayonnaise, strain the soup and whisk it in off the heat, then return the fish and vegetables to the soup. To serve, rub the bread on both sides with the cut garlic and divide among four to six soup bowls. Divide the mussels among the bowls and ladle the soup over them, along with the monkfish and vegetables. Garnish with the parsley.

Makes 4 to 6 servings

Hollandaise Sauce

Sauce Hollandaise

Although Hollandaise is not a Provençal sauce, my mother sometimes served it over eggs on Sunday mornings.

1 cup (2 sticks) unsalted butter (you can substitute margarine)
2 large egg yolks
1½ tablespoons water
½ teaspoon fresh lemon juice
Salt and freshly ground black pepper to taste

In a small, heavy saucepan over low heat, melt the butter.

In a medium-size, heavy pan over medium heat, combine the egg yolks and water and whisk continually until thickened, about 2 minutes. Add the butter slowly, whisking, until all the butter has been absorbed by the egg mixture. Pour into a bowl, discarding any unabsorbed butter on the bottom of the pan, and add the lemon juice, salt, and pepper, mixing well. The sauce will keep in the top of a double boiler over simmering water for up to 3 hours.

Makes about 1 cup

Green Sauce

Sauce Verte

These days it's probably safer to use prepared mayonnaise than it is to deal with uncooked eggs, so I include it in all the following mayonnaise-based sauces. Serve this green mayonnaise with cold meat or fish.

1 cup good-quality mayonnaise
6 fresh spinach leaves, well washed, tough stems removed, and coarsely chopped
2 teaspoons minced scallions, green part only
2 teaspoons minced fresh parsley
8 leaves fresh basil, coarsely chopped
1 clove garlic, peeled

Combine all the ingredients in a food processor and process until the vegetables are incorporated into the mayonnaise. May be refrigerated up to two days.

MAKES ABOUT 1½ CUPS

Saffron Mayonnaise

Sauce Rouille

In Provence rouille is the sauce that accompanies bouillabaisse. My version, based on mayonnaise, is easier than the traditional one, which is based on mashed potatoes.

1 cup good-quality mayonnaise
2 cloves garlic, smashed and minced
2 generous pinches crumbled saffron threads
½ teaspoon pastis or other anise-flavored liqueur

Generous pinch paprika
Salt and cayenne pepper to taste

Combine all the ingredients in a small bowl and refrigerate, covered, up to 2 days.

M<small>AKES ABOUT</small> 1½ <small>CUPS</small>

Provençal Touch Light Tomato Sauce

Sauce Tomate Légère

You don't need fresh tomatoes to create a fresh sauce—this earthy sauce looks and tastes as if its ingredients were just picked, even though it contains canned tomatoes and tomato juice. Its secret is lots of fresh herbs, along with some juicy onion. It is excellent over pasta, rice, vegetables, or any grilled fish or poultry.

1 small onion, thinly sliced
2 tablespoons extra virgin olive oil
4 cloves garlic, smashed and peeled
¼ large red bell pepper, seeded and minced (optional)
10 canned tomatoes, juice and seeds gently squeezed out and roughly
    chopped
2 cups canned tomato juice
2 tablespoons minced fresh parsley
1 teaspoon minced fresh thyme
1 teaspoon minced fresh basil
1 tablespoon minced scallions, white and tender green parts
Pinch freshly grated nutmeg
Pinch fennel seeds
Pinch ground cumin
1 bay leaf
Salt and freshly ground black pepper to taste

Combine the first four ingredients in a large pot and cook over medium-high heat 5 minutes. Reduce the heat to medium and add the remaining ingredients. Stir well and cook 15 to 20 minutes. This can be refrigerated, covered, for up to 1 week or frozen for up to 1 month.

MAKES ABOUT 4 CUPS

Uncooked Tomato Sauce

Coulis de Tomate Cru

Prepare this delicious cold sauce in the food processor (not the blender) in just a few seconds. Make it and use it right away—it doesn't keep.

    3 medium-size tomatoes, peeled, halved, juice and seeds gently squeezed
        out, and cut into wedges
    Pinch salt
    Generous pinch freshly ground black pepper
    2 tablespoons prepared tomato puree
    3 cloves garlic, peeled
    1 teaspoon chopped fresh basil
    1 cup extra virgin olive oil

Place all the ingredients except the olive oil in a food processor, turn on the motor, and add the oil in a thin stream. Process to a puree.

MAKES 2 CUPS

Fresh Tomato Fondue

Sauce Vierge

Add garden-fresh flavor to any entrée—meat, fish, or fowl—with this versatile uncooked sauce.

Juice of 1 lemon
Salt and freshly ground white pepper to taste
4 medium-size tomatoes, peeled, juice and seeds gently squeezed out, and
    finely chopped
6 fresh basil leaves, minced
1 clove garlic, smashed and minced
2 scallions, white and tender green parts, minced
¼ cup extra virgin olive oil

In a large bowl, combine the lemon juice with the salt and pepper. Add the tomatoes, basil, garlic, and scallions and whisk to combine thoroughly. Whisk in the olive oil. You can refrigerate the sauce up to 3 days but it is best served fresh.

MAKES ABOUT 2 CUPS

Orange Delight Sauce for Salmon

Sauce Légère à l'Orange

Here is another nonfat sauce for cold fish, cold seafood, salads—even your favorite pasta.

Juice of 3 medium-size oranges
1 medium-size tomato, seeded and roughly chopped into small dice (peel if desired)
2 tablespoons minced fresh parsley
1 teaspoon minced fresh rosemary
1 tablespoon seeded and minced red bell pepper
Grated zest of ¼ orange
1 small clove garlic, minced
Pinch freshly grated nutmeg
Pinch freshly ground black pepper
Salt to taste (optional)

In a small bowl, combine all the ingredients. This sauce is best served fresh.

MAKES 2 CUPS

Cold Provençal Sauce with Olive Oil

Sauce Provençale Froide à l'Huile d'Olive Vierge

Olive oil mixed with fresh lemon juice gives this sauce a beautiful golden color. Serve it with grilled or cold fish.

Juice of 1 lemon
Generous pinches salt and freshly ground black pepper
2 cloves garlic, smashed and minced
¾ cup extra virgin olive oil
2 medium-size tomatoes, halved, juice and seeds gently squeezed out, and
    roughly chopped into fine dice (peel if desired)
1 tablespoon minced fresh basil
1 tablespoon minced scallions, white and tender green parts
1 tablespoon minced fresh parsley

In a small bowl, combine the lemon juice, salt, pepper, and garlic. Add the olive oil and mix well. Add the remaining ingredients and mix well. Refrigerate, covered, for up to 3 days.

MAKES 2 CUPS

Nonfat Vinaigrette

Vinaigrette Légère

For people who prefer not to use any fat at all, this is a very good sauce for artichokes, asparagus, salads, or grilled fish.

3 tablespoons Dijon mustard
Juice of 2 medium-size lemons
2 tablespoons minced fresh parsley
Pinch freshly ground black pepper
1 teaspoon minced fresh thyme
1 clove garlic, minced (optional)

In a small bowl, combine all the ingredients. Refrigerate, covered, for up to 3 days. Thin with a few teaspoons of cold water, if necessary.

MAKES ¾ TO 1 CUP

Faire le civet d'avance et le réchauffer quand il
marinier.

Croûte aux truffes

Prenez un pain carré ou des rôties. Coupez en
des tranches minces, et faites les frire dans du
beurre très frais. Mettez dans la casserole de
la farine, puis ½ verre de vin que vous laissez bouillir
assez longtemps. Ajoutez autant d'eau et assaisonnez
de sel, poivre, feuille de laurier.
Coupez vos truffes en tranches et laissez-les cuire,
puis versez-les sur votre croûte pour les servir;
il peut que la croûte soit humectée par la sauce.

Œufs pochés Parmentière

Faire cuire au four de grosses pommes de terre.
Quand elles sont cuites, les vider sans briser l'enveloppe. Ajou-

en prenant seulement une bonne ouverture devant.
Pétrir la pulpe que vous avez retirée avec un bon
morceau de beurre frais, et assaisonner cette mixture
de sel et de poivre. Tapissez-en les parois des
pommes de terre et cassez dans chacune un œuf bien
frais. Faites cuire au four, et lorsque les œufs
sont cuits (pas trop), ajoutez dans chaque pomme de
terre une bonne cuillerée de belle crème (à défaut
de crème, on peut mettre de la béchamelle, mais c'est
moins bon). Saupoudrez de Gruyère râpé
et faites gratiner à four très vif.

Potage mousseline

Faire revenir au beurre une forte poignée
d'oseille épluchée et hachée, la mouiller avec
de l'eau, et y mettre quelques tranches de pain
grillées; laisser infuser cette panade environ
une heure. Au moment de servir, ajou-

CHAPTER 4

Vegetables

❧

Winter is short in Provence and the harvest season arrives with the warm breezes of early March. From spring through late fall, farmers from miles around converge on the small village of Saint-Étienne-du-Gres and set up their stalls in its spacious plaza. This market is especially well known for its early vegetables—*primeurs*— tender zucchini, eggplant, onions, peppers, melons, and beans. When I was a child, we harvested them every morning, packed them, still dewy, in large, open baskets without handles—*manes*—and offered them at the market in the late afternoon.

I went with my father to the market every day during harvest season, except for those times we concentrated on selling our flowers, which we did on the farm itself. We drove the ten miles from our farm to the village in his old Torpedo sedan, with the day's fruits, vegetables, and herbs on a flatbed trailer that the car pulled along. We had to leave home early each afternoon to get a good spot on the plaza. By mid-afternoon all our baskets were displayed colorfully under a spreading tree. Scores of farmers were arriving and unpacking all around us and the ground was soon covered with displays of ripe, red tomatoes, green parsley, shiny purple eggplants, *flageolets* (tiny kidney beans), green, red, and yellow beans, raspberries, strawberries, peaches, and herbs. Each farmer stood behind his collection of baskets as the prospective buyers walked about from one display to the next, and small children, myself included, played games of tag and catch around them.

There were a lot of kids like me—the fathers brought their children to the market and we enjoyed playing together. The atmosphere was very friendly, very nice. All the people spoke in a musical Provençal patois, more like singing than speech. A neighbor would ask, "Would you like some apricots?" and give them to me, and I would give him some strawberries or beans.

In one section of the plaza, loud squawking and clucking and musty barnyard smells announced that farmers were selling live chickens, ducks, and geese. In another, we breathed the sunny aroma of freshly pressed olive oil, black olives in large crocks, and strong, fresh herbs. In still another, we were surrounded by the mossy scent of small trees, bushes, and shrubs that were sold for transplanting. By the end of the day, all the smells came strongly together in an aromatic haze of warm flowers, fruits, vegetables, herbs, and creatures—the incense of the market.

This was a market for *expéditeurs*. Here, wholesalers, exporters, and producers from Paris and all over the country purchased vegetables, fruits, and other produce in large lots. People didn't come to Saint-Étienne-du-Gres to buy a kilo of beans. The buyers—very important men, in our eyes—came prepared to buy all that we had to offer. We had to be smart to get the best price for our goods. A lot of buyers would look over the crop and propose, "I will buy that for this price." Sometimes a farmer had to take a chance and say, "No," hoping for another offer. Sometimes he had to think fast and take the offer, realizing that no better bid would come up. There were days when we had six baskets of vegetables and sold only one, but most of the time we sold everything.

One afternoon during the harvest of salad greens: Grandmother Marguerite, Cousin Marie, myself, and my sister, Margo.

I enjoyed sitting beside my father and helping him, although occasionally, because I was more aggressive than he, he made me upset. My father was a nice man; he had a lot of friends. Often he seemed to me too nice, and even when I was little, it troubled me that he did not drive a harder bargain in selling his crops. But he was content, and after each market day ended, we stopped at the local café where the farmers enjoyed swapping stories and drinking pastis and the kids were treated to cool lemonade.

We usually came home from the market around seven or eight at night, and Mother would be waiting to see how the day had gone. Then she would serve us dinner, which often was soup, an omelette, a salad, and some big dishes of vegetables. There might be fried eggplant, covered with fresh tomato sauce, garlic, basil, parsley, and thyme and browned under a crust of cheese and bread crumbs; potatoes slowly cooked in chicken broth with onions, garlic, and leeks; or candied carrots with lime, sage, and parsley. Dessert was a custard—my mother made great custards—and bowls of fresh fruit and berries. It was a big meal, and usually meatless.

The three most popular vegetables on the Provençal table are eggplant, zucchini, and tomatoes—although many others are grown and enjoyed as staples of our menu. When eggplant season arrived each August, we treated the beautiful vegetables with respect bordering on veneration. Although eggplant originated in India, it has been cultivated in the south of France since the seventeenth century and in Provence it seems to have a place in almost every menu. My parents would build a big fire in our outdoor fireplace and after it had burned down to coals, put several whole eggplants among the embers, where they cooked slowly until they were very charred and soft, their caramelized fragrance perfuming the evening air. Then we peeled them, and in olivewood bowls, mashed the flesh with olivewood forks, mixing in fresh garlic, sage, and olive oil. Sitting around the fire, eating our eggplant, took on the feeling of religious ritual, our way of giving thanks for the fruits of the earth.

In Provence, zucchini may appear with eggplant or may be prepared alone— they are like cousins, very similar. The difference is the zucchini's skin becomes more tender in cooking, but the eggplant skin is tough. It's hard to believe that tomatoes, which often join the other two, once were suspected of being poisonous, because they have become absolutely basic to our cooking.

Vegetables are so central to Provençal cooking that the list of our favorites goes on and on, with leeks, fennel, celery, spinach, potatoes, broccoli, beans, lentils, endive, artichoke, carrots, peas, Swiss chard, beets—and, of course, onions and our divine garlic. For generations they have all thrived in the bright sunshine of Provence, giving their signature to our culture.

Artichokes with Herbs

Artichauts à la Barigoule

This stew combines golden onions and red tomatoes with green artichokes, basil, scallions, and parsley—many different shades of green are in the pot. Serve it as a main course, or as a side dish with grilled meat, fish, or poultry.

Whenever you use sautéed onions in a recipe, cook them until they are golden or brown, because their color gives the recipe a touch of personality.

For the artichokes

12 baby or small artichokes (you may use frozen)
1 tablespoon sea salt
½ teaspoon baking soda, optional

For the herb sauce

2 tablespoons corn or peanut oil
1 large onion, thinly sliced
6 cloves garlic, peeled and smashed
1 bay leaf
2 tablespoons minced scallions, white and tender green parts
4 plum tomatoes, cut in half lengthwise, juice gently squeezed out, and cut into ¼-inch slices
2 tablespoons minced fresh parsley
1 tablespoon minced fresh basil
Salt and freshly ground black pepper to taste
1 tablespoon all-purpose flour
2 cups homemade (page 82) or canned low-salt chicken broth
1 whole clove

To cook the artichokes, in a large saucepan over medium-high heat, combine the artichokes, salt, and baking soda with water to cover and bring to a boil. Reduce the heat to medium and cook at a steady boil until tender, about 20 minutes. Drain the artichokes, cut off the stems, coarse outer leaves, and prickly leaf tips, and cut in half lengthwise. (Or cook frozen artichokes according to package instructions.)

To prepare the herb sauce, in a large saucepan over medium-high heat, heat the oil, then sauté the onion until golden, about 5 minutes. Add the garlic and sauté 1 minute. Add the bay leaf and artichokes and stir gently (you don't want to separate the tender leaves). Add the scallions, tomatoes, parsley, basil, salt, and pepper, and cook 3 minutes. Add the flour and cook, stirring, 2 minutes. Add the chicken broth and clove, reduce the heat to low, and cook slowly, uncovered, until the sauce is thick and the artichokes are tender, 20 to 30 minutes.

MAKES 4 SERVINGS

Artichokes Baked with Cheese

Artichauts Gratinés

Three tablespoons may seem like a lot of oil, but it is used only to sear the surfaces of the artichokes, giving them a very special flavor. The onions are sautéed in the same oil. Make sure the oil is very hot, so it will not be absorbed by the vegetables.

Serve these golden-crusted artichokes as a garnish or as a main dish with a salad.

For the artichokes

12 baby or small artichokes (you may use frozen)
1 tablespoon sea salt
½ teaspoon baking soda, optional

For the gratin

3 tablespoons corn or peanut oil
1 large onion, thinly sliced
1 cup fresh bread crumbs, made from country bread
1 teaspoon minced fresh basil
3 tablespoons minced fresh parsley
1 tablespoon minced garlic
Extra virgin olive oil for drizzling

To cook the artichokes, in a large saucepan over medium-high heat, combine artichokes, salt, and optional soda with water to cover and bring to a boil. Reduce the heat to medium and cook at a steady boil until tender, about 20 minutes. Drain, cut off the stems, coarse outer leaves, and prickly leaf tips, and cut in half lengthwise. (Or cook frozen artichokes according to package instructions.)

Preheat the oven to 350°F. In a large skillet over medium-high heat, heat the corn oil until very hot, but not smoking. Place the artichoke halves in the oil cut side up and brown quickly, about 2 minutes on each side. Remove from the pan and drain on paper towels. Add the onion to the pan and sauté until colored, about 5 minutes. Drain on paper towels.

Combine the bread crumbs, basil, parsley, and garlic and set aside. On a gratin pan or ovenproof platter, arrange the artichoke halves, cut side up. Strew the onions over them, sprinkle the crumb mixture evenly on top, and drizzle with the olive oil. Bake until browned on top and heated through, about 20 minutes.

MAKES 4 SERVINGS

Cold Artichokes with Mustard Sauce

Artichaut Froid à la Sauce Moutarde

For this simple dish, simmer the artichokes until tender, then scoop out each center cleanly, leaving a container for the creamy mustard sauce. Or, if you like, fill the artichoke with your favorite tuna or shrimp salad.

4 large artichokes, stems trimmed, tough outer leaves removed, and top
    cut flat
2 tablespoons salt
⅓ teaspoon baking soda, optional
1 generous tablespoon Dijon mustard
Pinch each salt and freshly ground black pepper
Juice of 1 lemon
½ cup extra virgin olive oil

Combine the artichokes, salt, and the optional soda with water to cover in a large saucepan over medium-high heat and bring to a boil. Reduce the heat to medium and cook at a steady boil until the bases of the artichokes are soft and the bottom of an outer leaf is soft enough to eat, 45 minutes to 1 hour. Remove from the water and stand upside down to drain. Allow to cool to room temperature. Remove the choke, leaving a smooth cavity.

In a small bowl, combine the mustard, pinch of salt, the pepper, and lemon juice and stir together with a spoon or fork. Gradually add the olive oil, stirring, until the dressing resembles a soft mayonnaise.

To serve, divide the mustard sauce among the 4 artichokes, pouring it into their cavities. Serve at room temperature.

MAKES 4 SERVINGS

Bean Cake

Gâteau de Haricots

This elegant addition to your buffet table is all-vegetable, healthful, and delicious. Most important, it couldn't be simpler to make.

For the fresh tomato sauce

1 large tomato, halved, juice and seeds gently squeezed out, and finely
    chopped
½ cup extra virgin olive oil
1 tablespoon fresh lemon juice
Salt and freshly ground black pepper to taste
Grated zest of ½ lemon
½ teaspoon chopped fresh basil
1 clove garlic, smashed and minced

For the bean cake

¾ pound dried white beans, cooked according to the package instructions,
    with some water clinging to them
4 large eggs
Generous pinch freshly ground black pepper
Salt to taste (optional)
2 tablespoons chopped scallions, white and tender green parts

2 tablespoons chopped fresh parsley
1 teaspoon chopped fresh basil
4 cloves garlic, chopped
2 drops Worcestershire sauce
Generous pinch cumin seeds
⅛ teaspoon baking powder

Combine all the sauce ingredients in a small bowl and set aside.

Preheat the oven to 400°F. Lightly butter a 10-inch-round, 1-inch-high cake pan. Place all the cake ingredients in a food processor and puree. Pour into the pan and bake until firm and golden, 30 to 40 minutes. Serve accompanied by the sauce.

MAKES 6 TO 8 SERVINGS

Warm Bean Salad Marie-Thérèse

Salade de Haricots Marie-Thérèse

In the coldest part of the winter, while the mistral howled fiercely outside, we began preparing for spring planting. We children would sit around a big wooden table in my grandmother's warm living room, carefully sorting huge piles of dried beans. We removed little stones and bad beans and packed away the good beans to be used as seeds for the next year's crop. Grandmother always set aside some of the best for the family's food and my mother used them to make this warm bean salad. The beans were especially good because they were just a few months old. (Unfortunately, when you buy dried beans now, they may have been picked two years ago, or more.) Mother cooked the beans in a court bouillon rich with aromatic herbs and unpeeled onions and garlic—in the country, onion and garlic skins were used to add flavor.

The amounts of herbs and vegetables called for are flexible, since this salad was varied according to our provisions and my mother's whims.

For the beans

1 head garlic, unpeeled
1 or 2 onions, unpeeled
1 or 2 carrots, cleaned
Few sprigs fresh dill
Few sprigs fresh rosemary
Few sprigs fresh thyme
Few sprigs fresh oregano
1 or 2 whole cloves
3 or 4 allspice berries
One 2-inch square dried orange peel
3 to 4 tablespoons extra virgin olive oil
Sea salt to taste
1 tablespoon smashed black peppercorns (smashed in a mortar)
1 pound dried white beans, soaked or preboiled according to package instructions and drained

For the vinaigrette

1 teaspoon prepared mustard
1 teaspoon red wine vinegar
6 tablespoons extra virgin olive oil
Salt and freshly ground black pepper to taste

Fill a large pot three quarters full of water and add the garlic, onions, carrots, herbs, cloves, allspice, orange peel, olive oil, salt, and pepper. Bring to a boil over medium-high heat, then add the beans and cook until tender, about 45 minutes. Drain, cut the cooking vegetables into bite-size chunks, and combine the beans and vegetables in a large bowl.

In a small bowl, whisk together the mustard and vinegar, then add the oil very slowly, whisking until emulsified. Season generously with pepper and lightly with salt.

Serve the salad warm, with the vinaigrette sprinkled over individual portions.

MAKES 4 TO 6 SERVINGS

Lentil Salad with Anchovy Sauce

Salade de Lentilles Sauce Anchois

Delicious served warm for lunch or dinner, alongside Spring Zucchini (page 181). Anchovies provide all the salt the recipe needs.

For the lentils

½ pound dried lentils
½ onion, peeled
2 cloves garlic, unpeeled
½ large carrot
Pinch salt
Freshly ground black pepper to taste
3 tablespoons extra virgin olive oil
5 cloves garlic, smashed and minced
12 oil-packed anchovy fillets
2 tablespoons minced scallions, white and tender green parts
2 tablespoons minced fresh parsley
Pinch ground cumin
Pinch freshly grated nutmeg
1 teaspoon coarsely chopped fresh basil

For the croutons

2 tablespoons corn or peanut oil
2 slices white bread, crusts removed, cut into ¼-inch dice

In a large pot over medium-high heat, combine the lentils, onion, garlic, carrot, and salt with warm water to cover generously. Bring to a boil and cook at a steady boil until the lentils are tender, about 30 minutes. Add a little cold water to stop the cooking, then drain and cut the onion and carrot into 2-inch slices. Season generously with pepper and set aside.

In a small saucepan over low heat, mix the olive oil, minced garlic, and anchovies and season generously with pepper. Allow the mixture to warm slowly, then mix it well with a fork until the anchovies have melted into the oil. Keep over very low heat.

In a large bowl, combine the lentils and their cooking vegetables with the scallions and parsley. Add the anchovy mixture and mix well. Stir in the cumin, nutmeg, and basil.

To prepare the croutons, in a small skillet over medium-high heat, heat the oil until it sizzles when a piece of bread is immersed in it. Fry the bread until brown on all sides, about 30 seconds, and drain well in a strainer.

Serve the lentil salad in a soup bowl, garnished with the croutons.

MAKES 4 SERVINGS

White Bean Stew Farm Style

Ragoût de Haricots Blancs

This is a hearty main course we enjoyed on cold days at the farm. I prefer to add sea salt to the water when I boil beans, although many people do not and instead add salt to the beans later. This stew can be made with red or black beans or black-eyed peas, as well as white beans. Cooking time always will depend upon the size and age of the beans.

    1 pound white beans, soaked or preboiled according to package instructions and drained
    1 large carrot
    2 stalks celery, one cut in half lengthwise, the other cut into ¼-inch slices
    2 tablespoons sea salt (optional)
    2 tablespoons corn or peanut oil
    1 large onion, thinly sliced
    4 cloves garlic, thinly sliced
    4 plum tomatoes, cut into ¼-inch dice

3 cups homemade (page 82) or canned low-salt chicken broth or bean
 cooking water
Freshly ground black pepper to taste
Salt to taste, if beans were not cooked with salt
2 tablespoons minced scallions, white and tender green parts
2 tablespoons minced fresh parsley
2 bay leaves
¼ teaspoon coriander seeds
2 whole cloves
3 allspice berries, smashed
1 teaspoon grated lemon zest

In a large pot over medium-high heat, combine the beans, carrot, halved celery stalk, and sea salt with water to cover. Bring to a boil, then boil gently until the beans are tender, about 45 minutes, and drain.

In a medium-size saucepan over medium-high heat, heat the oil until very hot but not smoking, then sauté the onion until softened, about 3 minutes. Add the sliced celery, garlic, and tomatoes and sauté 2 minutes. Add the beans, broth, pepper, and salt and bring to a boil. Add the remaining ingredients and stir to combine. Reduce the heat to low and cook 15 minutes. Serve hot or at room temperature.

MAKES 4 TO 6 SERVINGS

Lentil Stew

Ragoût de Lentilles

Serve this aromatic vegetarian stew in your best tureen on the center of your table. It is a complete and satisfying main dish, needing just a slice of country bread to soak up the rich juices. Try to cook it with green French lentils, because American lentils often break down in cooking.

For the lentils

½ pound dried lentils
½ medium-size onion, sliced
2 cloves garlic, unpeeled
½ large carrot
Pinch salt

For the vegetables

2 tablespoons corn or peanut oil
1 large onion, thinly sliced
½ large or 1 small carrot, cut into ½-inch dice
5 cloves garlic, peeled and smashed
2 medium-size leeks, white and tender green parts, well washed, quartered
    lengthwise, and cut into 2-inch slices
2 plum tomatoes, cut into ½-inch dice
2 tablespoons minced scallions, white and tender green parts
6 large leaves fresh basil, coarsely chopped
2 tablespoons extra virgin olive oil
2 tablespoons prepared tomato puree
2 tablespoons minced fresh parsley
Salt and freshly ground black pepper to taste

To cook the lentils, combine all the ingredients in a large pot over medium-high heat with warm water to cover generously. Bring to a boil and cook at a steady boil until tender, 20 to 30 minutes. Add a little cold water to stop the cooking, then drain, reserving 4 cups of the cooking water.

Preheat the oven to 400°F. To prepare the vegetables, in a large skillet over medium-high heat, heat the oil, then sauté the onion 3 minutes. Add the carrot and sauté another 3 minutes. Add the garlic, leeks, tomatoes, scallions, and basil and sauté another 2 minutes. Add the lentils and mix well. Add the remaining ingredients and the reserved cooking water and mix well. Bring to a boil and cook at a steady boil for 15 minutes. Then place in the oven, uncovered, and cook another 15 minutes. Serve the stew in a soup bowl with its juices.

Makes 4 servings

Chick-Pea Stew

Ragoût de Pois Chiche

The colors in this stew are fantastic: red, green, glossy brown, gold, and tan. It makes a beautiful picture on your table and it is perfectly simple to prepare.

1 tablespoon corn or peanut oil
1 medium-size red onion, thinly sliced
1 tablespoon ¼-inch diced red bell pepper
1 tablespoon ¼-inch diced green bell pepper
1 plum tomato, cut into ¼-inch dice
One 19-ounce can chick-peas, drained
10 medium-size domestic mushroom caps, thinly sliced
Salt and freshly ground black pepper to taste
2 tablespoons minced fresh parsley
3 cloves garlic, smashed and minced
12 black olives marinated in olive oil and herbs (from Provence, Greece, or
    Italy), pitted and roughly chopped
1 tablespoon extra virgin olive oil
Pinch freshly grated nutmeg
1 bay leaf, crumbled

In a medium-size skillet over medium-high heat, heat the corn oil, then sauté the onion until softened but not colored, about 4 minutes. Add the remaining ingredients (be generous with the pepper) and cook until heated through, 5 to 10 minutes. Serve hot.

MAKES 4 SERVINGS

Broccoli Salad with Vinegar and Bacon

Salade de Brocolis au Vinaigre et Lard Fumé

Here is a dish for broccoli lovers, salad lovers, and lovers of spring. The last-minute addition of bacon, onions, and wine vinegar makes this a complex, unusual dish.

4½ teaspoons sea salt
4 teaspoons extra virgin olive oil
4 heads broccoli, florets only
Lettuce leaves to garnish
2 plum tomatoes, cut into ¼-inch dice
Salt and freshly ground black pepper to taste
3 tablespoons corn or peanut oil
2 slices country bread, crusts removed and cut into ¼-inch cubes
1 red onion, very thinly sliced
3 slices bacon, cut into ¼-inch pieces
2 tablespoons minced fresh parsley
¼ cup red wine vinegar

Fill a large pot two thirds full of water. Add the sea salt and olive oil and bring to a boil over high heat. Add the broccoli florets and boil 1 minute, then drain and place under cold, running water to stop the cooking. Mound in the center of a serving platter and surround with lettuce leaves. Scatter the plum tomatoes over the top, and sprinkle with salt and pepper. Set aside.

In a small skillet, heat 2 tablespoons of the corn oil over medium-high heat until

126 • COOKING PROVENCE

very hot but not smoking, and quickly sauté the bread cubes until lightly browned, about 30 seconds. Drain on paper towels and reserve, leaving 1 tablespoon of the oil in the pan.

Add the onion to the oil and sauté 2 minutes. Add the bacon, cook until brown, about 30 seconds, and drain the contents of the pan in a strainer. In the same pan, heat the remaining 1 tablespoon of corn oil until very hot but not smoking over medium-high heat, return the bacon and onions to the pan, add the parsley, and stir. Remove the pan from the heat, add the vinegar, and return to the heat for 30 seconds. Pour the contents of the pan over the tomatoes and broccoli and top with the croutons.

MAKES 4 SERVINGS

Broccoli Puree

Purée de Brocolis

I don't like to use butter or cream in this natural puree; instead, I lighten it with a little of the cooking water and some olive oil. It is delicious, with a lovely country feeling. This is a good way to cook broccoli stems when you use the florets for the broccoli salad on page 126 and it is a great dish for broccoli-resistant children—the light vegetable essence is hard to identify.

4 heads broccoli, stems only, cut into 1-inch slices
3 large potatoes, peeled, quartered lengthwise, and sliced ½ inch thick
3 cloves garlic, peeled and smashed
4½ teaspoons sea salt
¼ cup extra virgin olive oil
Salt and freshly ground black pepper to taste
Pinch freshly grated nutmeg

In a large pot, combine the broccoli stems, potatoes, garlic, sea salt, and 2 tablespoons of the olive oil. Cover generously with water, bring to a boil over high heat, and cook at a steady boil until the broccoli and potatoes are tender, 20 to 30 minutes.

Drain the vegetables in a strainer, reserving about 1 cup of the cooking water, and place them in a food processor with the remaining 2 tablespoons of olive oil, the salt, pepper, and nutmeg. Process to a puree (you may need to do this in several batches), using the reserved cooking water if too thick, and serve immediately.

MAKES 4 SERVINGS

Beets with Garlic and Parsley

Betterave à l'Ail et au Persil

I created this untraditional dish when I found some beautiful beets (a very popular vegetable in Provence) in my local market. It has an interesting combination of sweet, savory, and herbal tastes, and a purple color that looks lovely with the brown crumbs and green parsley. I use it to accompany grilled fish.

1 cup minced fresh parsley
2 tablespoons minced garlic
1 cup fresh bread crumbs
2 medium-size beets, cooked in boiling salted water to cover until tender,
    35 to 40 minutes, cooled, peeled, and sliced ¼ inch thick
Salt and freshly ground black pepper to taste
1 large egg, lightly beaten
2 tablespoons corn or peanut oil

In a small bowl, combine the parsley, garlic, and crumbs.

Sprinkle the beet slices with salt and pepper. Dip the slices into the beaten egg and dredge in the crumb mixture. Set aside.

In a large skillet over medium-high heat, heat the oil until it is very hot but not smoking. Add the beets and cook just until browned on each side, 30 to 60 seconds. Drain on paper towels and arrange on a serving platter. Serve hot.

MAKES 4 SERVINGS

Brussels Sprouts with Walnuts, Apples, and Raisins

Choux de Bruxelles aux Noix, Pommes, et Raisins

This green, fresh dish may be served with game or poultry. It is the perfect vegetable dish to accompany your Thanksgiving turkey.

1 tablespoon sea salt
10 ounces brussels sprouts, base and outer leaves removed
1 tablespoon corn or peanut oil
½ large onion, thinly sliced
1 clove garlic, thinly sliced
1 large Rome Beauty apple, cored and cut into 1-inch dice
Pinch sugar
½ teaspoon grated lemon zest
¼ cup shelled walnuts
¼ cup golden raisins
Pinch freshly grated nutmeg
Salt and freshly ground black pepper to taste
½ teaspoon unsalted butter

Fill a large pot three quarters full of water, add the sea salt, and bring to a boil over high heat. Add the brussels sprouts and boil steadily until tender but still green, about 10 minutes.

Meanwhile, in a medium-size skillet over medium-high heat, heat the oil until very hot but not smoking, then sauté the onion until it just starts to color, about 5 minutes. Add the garlic, apple, sugar, and lemon zest and mix well. Add the walnuts, raisins, nutmeg, salt, pepper, and butter and mix well.

Drain the cooked brussels sprouts and rinse in cold, running water. Cut them in half lengthwise, add them to the skillet, and cook 5 minutes. Serve hot.

Makes 2 servings

Little Provençal Cabbage Stew

Petite Potée Provençale au Chou

The authentic potée is a northern dish, but I do it Provençal fashion, with a lot of herbs. A touch of honey softens the flavor of the cabbage. For a spicy, winter variation, add 4 links of country sausage during the last 15 minutes of cooking.

2 tablespoons corn or peanut oil
1 large onion, thinly sliced
6 cloves garlic, peeled and smashed
1 large head green cabbage, about 3 pounds, cut into 8 wedges
2 leeks, white and tender green parts, well washed, cut into 3-inch
    sections, and quartered
1 stalk celery, cut into 3-inch sections
6 small red potatoes, cut in half
2 large tomatoes, each cut into 8 wedges
6 to 8 juniper berries
6 allspice berries
Pinch dried fennel
2 bay leaves
3 whole cloves
½ teaspoon dried thyme
10 to 12 cups homemade (page 82) or canned low-salt chicken broth, or to
    cover
Salt and freshly ground black pepper to taste
1 teaspoon honey
1 tablespoon extra virgin olive oil
½ lemon
Minced fresh parsley for garnish
1 tablespoon extra virgin olive oil for garnish

In a large soup pot over medium-high heat, heat the oil, then sauté the onion until softened, about 5 minutes. Add the garlic and stir. Arrange the cabbage wedges over the onions and garlic and strew the leeks and celery over the cabbage. Add all the remaining ingredients (squeeze the lemon, then add both the juice and the squeezed peel to the pot), except the garnishes, and press down gently so everything is covered by the stock. Bring to a boil. Cover with aluminum foil placed loosely over the vegetables, place in the oven, and cook until the vegetables are tender and the juices are glossy, 45 minutes to 1 hour.

To serve, arrange the vegetables in a soup bowl and ladle the broth over. Sprinkle with the parsley and olive oil.

MAKES 4 TO 6 MAIN-COURSE OR 8 SIDE-DISH SERVINGS

Spicy Carrot Pancake

Panequet de Carottes aux Épices

A simple, four-sided hand grater is the best kitchen machine you can have. Using it, you can grate all the carrots in seconds—less time than it would take you just to clean a food processor!

For this recipe, I use a generous mixture of spices, and I always use whole cloves, because they give me greater flavor control than powdered.

3 large carrots, grated
2 tablespoons minced fresh parsley
1 tablespoon minced scallions, white and tender green parts
½ tablespoon minced garlic
1 teaspoon minced fresh thyme, basil, rosemary, or other herb of choice
¼ teaspoon grated lemon zest (optional)
¼ teaspoon fennel seeds
1 bay leaf, cumbled
2 whole cloves, smashed
3 allspice berries, smashed
Pinch freshly grated nutmeg
Pinch ground cumin
Generous pinches salt and freshly ground black pepper
Generous pinch sugar
1 tablespoon extra virgin olive oil
3 large eggs, lightly beaten
2 tablespoons corn or peanut oil
1 teaspoon unsalted butter (optional)

In a large bowl, combine all the ingredients except the corn oil and butter.

Preheat the oven to 350°F. In a large skillet over medium-high heat, heat the oil until very hot but not smoking, then add the carrot mixture, pressing down slightly to form an even pancake. Cook, shaking the pan occasionally to prevent sticking, until browned on the bottom, about 5 minutes, then invert. If the surface of the pancake is dry, dot it with the butter. Place in the oven and bake until cooked through, 10 to 15 minutes.

MAKES 4 SERVINGS

Springtime Carrot Puree

Purée de Carottes Printanière

This puree of carrots and potatoes is given texture by the addition of crisp celery root. Make the puree with a food grinder, not a processor—this will give the mixture more character. Peas are the only vegetable I use frozen, because I believe the quality of frozen peas often surpasses that of fresh.

If you have leftovers, mix in 1 beaten egg and pour into a gratin dish. Then top with bread crumbs and grated cheese and bake until golden in a 400°F oven.

5 large carrots, cut in half lengthwise, then into 2-inch slices
1 medium-size celery root, peeled and cut into 1-inch chunks
2 large potatoes, peeled and cut into 1-inch chunks
1 tablespoon sea salt
2 cups frozen tiny peas
2 tablespoons sour cream
Salt and freshly ground black pepper to taste

Combine the carrots, celery root, potatoes, sea salt, and water to cover in a large saucepan and bring to a boil over medium-high heat. Boil steadily for 30 minutes. Add the peas and boil another 10 minutes.

Drain the vegetables and pass them through a food grinder fitted with a medium or fine blade. Place the puree in a large saucepan with the sour cream, mix well, and season with salt and pepper. Warm over low heat just until heated through.

MAKES 4 SERVINGS

Vegetables • 133

Candied Carrots Provençal

Carottes Glacées à la Provençale

These carrots are sweet, yet pleasantly peppery, with the unexpected tang of lime.

Pinch salt
3 large carrots, cut into ½-inch rounds, then trimmed into smooth ovals
2 tablespoons peanut oil
2 cloves garlic, smashed and minced
1 tablespoon sugar
Pinch grated lemon zest
Pinch grated lime zest
4 to 6 leaves fresh sage, minced
2 tablespoons minced fresh parsley

Fill a large saucepan three quarters full of water, add the salt, and bring to a boil over high heat. Add the carrots and boil until tender, about 30 minutes, then drain.

In a large skillet over high heat, heat the oil until sizzling, then add the carrots and cook, stirring, until they brown lightly. Add the sugar and shake the pan until the carrots are coated. Add the garlic and zests and cook, stirring, 2 minutes.

Place the carrots in a casserole or serving bowl and stir in the sage and parsley. Serve hot.

MAKES 4 SERVINGS

Carrot and Eggplant Stew with Lemon and Rosemary

Ragoût de Carottes, Aubergines, Citron, et Romarin

This vegetable stew is hearty but light, colorful, and aromatic. It goes well with any kind of fish, meat, or poultry or makes a fine meal by itself with just some salad and country bread.

2 tablespoons corn or peanut oil
1 large onion, thinly sliced
4 cloves garlic, peeled and smashed
3 large carrots, sliced ½ inch thick
Zest of 1 lemon, cut into large strips
2 plum tomatoes, cut in half lengthwise, then cut into thin wedges
4 cups homemade (page 82) or canned low-salt chicken broth
Pinch salt
Pinch freshly ground black pepper
1 tablespoon extra virgin olive oil
1 large eggplant, peeled, cut in half lengthwise, then cut into 1½-inch cubes
1 teaspoon minced fresh rosemary

In a large saucepan over medium-high heat, heat the oil until very hot but not smoking, then sauté the onion until golden, about 5 minutes. Add the garlic, carrots, lemon zest (twist and squeeze it a little to release the oils), and tomatoes and cook 1 to 2 minutes. Add 3 cups of the chicken broth, the salt, and pepper and bring to a boil. Reduce the heat to medium-low, add the olive oil, and cook at a slow boil, uncovered, for 30 minutes. Add the remaining stock, the eggplant, and rosemary and cook 15 minutes. Serve the vegetables on plates, surrounded by the broth.

MAKES 4 SERVINGS

Celery and Celery Root Served in a Marmite

Panaché de Céleris et Céleri-rave en Marmite

Celery root is a popular vegetable in Provence. Here it is combined with celery stalks and tomatoes and served in a tall earthenware pot called a marmite.

2 tablespoons corn or peanut oil
1 large onion, cut in half crosswise and thinly sliced
2 plum tomatoes, cut in half lengthwise, then into thin slivers
4 cloves garlic, peeled and smashed
2 medium-size celery roots, peeled, cut in half crosswise, then into ¼- by
    ½-inch slices
3 stalks celery, cut in half lengthwise, then into 1-inch slices
2 cups water
1 teaspoon grated orange zest
1 tablespoon extra virgin olive oil
Small pinch salt
Generous pinch freshly ground black pepper
4 sprigs fresh parsley
1 leek, white and tender green parts, quartered lengthwise and sliced 1
    inch thick

In a large saucepan over medium-high heat, heat the corn oil until it is very hot but not smoking, then sauté the onion until it colors, about 5 minutes. Add the tomatoes and garlic and cook 3 minutes. Add the celery root and stalks and stir, then add the water. Add the remaining ingredients and stir well. Reduce the heat to low and simmer for 40 minutes.

MAKES 4 SERVINGS

Celery Stew

Ragoût de Céleris

This main-dish stew treats celery like the interesting vegetable it is and makes it the centerpiece of a meal. Cook it without added salt because celery contains enough of its own, but add pepper generously. The light green celery is beautiful in a sauce of fresh tomato, sprinkled with bright green parsley.

2 tablespoons corn or peanut oil
1 large onion, thinly sliced
6 cloves garlic, smashed and minced
1 large tomato, cut into thin wedges
1 bunch celery, ends trimmed and outside leaves removed, cut into 2- to
    3-inch slices
1 tablespoon extra virgin olive oil
1 bay leaf
Pinch freshly grated nutmeg
Freshly ground black pepper to taste
1 cup tomato juice
1 cup homemade (page 82) or canned low-salt chicken broth
Few drops Worcestershire sauce
Pinch dried thyme
1 generous teaspoon minced fresh parsley for garnish
½ teaspoon extra virgin olive oil for garnish (optional)

Preheat the oven to 400°F. In a large saucepan over medium-high heat, heat the oil, then sauté the onion until lightly colored, about 5 minutes. Add the garlic, tomato, and celery and stir well. Add the remaining ingredients, except the garnishes, bring to a boil, and boil steadily for 5 minutes.

Place a square of aluminum foil directly on top of the vegetables, covering them loosely, and bake for 35 minutes. Place on a serving plate and sprinkle with the parsley and olive oil.

MAKES 4 SERVINGS

Baked Eggplant

Gratin d'Aubergines

Because the ingredients are cooked quickly, all the flavors in this colorful dish remain separate. This is what I like to do in all my cooking—keep the flavors fresh and clear. Delicious cold as well as hot, this is a good addition to a summer buffet.

For the eggplant

½ cup corn or peanut oil
2 large eggplant, about 2 pounds total, peeled and cut into ¼-inch slices
(about 18 slices)

For the tomato sauce

2 tablespoons corn or peanut oil
1 large onion, thinly sliced
3 cloves garlic, peeled and smashed
4 medium-size tomatoes, peeled (see note below), seeded, and coarsely
chopped
¼ cup prepared tomato puree
1½ teaspoons chopped fresh basil
Generous pinch salt
Generous pinch freshly ground black pepper, or to taste

To complete the dish

2 cloves garlic, thinly sliced
2 tablespoons minced fresh parsley
Salt and freshly ground black pepper to taste
½ teaspoon minced fresh thyme
2 tablespoons plain bread crumbs
Extra virgin olive oil for drizzling

Preheat the broiler. To prepare the eggplant, in a large skillet over high heat, heat the oil until it is very hot but not smoking. Cook the eggplant until deep brown, 1 to 2 minutes on each side, turning with tongs. Drain on paper towels.

To prepare the tomato sauce, wipe out the skillet and return it to high heat. Heat the oil until it is very hot but not smoking and sauté the onion until it just starts to color, about 4 minutes. Add the smashed garlic and continue cooking, stirring occasionally, until the onion turns the color of hazelnuts.

Add the tomatoes, tomato puree, basil, salt, and pepper. Cook 15 minutes— don't cook any longer or you will lose the fresh taste and texture of the tomatoes.

Brush the bottom of a casserole with olive oil and layer over it half the eggplant slices. Sprinkle with half the garlic slices and parsley. Layer the tomato sauce over the parsley and spread with a wooden spoon. Add another layer of eggplant slices, the remaining tomato sauce, garlic, and parsley. Sprinkle with salt, pepper, and thyme, top with the bread crumbs, and drizzle with olive oil. Brown quickly under a preheated broiler. Serve warm or cold.

MAKES 4 SERVINGS

NOTE: To peel tomatoes and garlic cloves, immerse them in boiling water for 30 seconds. The skins will slip off easily.

Gypsy Eggplant

Aubergines la Bohémienne

This is less a recipe than a method. My mother roasted eggplant in the embers of a wood fire and then, in an olivewood bowl, mashed the flesh with fresh garlic, herbs, and olive oil. Only in paradise can you eat that.

I have tried roasting the eggplant on the bottom of a gas oven, but it just doesn't work. To get the special tastes of smoke and olive oil and the somewhat candied consistency, there is no substitute for roasting in a real fire.

Always wash eggplant well before cooking, because it is treated with pesticides. On the farm, the young plants were preyed on by the *dorifaure,* a pest that was a bit larger than a ladybug, which it resembled.

  1 large eggplant
  1 clove garlic, minced
  2 tablespoons extra virgin olive oil
  Salt and freshly ground black pepper to taste

Prepare a wood or charcoal fire and let it burn down to embers. Bury the eggplant in the embers and roast 15 to 20 minutes, then turn and cook until the skin is thoroughly blackened and the flesh is soft, another 15 to 20 minutes. Holding the eggplant by the stem, peel off the skin with a sharp knife. Put the pulp in a bowl, add the garlic, olive oil, salt, and pepper, and mash together with a fork.

MAKES 1 SERVING

My Mother's Eggplant

Aubergines Marie-Thérèse

If you steam the eggplant before sautéing it, it will absorb less oil in the subsequent cooking. Sauté it in ½ cup of oil and you will find that a substantial amount will drain out easily after the eggplant has browned. It is very important to dry the eggplant thoroughly after its steaming; then be patient as it cooks in oil to an enticing shade of golden brown.

1 large or 2 medium-size eggplant, 1 to 1½ pounds total, peeled and cut
    into ½-inch dice
Salt and freshly ground black pepper to taste
1 tablespoon extra virgin olive oil
½ cup corn or peanut oil
6 cloves garlic, smashed and minced
1 medium-size tomato, cut into ½-inch dice
3 tablespoons minced fresh parsley

Season the diced eggplant with salt and pepper and drizzle with the olive oil. Place it in a steamer rack over boiling water and steam until softened, about 5 minutes, or place in a microwave-safe dish, cover, and steam in the microwave until softened, 2 to 3 minutes. Drain and pat dry with paper towels.

In a large skillet over medium-high heat, heat the corn oil until very hot. Add the eggplant all at once, stir well, and cook until brown on all sides, 5 to 10 minutes. Add the garlic and tomato, stir, and cook 1 to 2 minutes. Add 2 tablespoons of the parsley, season with salt and pepper, stir, and remove from the heat. Drain well in a strainer to remove the oil.

To serve, mound the drained eggplant on a serving dish and sprinkle with the remaining tablespoon of parsley.

MAKES 4 SERVINGS

Provençal Vegetable Stew

Ratatouille

Have ready a coarse strainer or colander set over a pot or bowl, so that after each vegetable is sautéed, you can drain it and reuse the cooking oil for the next vegetable. You will need 2 tablespoons of oil to cook each vegetable, except for the eggplant, which requires four. Do not soak or salt the eggplant before cooking—simply dicing it and cooking it quickly preserves its fresh flavor.

About 5 tablespoons corn or peanut oil
2 medium-size carrots, cut into ¼-inch dice
2 medium-size zucchini, cut into ¼-inch dice
½ medium-size red bell pepper, seeded and cut into julienne strips
½ medium-size green bell pepper, seeded and cut into julienne strips
Salt to taste
Generous pinch freshly ground black pepper
1 medium-size eggplant, peeled and cut into ¼-inch dice
1 large onion, cut into ¼-inch dice
4 cloves garlic, smashed and diced
1 large tomato, peeled, seeded, and medium-coarsely chopped
1 tablespoon minced fresh parsley
1 tablespoon chopped fresh basil

In a large skillet over high heat, heat 1 tablespoon of the oil until sizzling, then cook the carrots, stirring, until they start to brown, 2 to 4 minutes. They should be tender but firm. Drain, set aside the carrots, and pour the oil back into the pan, adding more oil if you need it. Repeat with the zucchini (it should be slightly browned, with a sweet smell) and the peppers (they should retain their crunch). Season with salt and pepper.

Add oil to make 4 tablespoons and heat until very hot but not smoking. Cook the eggplant, stirring, until softened and brown, 5 to 10 minutes. Drain, set aside, and pour 2 tablespoons of the oil back into the pan.

Sauté the onion 1 minute, then add the garlic and cook 1 minute more. Add the tomato, reduce the heat to medium, and cook, stirring, 3 minutes.

Return the cooked vegetables to the pan and cook, stirring, 3 to 4 minutes.

Remove from the heat and sprinkle with the parsley and basil. Drain any excess oil and serve hot or at room temperature with grilled meat or fish. Ratatouille can be prepared ahead and refrigerated for up to 4 days.

MAKES 4 TO 6 SERVINGS

Summer Salad of Endive, Beets, and Walnuts

Salade d'Endives, Betteraves, et Noix

Beets and endive are a refreshing summer combination and walnuts add a special flavor and crunch. This is my creation, using familiar vegetables.

For the dressing

2 tablespoons Dijon mustard
¼ teaspoon Worcestershire sauce
¼ cup red wine vinegar
¼ cup extra virgin olive oil
Grated zest of ½ lemon

For the salad

4 heads endive, cleaned and separated; halve large leaves lengthwise
1 large or 2 small beets, cooked in boiling salted water to cover until tender, 35 to 40 minutes, cooled, peeled, and cut into thin julienne strips
16 walnut halves, toasted if desired (see page 347)
2 tablespoons minced fresh parsley

In a small bowl, combine the dressing ingredients and mix well with a spoon. Arrange the endive leaves on four plates and scatter the beets over them. Top with the walnut halves and parsley. Spoon the dressing over the salads and serve.

MAKES 4 SERVINGS; 1 CUP DRESSING

Melted Endives

Fondue d'Endives

Sweet, peppery, and crunchy, these endives are delicious alone or served with Farm-Style Tomatoes Provençal (page 172) or pasta. The endive's core makes the vegetable bitter when cooked, so remove it.

    2 tablespoons corn or peanut oil
    4 large or 5 medium-size endives, cored and cut lengthwise into 6 to 8
        slices
    2 tablespoons sugar
    Salt and freshly ground black pepper to taste
    Grated zest of ½ lemon
    Juice of 1 lemon
    ¼ cup (½ stick) unsalted butter, melted

Preheat the oven to 400°F. In a large skillet over medium-high heat, heat the oil until very hot but not smoking, then add the endive. Sauté until softened, about 5 minutes. Sprinkle with the sugar and season lightly with salt and generously with pepper. Add the lemon zest, lemon juice, and butter. Cook the endive until colored, shaking the pan frequently to incorporate the other ingredients.

Remove the pan from the heat, cover with aluminum foil, and bake until tender and glossy, about 15 minutes.

MAKES 4 SERVINGS

Breaded Fiddlehead Ferns

Coeur de Fougères Panées

Heap these delicate spring vegetables on a platter and spear them with toothpicks, then pass them with drinks; or serve them as an unusual vegetable course. They taste a bit like asparagus and are available in gourmet markets for a short while during the spring or summer, depending on where you live. Though fiddleheads aren't common in Provence, this recipe successfully applies Provençal technique to their preparation.

Cooking the fiddleheads in strongly salted water will keep them green and eliminate the need for salting later.

3 to 4 tablespoons sea salt
1 pound fiddlehead ferns, stem tips cut off and rinsed
2 large eggs, lightly beaten
1 cup plain bread crumbs
Salt and freshly ground black pepper to taste
3 tablespoons corn or peanut oil
Juice of 1 lemon

Over high heat, bring to a boil a large saucepan of water with the sea salt. Add the fiddlehead ferns and boil until slightly softened, 30 to 60 seconds. Drain and rinse in cold running water.

In a large bowl, combine the fiddleheads and beaten eggs. Spread the bread crumbs over a flat plate and season with salt and pepper. Roll the fiddleheads in the crumbs until coated, and set aside.

In a large skillet over medium-high heat, heat the oil until very hot but not smoking, then sauté the ferns until brown on all sides, 30 to 60 seconds. Season generously with pepper. Place on a serving platter and squeeze the lemon juice over.

MAKES 4 APPETIZER SERVINGS

Peas Provençal Style

Petit Pois à la Provençale

Frozen tiny peas, petit pois, often are better than fresh and I use them freely. Although bacon is added to the vegetables, all its fat is drained off and only the smoky flavor remains. Serve this colorful dish in a pretty terra-cotta casserole.

    1 tablespoon corn or peanut oil
    1 small or ½ large onion, thinly sliced
    2 cloves garlic, peeled and smashed
    3 strips bacon, cut into ¼- to ½-inch pieces
    4 to 5 large lettuce leaves, cut into chiffonade (page 20)
    3 cups frozen tiny peas
    Salt and freshly ground black pepper to taste
    1 bay leaf, crumbled
    2 whole cloves

In a large saucepan over medium-high heat, heat the oil until very hot but not smoking, then sauté the onion until colored, about 5 minutes. Add the garlic and bacon and sauté until the fat part of the bacon becomes transparent, about 5 minutes. Pour the contents of the pan into a strainer and drain out all the fat, then return the vegetables and bacon to the pan.

Reduce the heat to low, add the lettuce, and cook, stirring, just until wilted, about 30 seconds. Add the peas, salt, pepper, bay leaf, and cloves and cook until the peas are cooked through, about 5 minutes.

MAKES 4 SERVINGS

Casserole of Peas and Tomatoes

Cassolette de Pois et Tomates

Serve this vegetable dish alone or accompany it with some rice for a light lunch. If it is to be thick, add a little chicken broth.

2 tablespoons corn or peanut oil
1 large onion, thinly sliced
1 stalk celery, cut in half lengthwise, then into ¼-inch slices
4 plum tomatoes, cut in half lengthwise, then into thin slivers
4 cloves garlic, smashed and peeled
5 sprigs fresh parsley, coarsely chopped
1 tablespoon extra virgin olive oil
3 cups frozen tiny peas
2 or 3 drops Worcestershire sauce
½ cup homemade or low-salt chicken broth, optional
Chopped fresh parsley for garnish

In a large saucepan over medium-high heat, heat the oil until very hot but not smoking, then sauté the onion until it begins to color, about 5 minutes. Add the celery, tomatoes, garlic, and parsley sprigs and sauté 5 minutes. Reduce the heat to low, add the olive oil, and mix. Add the peas and Worcestershire and mix. Add optional chicken broth. Cook 5 minutes, pour into a serving bowl, and garnish with the parsley.

MAKES 4 SERVINGS

Sautéed Snow Peas

Pois Gourmands Sautés

My mother prepared this beautiful stew of tender snow peas and served it with roasted pigeon or chicken. The peas are also delicious steamed, with just a touch of salt and pepper.

2 tablespoons corn or peanut oil
1 medium-size onion, thinly sliced
3 cloves garlic, smashed and minced
1 pound snow peas, strings removed
1 medium-size tomato, cut into ½-inch dice
1 bay leaf
Salt and freshly ground black pepper to taste
Pinch freshly grated nutmeg

In a large skillet over medium-high heat, heat the oil until very hot but not smoking and sauté the onion until it is soft but not colored, about 4 minutes.

Add the garlic and snow peas and cook 10 minutes. Add the remaining ingredients and cook another 5 minutes.

MAKES 4 SERVINGS

VARIATION: To prepare the peas en papillote, for each serving, arrange ¼ pound of peas on a square of aluminum foil and sprinkle with olive oil, salt, pepper, nutmeg, and 1 tablespoon dry white wine. Enclose in the foil and bake in a preheated 400°F oven until it puffs up, about 30 minutes.

Margo's Fresh Pepper Stew

Poivronade Margo

My sister, Margo, makes this traditional Provençal dish with the colorful fresh peppers that are so abundant at home. Put it in the middle of the table with a roast, grilled fish, or barbecue.

2 tablespoons corn or peanut oil
2 medium-size green bell peppers, seeded and cut into ½-inch julienne strips
2 medium-size red bell peppers, seeded and cut into ½-inch julienne strips
2 medium-size yellow bell peppers, seeded and cut into ½-inch julienne strips
Salt and freshly ground black pepper to taste
4 shallots, thinly sliced
6 cloves garlic, thinly sliced
1 plum tomato, cut into ½-inch wedges
Pinch sugar
¼ teaspoon paprika
1 tablespoon extra virgin olive oil

In a large skillet over medium-high heat, heat the oil until very hot but not smoking, then add the peppers and sprinkle with salt and pepper. Sauté until the peppers start to color, then reduce the heat to medium-low, add the remaining ingredients, and mix well. Cook slowly until soft and candied, 15 to 20 minutes.

Remove to a strainer and drain off the oil. Serve hot.

MAKES 4 TO 6 SERVINGS

Saint-Rémy-Style Potatoes

Pommes de Terre Saint-Remoise

This is how we prepared potatoes in Saint-Rémy-de-Provence. Hearty yet very subtle, they are almost a meal in themselves.

2 tablespoons corn or peanut oil
1 medium-size onion, thinly sliced
2 cloves garlic, smashed and peeled
1 small leek, white and tender green parts, well washed and thinly sliced
  crosswise
2 large potatoes, peeled and sliced ⅛ inch thick
2 cups homemade (page 82) or canned low-salt chicken broth
Salt and freshly ground black pepper to taste
Pinch grated lemon zest
Pinch freshly grated nutmeg
1 tablespoon extra virgin olive oil
2 tablespoons fine bread crumbs
2 tablespoons grated Swiss cheese
Extra virgin olive oil for drizzling

In a large skillet over high heat, heat the oil until sizzling, then sauté the onion until it begins to color, about 5 minutes. Add the garlic and leek, stir, and add the potatoes. Add the chicken broth, salt, and pepper and stir to combine. Add the lemon zest, nutmeg, and olive oil and stir. Cover tightly with aluminum foil, reduce the heat to medium, and cook until all the liquid has evaporated and the potatoes are glazed, 15 to 20 minutes.

Preheat the broiler. Combine the bread crumbs and cheese and sprinkle over the vegetables, drizzle with olive oil, and place under the broiler until the topping is browned. Serve hot.

MAKES 4 SERVINGS

Creamy Mashed Potatoes with Olive Oil and Garlic

Purée de Pommes de Terre à l'Huile d'Olive et à l'Ail

These potatoes must be prepared at the last minute and served immediately. Handle them as little as possible, mixing the ingredients quickly and with a light hand. The resulting dish will be a fragrant accompaniment to roasted or grilled chicken, meats, or fish.

2 large potatoes, peeled and thinly sliced
Pinch salt
2 tablespoons extra virgin olive oil
1 clove garlic, smashed and peeled
Pinch grated lime zest
3 to 4 drops Tabasco sauce

Place the potatoes, salt, and water to cover in a large saucepan over medium-high heat. Bring to a boil and boil steadily until tender, 25 to 30 minutes. Drain, reserving ½ cup of the water if needed for the puree.

Place the potatoes in a food processor and process just until mashed, about 20 seconds. Do not overprocess, or they will become gluey. Remove to a mixing bowl.

Quickly mix in the olive oil, being careful not to overmix. Add the garlic, lime zest, and Tabasco, stir to blend, and add additional cooking water if the mixture is too thick. Serve immediately.

MAKES 2 SERVINGS

Provençal Mashed Potatoes with Vegetables

Hachis Parmentier

When Antoine-August Parmentier introduced the potato into France in the eighteenth century, he not only added a delicious element to our cuisine, he offered the world a staple that was to save many people from starvation. His name signifies potatoes, here combined with sautéed vegetables in a hearty casserole. A bonus is the water in which you boiled the potatoes. In Provence, we drank it as a flavorful broth and also believed in its medicinal properties—it was supposed to cure cholera.

A word about kitchen equipment: I prefer to slice the potatoes and other vegetables on a mandoline, which treats them more tenderly than a food processor does. You don't have to buy an expensive import; inexpensive plastic mandolines are available. I also prefer to pass the cooked potatoes through a food grinder, rather than puree them in a processor.

4 large potatoes, peeled, cut in half, and sliced ½ inch thick on a
    mandoline
¼ cup extra virgin olive oil
3 cloves garlic, peeled
2 bay leaves
1 tablespoon sea salt
Salt and freshly ground black pepper to taste
2 tablespoons corn or peanut oil
1 carrot, sliced medium thick on a mandoline
2 leeks, white part only, well washed and cut into 4-inch-long julienne
    strips
1 medium-size zucchini, green peel and part of the white flesh only, sliced
    medium thick on a mandoline (rotate zucchini until all the green is
    sliced, then discard the core)
2 stalks celery, cut into 4-inch-long julienne strips
2 medium-size tomatoes, roughly chopped
3 shallots, coarsely chopped
4 large or 5 medium-size cloves garlic, smashed and minced

1 teaspoon chopped fresh basil
2 tablespoons chopped fresh parsley
1 large egg yolk beaten with 1 tablespoon water
2 tablespoons plain bread crumbs

Preheat the oven to 400°F. Place the potatoes, water to cover, 2 tablespoons of the olive oil, the garlic, bay leaves, and sea salt in a large saucepan over medium-high heat and bring to a boil. Cook, uncovered, at a steady boil until tender, 30 to 40 minutes. Drain, reserving the water. Discard the bay leaf and put the potatoes and garlic through the medium blade of a food grinder. Spoon into a mixing bowl and add the remaining olive oil and enough of the reserved cooking water (about ½ cup) to make a thick but manageable mixture. Season with salt and pepper.

Meanwhile, in a large skillet over medium-high heat, heat the corn oil, then sauté the carrot about 1 minute. Add the leeks, zucchini, celery, and tomatoes, reduce the heat to medium, and sauté 10 minutes. Add the shallots, garlic, basil, and parsley, cook 1 minute more, and season with salt and pepper.

Oil a medium-size gratin dish and place half the potato puree in the bottom. Add the vegetables in a smooth layer and cover with the remaining puree. Paint with the egg wash and sprinkle with the bread crumbs. Place in the oven until well cooked and golden brown on top, about 30 minutes.

MAKES 4 SERVINGS

Potatoes with Vinegar

Pommes de Terre au Vinaigre

Tarragon and red wine vinegar are like Romeo and Juliet in this million-dollar recipe. The dish is brown, green, and golden, with surprisingly intense flavor. Serve it as an accompaniment, or double the quantity and serve it as a main dish with a salad.

    2 tablespoons corn or peanut oil
    12 medium-size red potatoes, peeled and quartered lengthwise
    1 medium-size red onion, cut in half crosswise, then thinly sliced
    4 cloves garlic, thinly sliced
    1 tablespoon minced fresh tarragon
    2 tablespoons minced fresh parsley
    Salt and freshly ground black pepper to taste
    ¼ cup red wine vinegar

In a large skillet over medium-high heat, heat the oil until it sizzles when a bit of potato is immersed. Add the potatoes and cook for 5 minutes. Shake the pan or stir often to move the potatoes around in the oil.

Add the onion and cook, still shaking the pan, until the potatoes are brown on all sides and the onion has colored, another 5 minutes. Add the garlic, tarragon, and parsley and cook 1 minute. Season with salt and pepper.

Remove the pan from the heat and add the vinegar, mixing well. Return to the heat for 1 minute to heat through, and serve.

MAKES 4 SERVINGS

Potatoes with Lemon and Saffron

Pommes de Terre au Citron et Safran

Undertones of lemon, saffron, and paprika turn the humble potato into something exotic in this fragrant dish. It is so rich in flavor that it makes a satisfying main course.

    4 large potatoes, peeled and sliced ¼ inch thick
    2 tablespoons extra virgin olive oil
    Grated zest of 1 lemon
    Juice of 2 lemons
    3 cloves garlic, minced
    3 tablespoons minced fresh parsley
    Generous pinch saffron threads
    Generous pinch paprika
    Salt and freshly ground black pepper to taste
    1 cup coarsely grated Swiss cheese
    1 tablespoon minced fresh thyme or parsley

Place all the ingredients, except the cheese and thyme, in a large saucepan with hot water to cover over medium-high heat and bring to a boil. Reduce the heat to medium, cover with aluminum foil, and cook at a steady boil until the potatoes are tender, about 10 minutes.

Preheat the broiler. Uncover the pan and cook another 10 minutes. Drain the contents of the pan, pour into a lightly oiled medium-size gratin dish, and top with the grated cheese. Place under the broiler just until the cheese is melted and brown, then sprinkle with the thyme and serve immediately, spooning some of the juices over each serving.

MAKES 4 SERVINGS

Potatoes with Leeks, Anchovies, and Olives Marie-Thérèse

Pommes de Terre Marie-Thérèse au Poireaux, Anchois, et Olives

This is a totally satisfying vegetable dish and its colors are fantastic. On the farm, we let the anchovies melt in a pot on a warm corner of our wood-burning stove, but in modern kitchens they can be put over a very low flame and allowed to take their time.

Look for imported black olives that are packed in oil and herbs; they add a lot of flavor. Salt the dish very lightly, if at all, because the anchovies will contribute their salt.

2 tablespoons corn or peanut oil
1 large red or white onion, very thinly sliced
1 bay leaf
4 large potatoes, peeled, quartered lengthwise, and sliced ½ inch thick
2 large or 3 medium-size leeks, white and tender green parts, well washed, quartered lengthwise, then cut into ½-inch slices
¼ cup extra virgin olive oil
Salt and freshly ground black pepper to taste
Pinch ground nutmeg
6 oil-packed anchovy fillets
3 cloves garlic, smashed and minced
24 small black olives, pitted
1 plum tomato, cut into ¼-inch dice
1 tablespoon brine-packed capers, drained
Grated zest of 1 lemon
2 tablespoons minced fresh parsley

In a large saucepan over medium-high heat, heat the corn oil until hot but not smoking and add the onion and bay leaf. Cook until the onion is golden, about 5 minutes, then add the potatoes and leeks, mix well, and cook 30 seconds. Add water to cover, 3 tablespoons of the olive oil, a small pinch of salt, pepper, and nutmeg and bring to a boil. Reduce the heat to medium and cook until the potatoes are tender, 20 to 30 minutes.

Meanwhile, in a small saucepan over low heat, combine the anchovies with the garlic, the remaining olive oil, and a pinch of pepper and allow to warm slowly and then melt. Don't allow the mixture to cook. Mix well and keep warm.

When the potatoes are done, discard the bay leaf, add the anchovy mixture, and stir well. Add the olives, tomato, capers, lemon zest, and parsley and stir well. Cook just to warm through, about 30 seconds. To serve, spoon into a soup bowl and pour some of the juices over all.

MAKES 4 TO 6 SERVINGS

Sautéed Potatoes

Pommes de Terre Sautées

Prepare this simple accompaniment while your main dish is cooking and serve it hot and fragrant.

¼ cup corn or peanut oil
3 medium-size Idaho potatoes, peeled, quartered lengthwise, and cut into
    ½-inch slices
Salt and freshly ground black pepper to taste
4 shallots, finely diced
1 tablespoon minced fresh parsley

In a large skillet over medium-high heat, heat the oil until it begins to smoke, then cook the potatoes until golden around the edges and on the bottom, 4 to 5 minutes. Sprinkle with salt and pepper, turn, add the shallots, and cook until browned and tender, 4 to 5 minutes. Before serving, sprinkle with the parsley and shake the pan to mix.

MAKES 4 SERVINGS

Potatoes with Sweet Garlic

Pommes de Terre à l'Ail Doux

Caramelized garlic adds delicate sweetness to this combination of potatoes, tomatoes, and herbs. In Provence we could not live without potatoes and garlic!

3 tablespoons corn or peanut oil
4 large potatoes, peeled and cut into 1-inch dice
Salt and freshly ground black pepper to taste
2 plum tomatoes, cut into ¼-inch dice
5 cloves garlic, thinly sliced
Grated zest of ½ lemon
1 tablespoon minced fresh rosemary
2 tablespoons minced fresh parsley
2 tablespoons sugar

In a large skillet over medium-high heat, heat the oil until a piece of potato sizzles when immersed. Sauté the potatoes until golden on all sides, about 8 minutes. Season with a small pinch of salt and a generous pinch of pepper.

Add the tomatoes carefully, since they will splatter. Add the garlic, lemon zest, rosemary, parsley, and sugar and mix well. Cook 30 seconds to 1 minute, drain, and place on a serving platter.

MAKES 4 SERVINGS

Country Casserole

Gratin du Paysan

Here is a simple combination of ingredients with a country feeling. The creamy potatoes and cheese are accented by gentle seasonings and are flecked with bright green parsley.

4 large potatoes, peeled and very thinly sliced on a mandoline
3 cups regular or low-fat milk
4 cloves garlic, smashed and peeled
Pinch freshly grated nutmeg
Salt and freshly ground black pepper to taste
1 cup coarsely grated Swiss cheese
2 tablespoons minced fresh parsley

Preheat the broiler. In a large saucepan over medium-high heat, combine all the ingredients, except the cheese and parsley, and bring to a boil. Reduce the heat to medium and cook at a medium boil until the potatoes are tender, about 10 minutes. Drain and set aside.

Lightly butter a medium-size gratin dish, pour in the potatoes, and top with the grated cheese. Place under the broiler just until the cheese melts and turns golden. Garnish with the minced parsley.

MAKES 4 SERVINGS

Potato Stew Marie-Thérèse

Ragoût de Pommes de Terre Marie-Thérèse

This hearty, colorful stew makes a wonderful vegetable main course. If you want a meat flavor, you can easily add a lamb bone to the pot, but why complicate this classic?

2 tablespoons corn or peanut oil
1 large onion, cut into 1-inch dice
4 large potatoes, peeled and cut into 2-inch dice
3 cloves garlic, minced
2 plum tomatoes, cut into 1-inch dice
1 tablespoon minced fresh thyme
2 tablespoons minced fresh parsley
1 bay leaf
1 whole clove
Generous pinch ground cumin
1 tablespoon extra virgin olive oil
3 cups homemade (page 82) or canned low-salt chicken broth
Salt and freshly ground black pepper to taste

In a large saucepan over medium-high heat, heat the oil, then sauté the onion until golden, about 5 minutes. Add the potatoes, garlic, tomatoes, thyme, and parsley and mix well. Add the bay leaf, clove, and cumin. Add the olive oil and chicken broth, season with salt and pepper, and bring to a boil. Reduce the heat to medium and cook until the potatoes are tender, about 20 minutes.

To serve, spoon the potatoes into a soup bowl and surround with the vegetables and broth.

MAKES 4 MAIN-COURSE SERVINGS

Thin Potato Pancakes

Crêpes de Pommes de Terre

❧❧❧

Serve these delicate pancakes with a main course of roasted meat or chicken. Beer in the batter keeps the crêpe from sticking, so when it turns brown around the outer edge, you can flip it over easily.

⅓ cup regular or low-fat milk
½ cup beer
2 large eggs
3 tablespoons all-purpose flour
2 tablespoons minced fresh parsley
3 cloves garlic, smashed and minced
Pinch freshly grated nutmeg
Salt and freshly ground black pepper to taste
2 large baking potatoes, peeled and coarsely grated
2 to 4 tablespoons corn or peanut oil

In a mixing bowl, combine the milk, beer, eggs, flour, parsley, garlic, nutmeg, salt, and pepper and whisk together well. Add the potatoes and mix well.

In a seasoned crêpe pan or nonstick 8-inch skillet, heat 1 tablespoon of the oil over medium-high heat until very hot but not smoking, then add one quarter of the potato batter, patting it down to form an even pancake. Cook, shaking the pan, until the edges brown, about 2 minutes, then turn. Reduce the heat to medium and cook the other side 5 minutes. Reserve and keep warm.

Repeat with the remaining batter, adding more oil as needed. Alternatively, you can heat 2 tablespoons oil in a large skillet and fry two or more pancakes at once.

MAKES 4 SERVINGS

Provençal Doormat

Paillasson Provençal

These flat potato cakes, which look like little doormats, are crisp on the outside and very creamy inside. Because they cook so quickly, their taste is garden-fresh. They contain nothing more than potatoes, herbs, and seasonings and make a light accompaniment to any main dish.

4 large potatoes, peeled and grated medium
2 large eggs, lightly beaten
Salt and freshly ground black pepper to taste
2 cloves garlic, minced
3 tablespoons minced fresh parsley
Generous pinch freshly grated nutmeg
4 teaspoons corn or peanut oil

In a large bowl, combine all the ingredients except the corn oil.

In a small skillet or a crêpe pan over medium-high heat, heat 1 teaspoon of the oil until a drop of the potato mixture sizzles when immersed. Place one quarter of the mixture in the pan and fry until brown around the edges, about 2 minutes. Reduce the heat to medium and cook until golden on the bottom, another 2 minutes, then turn. Raise the heat to medium-high and cook 30 seconds, then reduce to medium and cook until golden, 2 to 4 minutes. Repeat with the remaining potato mixture to make three more pancakes. You also can make smaller individual cakes in a large pan.

MAKES 4 SERVINGS

Potato Fritters

Beignets de Pommes de Terre

These fritters make a fine accompaniment to fish, meat, or barbecue. Or serve them with just a salad, for a satisfying lunch.

4 large potatoes, peeled and cut lengthwise into quarters
1 large egg, lightly beaten
2 tablespoons minced fresh parsley
2 cloves garlic, minced
Grated zest of ½ lemon
Pinch freshly grated nutmeg
Salt and freshly ground black pepper to taste
¼ cup corn or peanut oil

Put the potatoes through a food grinder fitted with a medium blade, or grate coarsely on a grater. In a mixing bowl, combine the ground potatoes with the remaining ingredients, except the corn oil, and mix well.

In a large skillet over medium-high heat, heat the oil until it sizzles when a drop of batter is immersed in it. Drop the batter by tablespoonsful into the hot oil, making sure that the fritters do not touch one another. Sprinkle lightly with salt. Fry until golden, about 2 minutes per side. Drain well on paper towels.

MAKES 4 SERVINGS AS AN ACCOMPANIMENT

Cold Potato Salad Provençal

Salade de Pommes de Terre Provençale

This is a salad of crisp, colorful vegetables combined with potatoes, hard-boiled eggs, and a bracing mustard vinaigrette. You may refrigerate it ahead of time, as long as you bring it to room temperature 30 minutes before serving.

For the salad

16 small or 12 medium-size red potatoes
1 tablespoon sea salt
¼ green bell pepper, seeded and cut into ⅛-inch julienne strips
¼ red bell pepper, seeded and cut into ⅛-inch julienne strips
2 medium-size tomatoes, cut in half, then cut into ¼-inch slices
12 black olives marinated in olive oil and herbs (from Provence, Greece, or Italy), drained and pitted
2 large hard-boiled eggs, shelled and quartered
2 tablespoons minced fresh parsley
2 tablespoons minced scallions, white and tender green parts
2 cloves garlic, very thinly sliced
4 oil-packed anchovy fillets
Salt and freshly ground black pepper to taste

For the vinaigrette

1 teaspoon Dijon mustard
1 tablespoon red wine vinegar
¼ cup extra virgin olive oil
Salt and freshly ground black pepper to taste

Place the potatoes, water to cover generously, and the sea salt in a large saucepan over medium-high heat and bring to a boil. Cook at a steady boil until tender, 30 to 40 minutes, and drain. When cool enough to handle, slice the potatoes ½ inch thick and place in a large salad bowl. Add the remaining salad ingredients to the potatoes.

In a small bowl, whisk together the mustard and vinegar, then add the oil very slowly, whisking until emulsified. Season generously with pepper and lightly with salt, pour over the salad, and toss to combine. Serve at room temperature.

MAKES 4 TO 6 SERVINGS

Warm Potato Salad with Basil and Sweet Garlic

Salade de Pommes de Terre au Basilic et Ail Doux

This recipe is my own creation, using the simple ingredients that were available on our farm.

8 small red potatoes
Large pinch sea salt
Freshly ground black pepper to taste
6 fresh basil leaves, coarsely chopped
3 tablespoons extra virgin olive oil
Grated zest of ½ lemon
1 tablespoon corn or peanut oil
6 cloves garlic, cut in half lengthwise
2 tablespoons sugar
2 tablespoons minced fresh parsley

In a large saucepan over medium-high heat, combine the potatoes with water to cover and the salt and bring to a boil. Boil steadily until tender, 30 to 40 minutes. Drain and when the potatoes are cool enough to handle, cut into halves, then cut each half into thirds.

Place in a large bowl and sprinkle generously with the pepper. Add the basil, 2 tablespoons of the olive oil, and the lemon zest.

In a small skillet over medium-high heat, heat the corn oil, then cook the garlic, shaking the pan, until golden, about 1 minute. Sprinkle with the sugar and cook 30 seconds. Remove the garlic and discard the cooking oil.

Add the garlic to the potatoes. Add the remaining tablespoon of olive oil and the parsley and mix well.

MAKES 4 SERVINGS

Candied Shallots

Échalotes Glacées à la Provençale

The delicate sweetness of this vegetable dish makes it a good foil for game.

    2 tablespoons corn or peanut oil
    24 shallots, peeled
    1 tablespoon sugar
    3 tablespoons water

In a small skillet over medium-high heat, heat the oil until very hot but not smoking, then sauté the shallots until golden, about 2 minutes. Reduce the heat to medium and sauté until golden brown on all sides, about 5 minutes.

Sprinkle the sugar over the shallots and mix well. Add the water, reduce the heat to low, and cook slowly until the shallots are tender and a golden syrup forms, about 20 minutes. Serve warm or cold.

MAKES 1½ TO 2 CUPS

Spinach Cake

Gâteau d'Épinard

This is an unusual dish, with a peppery spinach taste. Serve it with diced fresh tomatoes on top.

2 tablespoons corn or peanut oil
2 pounds fresh spinach, well washed and tough stems removed, to yield
    1 pound leaves
Salt and freshly ground black pepper to taste
1 tablespoon minced shallots
3 cloves garlic, smashed and peeled
Pinch grated lemon zest
Pinch freshly grated nutmeg
2 tablespoons minced fresh parsley
¼ cup all-purpose flour
¼ cup regular or low-fat milk
2 large eggs
1 teaspoon unsalted butter or margarine, softened

Lightly oil a 10-inch round cake pan. Preheat the oven to 400°F.

In a large skillet over medium-high heat, heat the oil until very hot but not smoking.

Cut the spinach leaves into chiffonade and drop them into the hot oil. Season with salt and pepper. Add the shallots, garlic, lemon zest, nutmeg, and parsley, and cook, stirring, until the spinach has wilted, about 1 minute.

Still over medium-high heat, add the flour and mix well; add the milk and eggs and mix well. Remove from the heat and stir in the butter. Pour into the prepared pan and press down evenly with a spoon. Bake until firm and lightly browned, about 10 minutes.

MAKES 4 TO 6 SERVINGS

Spinach Gratin

Gratin d'Épinard

A beautiful golden crusty top covers green spinach in a creamy sauce in this traditional farmhouse recipe.

For the béchamel

2 tablespoons unsalted butter
½ cup all-purpose flour
3 cups whole milk
Freshly ground white pepper or Tabasco sauce to taste
Pinch freshly grated nutmeg

For the vegetables

2 tablespoons corn or peanut oil
1 large onion, thinly sliced
2 pounds fresh spinach, well washed and tough stems removed, to yield
    1 pound leaves, then cut into chiffonade

To complete the dish

½ cup grated Swiss cheese

Preheat the oven to 400°F; preheat the broiler, if separate. Lightly butter a medium-size baking dish.

In a medium-size saucepan over medium-high heat, melt the butter. Sprinkle the flour over it, then add the milk, pepper, and nutmeg and whisk until thickened and well combined, 3 to 4 minutes. Set aside.

In a large skillet over medium-high heat, heat the oil until very hot but not smoking. Sauté the onion until soft and golden, about 3 minutes. Add the spinach and cook, stirring or shaking the pan, until wilted, 1 to 2 minutes. Pour the mixture into a strainer and drain well, then pour into the prepared gratin dish.

Pour the béchamel over the spinach and smooth the top. Scatter the cheese over the béchamel. Bake 10 minutes, then put under the broiler until browned.

MAKES 4 TO 6 SERVINGS; 1 CUP BÉCHAMEL

Sweet Potato Casserole

Gratin de Pommes de Terre Douce

Like many farm dishes, this gratin is very simple to prepare, yet it makes a beautiful appearance and tastes heavenly.

3 medium-size sweet potatoes, peeled, quartered lengthwise, and sliced
    1 inch thick
1 tablespoon sea salt
2 tablespoons unsalted butter
1 tablespoon sour cream
1 large egg
Pinch ground cumin
Pinch freshly grated nutmeg
1 cup grated Swiss cheese
2 tablespoons minced fresh parsley
1 tablespoon plain bread crumbs

In a large pot over medium-high heat, combine the potatoes, salt, and 1 tablespoon of the butter, cover generously with water, and bring to a boil. Boil steadily until the potatoes are tender, about 45 minutes. Drain.

Preheat the oven to 350°F. In a large bowl, combine the sweet potatoes, sour cream, egg, cumin, and nutmeg and mash with a fork, leaving the mixture somewhat chunky. Mix in ½ cup of the grated cheese and the parsley.

Lightly oil an 8-inch gratin or Pyrex baking dish and add the sweet potato mixture. Top with the remaining grated cheese and the bread crumbs and dot with the remaining butter. Bake until firm and golden brown, 20 to 30 minutes.

MAKES 4 SERVINGS

Swiss Chard Sauté

Blettes Sautées

This is a natural sauté with no extra ingredients, just vegetables and herbs. First boil the chard to soften it and remove any bitterness.

1 tablespoon sea salt
1 pound Swiss chard, cut to separate the white from the green, cleaned by immersing in a large bowl of cold water, and then squeezed dry
2 tablespoons corn or peanut oil
1 medium-size or ½ large onion, thinly sliced
4 cloves garlic, thinly sliced
2 medium-size very red, ripe tomatoes, halved, juice and seeds gently squeezed out, and roughly chopped
½ teaspoon minced fresh rosemary
Salt and freshly ground black pepper to taste

Fill a large pot three quarters full of water, add the sea salt, and bring to a boil over medium-high heat. Add the Swiss chard and boil 3 minutes, then drain in a strainer and set aside.

In a large skillet over medium-high heat, heat the oil until very hot but not smoking, then sauté the onion until golden, about 5 minutes. Add the garlic, tomatoes, and rosemary and sauté 2 minutes. Add the Swiss chard, salt, and pepper, stir well, and sauté 5 minutes. Serve hot.

MAKES 4 SERVINGS

Green Swiss Chard Tart

Tarte au Vert de Blette

Swiss chard leaves will keep their green color if sautéed until they wilt before being baked in the tart. The finished tart, lighter than a traditional quiche, is puffy and golden brown, with flecks of bright green chard.

Reserve the leftover Swiss chard stems for use in White Swiss Chard Omelette Marie-Thérèse (page 41).

2 tablespoons corn or peanut oil
1 large onion, cut in half crosswise and thinly sliced
3 or 4 cloves garlic, thinly sliced
6 packed-down cups Swiss chard leaves cut into 1-inch chiffonade, rinsed
  in a large bowl of cold water, and gently squeezed to remove the water
  (use about 1 pound Swiss chard)
Pinch freshly grated nutmeg
Salt and freshly ground black pepper to taste
2 large eggs, lightly beaten
½ cup heavy cream
1 sheet frozen puff pastry, thawed and rolled out to half its original thickness

In a large skillet over medium-high heat, heat the oil until very hot but not smoking, then sauté the onion until golden brown, about 5 minutes. Add the garlic and cook about 30 seconds. Add the Swiss chard leaves, nutmeg, salt, and pepper, toss or stir to combine, and cook, stirring, until the chard is wilted, 5 to 8 minutes. Drain in a strainer and allow to cool to room temperature. (It will cool faster if spread thin on a large platter or tray.)

Preheat the oven to 400°F. In a small bowl, combine the eggs and cream, season with salt and pepper, and whisk well. Fit the puff pastry into an 8-inch tart pan with a removable bottom and crimp the edges. Spoon the chard mixture into the pastry shell and pour the egg mixture over it. Bake until puffed and brown, about 40 minutes.

MAKES 4 TO 6 SERVINGS

Farm-Style Tomatoes Provençal

Tomates Provençales comme à la Ferme

Here are a few rules to follow in preparing this easy dish: scoop the centers out of the tomatoes carefully, so that you don't break the thin outer shell. Don't let the cooking oil become too hot, or it will splatter when you add the tomatoes. Don't use a high-sided skillet, because it will be difficult to work with the tomatoes (you will stuff them in the pan).

Quickly browning the tomato halves in oil is a simple first step that does a lot for the taste. Serve this colorful garnish with fish, poultry, grilled meat, or rice. It is also delicious served alongside Melted Endives (page 144).

    1 tablespoon corn or peanut oil
    8 small plum tomatoes, ends cut off so they can stand up, seeds and pulp
        removed and reserved
    8 tablespoons fresh bread crumbs
    2 tablespoons minced fresh parsley
    2 tablespoons minced scallions, white and tender green parts
    4 cloves garlic, smashed and minced
    Salt and freshly ground black pepper to taste
    1 teaspoon extra virgin olive oil

Preheat the oven to 400°F. In a large skillet over medium-high heat, heat the oil to moderately hot. Place the tomatoes in the pan cut side down and cook until they color around the edges, about 1 minute.

In a small bowl, combine the reserved tomato pulp, the bread crumbs, parsley, scallions, garlic, salt, and pepper. Remove the skillet from the heat, turn over the tomatoes, and stuff them generously with the mixture. Drizzle with the olive oil and season lightly with salt and pepper.

Place the skillet in the oven and cook until the stuffing has browned, about 15 minutes.

MAKES 4 SERVINGS

Fresh Tomatoes with Thyme

Tomates au Thym

When it was tomato season on the farm, my mother would send me to the fields to pick a few. I would run among the plants, which were taller than I, and inhale their strong, warm aroma. Mother took the tomatoes I picked and buried them in the embers of our outdoor fireplace until their skins split. Then we used a fork to mash them on our plates with a little olive oil and minced garlic. Try it yourself on your barbecue, and try this dish of fresh tomatoes and herbs in your kitchen.

2 tablespoons corn or peanut oil
2 large tomatoes, cut into 3 slices each (first cut off the ends)
Salt and freshly ground black pepper to taste
2 cloves garlic, thinly sliced
3 or 4 tablespoons tomato juice
Pinch dried thyme
1 teaspoon minced fresh thyme
1 tablespoon minced fresh parsley
Few drops extra virgin olive oil
12 very thin slices Swiss cheese (shave the cheese on a grater or cheese shaver)
1 tablespoon plain bread crumbs

Preheat the broiler.

In a large skillet over medium-high heat, heat the oil until very hot but not smoking and cook the tomatoes just until colored, about 1 minute on each side. Drain on a paper towel-lined platter and sprinkle with salt and pepper. Add the garlic to the pan and cook just until colored, about 30 seconds (don't let it burn).

Spoon the tomato juice along the bottom of an ovenproof tray or baking dish large enough to accommodate the tomato slices. Place the tomatoes on top and sprinkle with the garlic, herbs, and olive oil. Top with the cheese and sprinkle with the bread crumbs. Place the dish under the broiler just until the cheese is melted and the crumbs are browned. Serve warm or cold.

MAKES 4 SERVINGS AS A SIDE DISH

Fresh Tomato Cake

Gâteau de Tomate

This unusual pancake will be soft when you remove it from the pan, but it will become firm as it cools. This is not a traditional recipe, but an example of how you can cook if you have Provence in your heart.

2 tablespoons corn or peanut oil
1 large onion, thinly sliced
3 or 4 cloves garlic, thinly sliced
8 ripe plum tomatoes, roughly chopped
Grated zest of ¼ lemon
Salt and freshly ground black pepper to taste
1 teaspoon minced fresh thyme
½ teaspoon minced fresh basil
2 tablespoons minced fresh parsley
2 tablespoons thinly sliced scallions, white and tender green parts
Pinch freshly grated nutmeg
Small pinch fennel seeds
3 allspice berries, smashed
2 whole cloves
1 bay leaf
3 tablespoons prepared tomato puree
2 large eggs
1 teaspoon sugar
3 tablespoons all-purpose flour

Preheat the oven to 400°F.

In a large skillet over medium-high heat, heat the oil until very hot but not smoking and sauté the onion until golden, about 5 minutes. Add the garlic and sauté 30 seconds. Add the tomatoes, lemon zest, salt, a generous amount of pepper, and the herbs and spices. Cook until softened and combined, about 10 minutes. Just before the vegetables are done, mix in the tomato puree.

In a small bowl, beat the eggs lightly with the sugar and flour. Pour over the tomato mixture in the pan, remove from the heat, and mix well. Place in the oven until brown and slightly firm, about 10 minutes. Serve hot or cold.

MAKES 4 SERVINGS

Tomato Stew

Ragoût de Tomates

This is the kind of dish you would throw together in a Provençal kitchen, using fresh vegetables and a bit of free-flowing inspiration.

2 tablespoons corn or peanut oil
1 large onion, thinly sliced
8 plum tomatoes, quartered lengthwise
5 cloves garlic, thinly sliced
Salt and freshly ground black pepper to taste
1 teaspoon minced fresh basil
½ teaspoon minced fresh thyme
3 tablespoons minced fresh parsley
1 bay leaf
Pinch freshly grated nutmeg
Grated zest of ¼ lemon

In a large skillet over medium-high heat, heat the oil until very hot but not smoking and sauté the onion until colored, about 5 minutes. Add the remaining ingredients and cook until the tomatoes are cooked through but still firm, about 10 minutes. Serve hot.

MAKES 4 SERVINGS

Warm Salad of Tomato and Cucumber

Salade Chaude de Tomates et Concombres

In France we like to cook cucumber, as well as to serve it raw with a vinaigrette. This cooked dish combines the refreshing flavors of lemon, cucumber, tomato, and herbs.

2 tablespoons corn or peanut oil
6 shallots, thinly sliced
1 large cucumber, peeled, halved lengthwise, seeded, and thinly sliced crosswise
2 large tomatoes, cut into thin wedges
3 cloves garlic, thinly sliced
Salt and freshly ground black pepper to taste
1 teaspoon minced fresh basil
3 tablespoons minced fresh parsley
Grated zest of ¼ lemon
Juice of 1 lemon

In a large skillet over medium-high heat, heat the oil until very hot but not smoking and sauté the shallots until just softened, about 30 seconds. Add the cucumber, tomatoes, garlic, salt, a generous amount of pepper, the basil, 2 tablespoons of the parsley, the lemon zest, and lemon juice. Toss or stir to mix all the ingredients and remove from the heat.

Place in a serving bowl and sprinkle with the remaining parsley.

MAKES 4 SERVINGS AS A SIDE DISH OR 2 AS A VEGETABLE

Provençal Couscous Salad

Tabbouleh Provençal

This cool, colorful, herbaceous salad is a perfect centerpiece for your buffet or luncheon table.

One 10-ounce box instant couscous
2 tablespoons extra virgin olive oil
1 cup hot water
Salt and freshly ground black pepper to taste
2 large ripe tomatoes, halved, juice and seeds gently squeezed out, and cut into small dice
1 tablespoon minced fresh basil
2 tablespoons chopped scallions, white and tender green parts
2 tablespoons chopped fresh parsley
3 to 4 cloves garlic, minced
Grated zest and juice of 1 lemon
12 to 14 black olives marinated in olive oil and herbs (from Provence, Greece, or Italy), pitted and cut in half
2 to 3 oil-packed anchovy fillets, mashed (optional)
1 tablespoon pignoli (pine nuts)

Put the couscous, olive oil, and water in a large pan and stir to combine. Season with salt and a generous amount of pepper. Cover and set aside until the couscous has absorbed all the water, about 5 minutes.

Add the remaining ingredients and mix well. Serve at room temperature.

MAKES 6 TO 8 BUFFET SERVINGS

Zucchini Salad

Salade de Courgettes

Nothing could be simpler than this warm salad of tender, fresh zucchini, ripe tomatoes, and Provençal herbs, served with plain garlic toast.

For the salad

2 medium-size zucchini, very thinly sliced on a mandoline or by hand (do not use a food processor)
1 teaspoon extra virgin olive oil
Salt and freshly ground black pepper to taste
1 medium-size tomato, diced
2 tablespoons seeded and diced red bell pepper
1 teaspoon minced fresh rosemary
1 teaspoon minced fresh thyme
1 large clove garlic, thinly sliced

For the vinaigrette

1 teaspoon prepared mustard
1 teaspoon red wine vinegar
6 tablespoons extra virgin olive oil
Salt and freshly ground black pepper to taste

For the garlic toast

4 slices country bread
1 clove garlic, halved

Drizzle the zucchini slices with the olive oil and sprinkle with salt and pepper. Steam over boiling water until the zucchini is still crisp, 2 to 3 minutes. Drain.

To make the vinaigrette, in a small bowl, whisk together the mustard and vinegar, then add the oil very slowly, whisking until emulsified. Season generously with pepper and lightly with salt. Toast the bread slices and rub both sides with the cut side of the garlic clove.

For each serving, arrange one quarter of the zucchini slices on a plate and sprinkle with one quarter of the tomato, bell pepper, rosemary, thyme, and garlic. Drizzle with one quarter of the vinaigrette and serve with 1 slice of garlic toast.

MAKES 4 SERVINGS

Baked Zucchini
Gratin de Courgettes

2 tablespoons corn or peanut oil
1 large onion, thinly sliced
4 large zucchini, ends cut off, cut into 3-inch lengths, then halved length-
    wise and each half-section cut into 2 or 3 wedges
6 cloves garlic, peeled and smashed
2 medium-size tomatoes, halved, juice and seeds gently squeezed out, and
    cut into 8 wedges each
2 tablespoons minced scallions, white and tender green parts
1 generous tablespoon minced fresh thyme
1 tablespoon extra virgin olive oil
Salt and freshly ground black pepper to taste
1 cup grated Swiss cheese

Preheat the broiler. In a large saucepan over medium-high heat, heat the oil and sauté the onion until lightly colored, about 5 minutes. Add the zucchini, stir well, and sauté 5 minutes. Add the garlic and tomatoes and cook 2 minutes. Add the remaining ingredients, except the cheese, and mix well. Place a sheet of aluminum foil placed directly over the vegetables, reduce the heat to low, and cook 15 minutes, stirring occasionally.

Lightly oil a medium-size gratin dish and spoon in the vegetable mixture. Top with the grated cheese and place under the broiler until melted.

MAKES 4 SERVINGS

Zucchini and Tomatoes with Dill and Garlic

Courgettes et Tomates à l'Hanet et à l'Ail

You may need a little more zucchini if you decide to use a slightly larger baking dish, such as a 10-inch square. This is a very free-form recipe—increase or decrease the amounts according to your needs.

1 medium-size zucchini, very thinly sliced (about ⅛ inch)
4 plum tomatoes, not too ripe, very thinly sliced (about ⅛ inch)
3 tablespoons warm water
6 cloves garlic, minced
2 tablespoons minced fresh dill feathers (no stems)
Salt and freshly ground black pepper to taste
3 tablespoons extra virgin olive oil
Few drops Worcestershire sauce (optional)

Preheat the oven to 400°F. Lightly butter a medium-size gratin dish. Starting at one narrow end of the dish, arrange a row of zucchini slices standing on end along the edge. Follow that with a row of tomato slices, standing them on end up against the zucchini. Continue layering the vegetables until the dish is full and the layers are pressed close against each other. Pour the warm water over the vegetables.

In a small bowl, mix together the garlic, dill, salt, pepper, and olive oil. Spoon the mixture evenly over the zucchini and tomatoes. Sprinkle the top with a little more olive oil and the Worcestershire. Cover tightly with aluminum foil and bake until tender, 30 to 40 minutes.

MAKES 4 SERVINGS

Pasta Salad with Rose Petals *(Pâtes aux Pétales de Rose)*, page 52.

Provençal Vegetable Soup *(Soupe au Pistou)*, page 86.

Clockwise from top left, Gruyère and Nutmeg Bread *(Pain au Gruyère et Noix de Muscade),* page 359; Provençal Flat Bread *(Fougasse),* page 357; Country Bread *(Pain Maison),* page 358; and Olive and Rosemary Bread *(Pain aux Olives et Romarin),* page 360.

Sardines with Spinach *(Sardines aux Épinards)*, page 218.

Bean Cake *(Gâteau de Haricots),* page 118, and Zucchini and Tomatoes with Dill and Garlic *(Courgettes et Tomates à l'Hanet et à l'Ail),* page 180, with sautéed potatoes.

Rack of Lamb Farm Style *(Carré d'Agneau Comme à la Ferme),* page 249,
and Artichokes with Herbs *(Artichauts à la Barigoule),* page 114.

Almond and Hazelnut Soufflés *(Soufflés Macaron),* page 330.

Grandma Cake with Apples and Rosemary *(Gâteau de Grand-mère aux Pommes et Romarin)*, page 332; Orange Cookies *(Biscuits à l'Orange)*, page 351; and Upside-Down Apple Tart with Rosemary *(Tarte Tatin aux Romarin)*, page 346.

Spring Zucchini

Courgettes Printanières

This is a magnificent dish, colorful, delicious, and perfumed with the herbs and vegetables of Provence. It is the perfect do-ahead vegetable course—a boon for any hostess.

Dry the zucchini halves with paper towels before cooking them in oil to avoid splattering. Slice the leeks on an angle for an attractive presentation.

5 large zucchini
¼ cup corn or peanut oil
1 large onion, thinly sliced
4 large or 5 medium-size cloves garlic, smashed and minced
3 leeks, white and tender green parts, well washed, halved lengthwise, and
    cut on an angle into ½-inch slices
2 tablespoons minced scallions, white and tender green parts
1 medium-size red bell pepper, quartered, seeded, and cut into ½-inch dice
4 plum tomatoes, halved lengthwise and cut into ½-inch slices
3 tablespoons minced fresh parsley
1 teaspoon minced fresh basil
1 teaspoon minced fresh rosemary
1 teaspoon minced fresh thyme
6 black olives marinated in olive oil and herbs (from Provence, Greece, or
    Italy), drained and pitted
2 tablespoons extra virgin olive oil
Salt and freshly ground black pepper to taste
1 cup coarsely grated Swiss cheese

Preheat the oven to 400°F. Cut the zucchini in half lengthwise. Scoop out the center core of one halved zucchini, discarding the pulp, and cut the green shell into ¼-inch slices.

In a large skillet over medium-high heat, heat 2 tablespoons of the corn oil until very hot, but not smoking. Cook the zucchini halves in the oil until browned, about

2 minutes on each side. Then place the skillet in the oven and roast the zucchini for 10 minutes. Remove from the oven and set aside.

Meanwhile, in another large skillet over medium-high heat, heat the remaining 2 tablespoons of corn oil until very hot, but not smoking, and sauté the onion until colored, about 5 minutes. Add the garlic and cook 1 minute. Add the sliced zucchini, leeks, scallion, bell pepper, and tomatoes. Add 2 tablespoons of the minced parsley, the basil, rosemary, thyme, olives, olive oil, salt, and pepper and sauté until all the vegetables are softened, 8 to 10 minutes.

Preheat the broiler. Lightly oil a medium-size gratin dish and arrange the roasted zucchini halves in it skin side down. Drain the vegetable mixture in a strainer and spoon it over the zucchini. Sprinkle with the grated Swiss cheese and the remaining tablespoon minced parsley. Place under the broiler until the cheese melts and browns slightly, 3 to 4 minutes.

To serve, place 2 zucchini halves, with vegetables and cheese, on each plate.

Makes 4 servings

Stuffed Vegetables

Les Farcis

My grandmother made stuffed farm-fresh vegetables, one of the most famous dishes in the south of France, in the spring and summer, when a variety of colorful produce was available. Of course, this can easily be made any time of the year. When you bring the bubbling casserole to the table, fragrant after an hour in the oven, it makes a fantastic main course. Serve farcis hot with a salad and some country bread, or as a cold dinner or lunch in the summertime. If you like, you can vary the stuffing, using sausage or chopped vegetables to make about 3 cups.

For the vegetables

- 4 small red potatoes, halved crosswise and a shallow depression scooped out of the flesh of each half
- 4 plum tomatoes halved crosswise, juice squeezed out and reserved, and pulp scraped out and reserved

2 small zucchini, cut into 2-inch lengths and a shallow depression scooped
    out of the top of each section
1 small red bell pepper, seeded, bottom cut off to make 1-inch-high cup
1 small green bell pepper, seeded, bottom cut off to make 1-inch-high cup
    (peppers also can be halved lengthwise and seeded to make "cups")
1 small eggplant, cut into 2-inch lengths and a shallow depression scooped
    out of the top of each section

For the stuffing

4 chicken breast halves, skinned and boned
2 chicken livers
6 cloves garlic, peeled
6 shallots, peeled
Salt and freshly ground black pepper to taste
2 tablespoons minced scallions, white and tender green parts
3 tablespoons minced fresh parsley
1 tablespoon minced fresh thyme
2 large eggs

For the broth

2 tablespoons corn or peanut oil
1 large onion, thinly sliced
4 cloves garlic, thinly sliced
2 bay leaves, lightly crumbled
4 cups homemade (page 82) or canned low-salt chicken broth

For the topping

½ cup plain bread crumbs
2 tablespoons extra virgin olive oil

Arrange the vegetables scooped sides up in a lightly oiled, high-sided ovenproof
pan or casserole. Cut a small slice off the bottom of each, if necessary, to help them
stand steadily. Preheat the oven to 350°F.

Combine the chicken, livers, garlic, shallots, and the reserved tomato juice and
pulp and pass the mixture through a food grinder equipped with a large-holed disk

(don't do this with a food processor; you won't get the right texture). In a large bowl, combine the mixture with the salt, pepper, scallions, parsley, thyme, and eggs. Spoon the stuffing loosely into the prepared vegetables.

In a large skillet over medium-high heat, heat the oil until very hot but not smoking and sauté the onion until golden, about 4 minutes. Add the garlic and bay leaves and sauté 1 minute. Add the broth and bring to a boil. Pour over the vegetables. Sprinkle the bread crumbs over the top of the vegetables and drizzle with the olive oil. Sprinkle with salt and pepper.

Bake until the vegetables are softened, the stuffing is golden, and the broth is bubbling and aromatic, about 1 hour. Halfway through the baking, cover with aluminum foil. To serve, put a selection of vegetables on each plate and spoon the broth over and around them. Serve hot or cold. Can be refrigerated up to 3 days.

MAKES 4 SERVINGS

Creamy Polenta Pancakes

Petits Penaquets Cremeux de Polenta

At home, we warmed the ripe tomato garnish for these cakes by setting the pot on a warm spot on the stove.

These are a good side dish for any meat course.

For the pancakes

4 cups whole or low-fat milk
1½ cups cornmeal
1½ cups coarsely grated Swiss cheese
Salt and freshly ground pepper to taste
Pinch grated nutmeg
1 large egg, lightly beaten
1 tablespoon extra virgin olive oil

1 tablespoon minced fresh marjoram or oregano
2 tablespoons corn or peanut oil

For the tomato garnish

3 ripe plum tomatoes, halved, juice and seeds gently squeezed out, flesh
    cut in medium dice
1 tablespoon extra virgin olive oil
Salt and freshly ground pepper to taste
1 tablespoon minced parsley
1 clove garlic, minced

In a large saucepan over medium-high heat, bring the milk to a boil. Add the cornmeal and whisk until combined.

Remove the pan from the heat and whisk in the Swiss cheese, salt, pepper, nutmeg, egg, olive oil, and marjoram. Cover and let stand at room temperature 10 to 15 minutes. The mixture will become quite firm.

Meanwhile, in a small saucepan, combine the tomatoes, olive oil, parsley and garlic, salt, and pepper and place over low heat until fragrant and warm, but not cooked through, 10 to 15 minutes.

In a large skillet over medium-high heat, heat the corn oil until very hot but not smoking and drop in the polenta mixture by tablespoons, being careful not to crowd the cakes. Cook until brown and crisp, and creamy in the middle, 3 to 4 minutes on each side. Drain on paper towels and serve garnished with tomato mixture.

MAKES 12 CAKES, SERVING 4

Farm-Style Gratin of Polenta
with Fresh Vegetable Sauce

Polenta en Gratin Fermier à la Sauce de Légumes

This exceptionally delicate polenta is easily reheated. Served with its colorful, aromatic fresh vegetable sauce, it makes a complete lunch or dinner.

    5 cups regular or low-fat milk
    2 cups yellow cornmeal
    ½ medium-size red bell pepper, seeded and cut into ¼-inch dice (reserve
        the other half pepper for the vegetable sauce)
    2 cloves garlic, smashed and peeled
    1 teaspoon grated lemon zest
    Salt and freshly ground black pepper to taste
    1 cup grated Swiss cheese
    2 large eggs, lightly beaten
    3 tablespoons fresh bread crumbs
    Extra virgin olive oil for drizzling
    Chopped fresh parsley for garnish
    Fresh Vegetable Sauce (recipe follows)

Preheat the oven to 400°F. In a large saucepan over medium-high heat, bring the milk to a boil, then add the cornmeal, whisking briskly to combine. Cook, whisking, 2 minutes. Whisk in the bell pepper, garlic, lemon zest, salt, and pepper.

Reduce the heat to medium and whisk in the cheese and the eggs. Cook 30 seconds (just to cook the eggs) and pour into a lightly oiled medium-size gratin pan. Sprinkle with the bread crumbs and the olive oil and bake until firm and golden, about 30 minutes. Serve sprinkled with chopped parsley, with the fresh vegetable sauce alongside.

MAKES 8 SERVINGS

Fresh Vegetable Sauce

Sauce de Légumes

This sauce transforms even the saddest of winter tomatoes. All the vegetables share fresh herbal flavor and color when cooked together and they are a perfect accent to the gratin of polenta. Try the sauce on rice or pasta as well.

2 tablespoons corn or peanut oil
1 large onion, thinly sliced
3 large tomatoes, halved, juice and seeds gently squeezed out, and coarsely chopped
½ medium-size red bell pepper, seeded and cut into ¼-inch dice
6 cloves garlic, smashed and minced
Salt and freshly ground black pepper to taste
1 tablespoon minced fresh thyme
2 tablespoons minced fresh parsley
2 tablespoons chopped scallions, white and tender green parts
1 tablespoon extra virgin olive oil
1 cup water

In a large skillet over medium-high heat, heat the oil until hot but not smoking, then sauté the onion until golden, about 5 minutes. Add the tomatoes, bell pepper, garlic, salt, and pepper and sauté until all the vegetables are soft, about 5 minutes.

Add the thyme, parsley, and scallions and mix well. Stir in the olive oil, cook 30 seconds, and add the water. Reduce the heat to low and cook slowly until soft and thickened, 20 to 30 minutes.

MAKES 8 SERVINGS

Garden-Fresh Vegetable Condiment

Les Condiments Frais du Jardin

My grandmother filled a large glass bowl with these crisp, colorful, lightly pickled vegetables and kept it in the center of the kitchen table. With big wooden pincers, we picked out our favorite vegetables to snack on or to accompany meals. The mixture got better every day.

This makes a large pot of vegetables, and you may want to cool several portions in a hurry. Simply pack the condiment in a jar, close tightly, and submerge in a bowl or sink full of cold water.

1 head garlic, separated into cloves but left unpeeled
1 tablespoon fennel seeds
1 tablespoon cumin seeds
1 tablespoon coriander seeds
6 to 8 whole cloves
6 to 8 allspice berries
3 tablespoons black peppercorns
3 large or 4 medium-size bay leaves
1 large onion, roughly sliced
1 medium-size yellow squash, outside flesh cut into ½-inch-wide julienne
    strips (discard the center portion containing the seeds)
1 medium-size cucumber, peeled and cut into ½-inch slices
Florets from 2 stalks broccoli
1 broccoli stalk, cut into ½-inch slices
½ medium-size cauliflower, separated into florets
2 medium-size green tomatoes, cut into 1-inch slices
4 asparagus spears, tough bottom portions snapped off and spears cut into
    2-inch pieces
3 medium-size carrots, cut into ½-inch slices
2 leeks, white part only, well washed, cut in half lengthwise, then cut into
    2-inch slices
1 medium-size yellow bell pepper, seeded and cut into ½-inch wide strips
1 medium-size red bell pepper, seeded and cut into ½-inch-wide strips

1 medium-size green bell pepper, seeded and cut into ½-inch-wide strips

3 plum tomatoes, not too ripe, quartered

3 stalks celery, leaves included, cut in half lengthwise, then cut into 2-inch slices

Small bunch fresh dill

6 to 8 fresh basil leaves

4 or 5 sprigs fresh parsley

3 sprigs fresh rosemary

3 sprigs fresh thyme

Peel of 1 lemon, in large pieces

10 cups white vinegar

2 tablespoons sea salt

2 tablespoons extra virgin olive oil

Divide the vegetables and herbs among three bowls. In bowl one, combine the garlic, fennel, cumin, coriander, cloves, allspice, peppercorns, bay leaves, and onion. In bowl two, combine the squash, cucumber, broccoli, cauliflower, green tomatoes, asparagus, carrots, and leeks. In bowl three, combine the peppers, plum tomatoes, celery, dill, basil, parsley, rosemary, thyme, and lemon peel.

In a large saucepan over high heat, combine the contents of bowls one and two with the vinegar, sea salt, and oil and bring to a boil. Let boil 10 minutes. Add the contents of bowl three and let boil 5 minutes. Remove from the heat and allow to cool in the pot. Store at room temperature in a large glass bowl, or in the refrigerator for up to 1 month.

MAKES ABOUT 1 GALLON

Camargue Rice

Riz Camarguais

A lot of rice is grown in the Camargue and this is one typical way of preparing it, mixed with garlic, onion, tomatoes, and olives. I prefer to leave the pits in the olives, for an authentic touch, but it is a good idea to warn your guests.

6 tablespoons extra virgin olive oil
1 large onion, halved and thinly sliced
6 cloves garlic, smashed and peeled
2 large ripe tomatoes or 4 to 6 plum tomatoes, roughly chopped
2 to 3 bay leaves
1 pound (2¼ cups) long or short grain rice, rinsed
Salt and freshly ground black pepper to taste
½ cup black olives marinated in olive oil and herbs (from Provence, Greece, or Italy), pitted (optional)
5⅔ cups water, chicken broth, or an equal mixture of both, to equal 2½ times the volume of the rice
Small sprig fresh rosemary
½ teaspoon cumin seeds
3 leeks, white and tender green parts, well washed, quartered lengthwise, and sliced 1 inch thick
1 celery stalk, sliced 1 inch thick
1 medium-size carrot, halved lengthwise and sliced ¼ inch thick
Grated zest of ½ lemon

In a large soup pot over medium-high heat, heat 2 tablespoons of the oil until very hot but not smoking and cook the onion until softened and golden, about 5 minutes. Add the garlic, tomatoes, and bay leaves and stir. Add the rice and the remaining oil. Sprinkle with the salt and pepper. Add the olives and water, stir well, and bring to a boil.

Add the rosemary, cumin, leeks, celery, carrot, and lemon zest, reduce the heat to low, and cover with a sheet of aluminum foil pressed down over the rice. Cook slowly 45 minutes until the grains are soft and separate, and serve hot.

MAKES 8 TO 10 SERVINGS

Bien mélanger le tout et l'étendre en petits tas sur une plaque beurrée. Dès qu'ils ont pris couleur, les rouler tout chaud sur un doigt en forme de tuile.

Bouillabaisse

Mettre dans une casserole de l'huile d'olive, y émincer oignons poireaux carotte et quelques gousses d'ail. Que ce soit passé bien frit. Y revenir le poisson, couvrir d'eau bouillante et laisser cuire un bon quart d'heure. Ajouter sel poivre, safran persil girofle, fenouil. Servir le poisson dans un plat et passer le bouillon sur des tranches de pain qu'on aura laissé un moment au feu.

Sauce Mousseline

Mettez dans une petite casserole trois jaunes d'œufs, une noisette de beurre et une cuillerée à café de jus de citron. Placez la casserole au bain marie, puis avec un fouet mélangez fortement son contenu jusqu'à ce que ce soit épais comme une mayonnaise. Incorporez alors à cette sauce peu à peu et toujours en fouettant 125 gr de beurre divisé en petits fragments. Assaisonnez cette sauce avec sel et poivre. Une fois le moment venu d'y ajouter au dernier moment sous le feu incorporez deux cuillerées à bouche de crème fouettée.

Sauce Hollandaise

Mettez dans une casserole deux ou trois

CHAPTER 5

Fish and Shellfish

After my apprenticeship at La Riboto de Taven, I was lucky enough to work in L'Escale, in the little seaport town of Carry-le-Rouet, near Marseille, which received two Michelin stars and was considered one of the finest fish restaurants in the world. It was on the bay, where the water was so quiet and clean, you could see the colored pebbles on the bottom. I remember there was a fisherman who went out every morning and came back with a huge basket filled with colorful tiny fish that were still alive—turquoise, pink, green, gray, and red. They were so beautiful, jumping and wiggling in the sunlight.

Here I learned to prepare fish from Charles Berot, a superb chef and teacher, whose kitchen was a joyful place to be in. We did a spectacular bouillabaisse using fish from the Mediterranean: rascasse, galinette, monkfish, St. Peter's fish, and reyniere. We put them in a pot of water with saffron, anise, pastis, garlic, and herbs and poached them with a thin slice of potato. When the potato was cooked, the bouillabaisse was done. It was an elixir of God! In the chapter on soups, I include a recipe that comes very close to the original (page 102).

Everyone seems to have an explanation for the origin of the word *bouillabaisse.* There is a story in Marseille that says when the fishermen had caught enough fish, they cooked the dish immediately on the boat. Their only rule was "When it boils, turn it down" or *"Quand sa bouille, abess."*

Before my professional training, I had learned about fish from my grandmother and mother, who served it every Friday without fail. They could buy fresh fish in several outdoor markets near Saint-Rémy, but their favorite was the one on Wednesdays, which specialized in fish and exotic fruit. There the fish came from Marseille, which was the biggest wholesale fish market, and there were baskets full of freshly caught codfish, whitefish, monkfish, and daurade, a fish like red snapper. Mediterranean fish is the best, with the briny taste of the sea, because it has a lot of iodine. It is very well known for this taste.

All our fish dishes are complex, subtle, and imaginative. We don't hesitate to combine fish with generous amounts of garlic and herbs and to season it aggressively. I am always surprised by people who expect fish to be boring or bland—it's never that way in Provence.

Cod is our most popular fish—it is the ambassador of Provençal cooking, carrying its message everywhere. It is the one fish that seems to marry perfectly with all vegetables and herbs, especially anise, the licorice flavor present in pastis, our popular aperitif. It is an affordable fish, with a very subtle consistency, like velvet. Many traditional recipes my mother prepared call for dried or salted cod, but I prefer to use fresh cod, which is easy to find in most fish markets. In Provence tiny fresh sardines also are popular, as are red snapper and monkfish. They all combine sublimely with a variety of vegetables. Neither bluefish nor salmon is common in our markets, but I have cooked them here, and I find them natural partners to Provençal herbs and seasonings.

When you shop for a whole fish, look at its eyes, which should be shiny and bulging, not flat or concave. Open the mouth, which should feel moist (or let the fishmonger do this). The gills should have a little trace of blood, and shouldn't be dry or brown.

Whether you cook whole fish or fillets, it is easy to recognize when they are done. Just take the skillet off the heat and spread the fish apart with two forks or a fork and spoon—the flesh should be the same color throughout. If it is raw in the middle, just cook a little more. Remember that even if the fish is not completely done, it will continue to cook from its own heat for another five minutes.

Something else we all enjoyed was snails. When the entire family gathered for Christmas Eve dinner, my grandfather Joseph was in charge of collecting them and my grandmother Marie was in charge of preparing them. This was a process that began long before they were to be served.

After the first rain of autumn, snails by the hundreds would crawl out of the nearby brook onto dry land. This was when Grandfather, my sister, and I would scoop them into a big basket, bring them home, and transfer them to a large wire cage. From that day until Christmas, we did not feed them, so they could disgorge all the mud, pebbles, and other unpleasant stuff they had swallowed. But we filled the cage with thyme and rosemary and they slowly took on those subtle flavors. Snails protect themselves by forming a skin, which we removed a day before they were to be cooked. Then we soaked them overnight in a mixture of vinegar and sea salt for a final cleaning. The next day, Grandmother boiled them two or three hours with leeks, carrots, and unpeeled garlic and onions—the unpeeled vegetables lent a special hearty taste. Then she strained them and put them in a sauce made with onions, unsmoked bacon, fresh tomatoes, tomato paste, flour, water, and a lot of garlic. She had to make a great deal of sauce, because a snail is like a sponge—when you put it in liquid, it soaks up huge amounts. After this introduction, you know why I haven't given my grandmother's recipe in this chapter, but I have included a simple and delicious dish made with canned snails and Provençal herbs.

Codfish with Mayonnaise Sauce

Morue à la Rouille

Cod is the most popular Provençal fish, marrying perfectly with the flavors of local herbs and vegetables. Fresh codfish is wonderful, very light and good; I much prefer it to the salted variety, which isn't as popular in Provence as it once was.

Poaching in a court bouillon is the traditional way of cooking codfish in the farm kitchens of the south. The bouillon is flavored only by vegetables and contains no wine, yet the fish emerges with a sweet flavor and a velvety texture. I suggest using four cloves of garlic in the broth, but you may use more or fewer, according to your own taste. You may even prepare it without any garlic. If you are watching your diet, serve the codfish with just the broth and its vegetables, without any other sauce.

For the sauce

1 cup good-quality mayonnaise
1 generous teaspoon Spanish paprika
Few drops Tabasco sauce
Generous ½ teaspoon saffron threads
2 to 3 cloves garlic, smashed and minced (optional)
1 tablespoon minced fresh parsley

For the court bouillon

1 large carrot, thinly sliced
½ onion, thickly sliced
1 leek, white and tender green parts, well washed and thickly sliced
4 cloves garlic, peeled
Pinch saffron threads
1 whole clove
1 bay leaf
2 tablespoons extra virgin olive oil

1 tablespoon fresh parsley leaves
¼ teaspoon freshly ground black pepper
¼ teaspoon salt

To finish the dish

2 pounds cod fillets
8 small red potatoes, halved
8 sprigs fresh basil for garnish
4 wedges lemon for garnish

One hour before serving, prepare the sauce. Combine all the ingredients in a small bowl and refrigerate (the saffron will give it a warm orange-gold color).

To prepare the court bouillon, in a large saucepan over medium-high heat, combine all the ingredients with water to cover generously, and bring to a boil. Reduce the heat to medium and continue cooking for 10 minutes.

Place the cod in the simmering court bouillon and cook until firm, white, and shiny, about 10 minutes.

Meanwhile, prepare the potato garnish. Place the potatoes in a small saucepan with water to cover and bring to a boil over medium-high heat. Reduce the heat to medium and continue cooking until the potatoes are tender, about 15 minutes. Drain and set aside.

To serve, divide the fish among four dishes. Spoon the vegetables and a little broth over the fish, scatter the potatoes on individual plates, and garnish with the basil. Place a spoonful of the mayonnaise sauce and a lemon wedge alongside the fish.

MAKES 4 SERVINGS

Provençal Poached Cod and Vegetables with Garlic Sauce

Aïoli Garnit

Aïoli, the steaming, fragrant combination of codfish, garlic, fresh vegetables, and herbs, is the signature dish of Provence. In some towns, hundreds of people join in an aïoli feast, consuming gigantic pots of the stew and singing beautiful Provençal songs. When the dish cooks, you can smell garlic all over the place—garlic is not only a flavor, it is the secret of happiness. I believe garlic is the reason people in the south of France live to be a hundred!

My recipe calls for fresh fish, although aïoli traditionally is made with salt cod, and I add a pinch of saffron—my own little note.

For the court bouillon

2 large carrots, cut into thirds crosswise and halved lengthwise
6 small red potatoes or 3 large potatoes
2 turnips, peeled and quartered
1 head garlic, unpeeled, cut in half crosswise
1 large onion, roughly chopped
Bouquet garni made of 2 sprigs each fresh sage, parsley, rosemary, and
    thyme and 2 bay leaves, tied together with kitchen string
1 tablespoon sea salt
¼ teaspoon black peppercorns
4 allspice berries
3 whole cloves
8 cups boiling water
2 cups dry white wine

For the fish

2 pounds cod, snapper, or striped bass fillets
Pinch saffron threads
2 large zucchini, cut into 3-inch lengths and then quartered lengthwise
3 or 4 leeks, white and a bit of the tender green parts, well washed and cut
    into 3-inch lengths
4 plum tomatoes, halved
1 stalk celery, cut into 3-inch lengths
Two 1-inch slices red bell pepper
Two 1-inch slices green bell pepper
4 scallions, white and tender green parts
2 tablespoons extra virgin olive oil

For the sauce aïoli

1 cup mayonnaise
4 cloves garlic, smashed and minced
2 tablespoons extra virgin olive oil
Freshly ground black pepper to taste

In a large soup pot over high heat, combine the court bouillon ingredients and bring to a boil. Reduce the heat to medium-high and cook until the carrots are almost tender, about 20 minutes.

Add the ingredients for the fish, making sure that everything is covered by the broth. Reduce the heat to low and cook until the fish is opaque all the way through and can be flaked, about 15 minutes.

In a small bowl, combine the mayonnaise and garlic. Add the olive oil in a steady stream, mixing well. Sprinkle with pepper generously.

To serve, remove the fish and vegetables from the pot with a slotted spoon and place on individual plates. Moisten with a little broth and garnish with the aïoli.

MAKES 4 TO 6 SERVINGS

Poached Cod with Sweet Garlic

Filet de Morue à l'Ail Doux

Here the poached fish is served with a highly flavored sauce, and a little sauce goes a long way. If you prefer more sauce, just double the amounts below. Served with ratatouille (page 142), this makes a delicious, rustic meal.

1 recipe Court Bouillon (page 198)
2 pounds cod fillets
Sprigs fresh thyme for garnish

For the sweet garlic sauce

2 tablespoons corn or peanut oil
10 cloves garlic, cut lengthwise into halves or quarters
2 tablespoons sugar
1 large tomato, roughly diced
½ teaspoon grated lemon zest
½ teaspoon minced fresh rosemary
Salt to taste
¼ cup dry white wine

In a large saucepan over high heat, bring the court bouillon to a boil. Add the cod, lower the heat to medium, and simmer until firm, white, and shiny, about 10 minutes, then drain and set aside.

Meanwhile, prepare the garlic sauce. In a large skillet over medium-high heat, heat the oil to medium-hot and sauté the garlic until golden, about 2 minutes. Add the sugar and cook another 3 minutes, stirring.

Drain the garlic and return to the pan. Add the tomato, lemon zest, and rosemary and season with salt. Sauté until softened, about 5 minutes. Add the wine, raise the heat to high, and reduce to a syrup.

Divide among four plates. Top with the sauce and garnish with the thyme.

MAKES 4 SERVINGS

Codfish Baked with Potatoes

Gratin de Morue et de Pommes de Terre

This farm dish is very easy to make and so colorful, with brown potatoes, golden broth, and green parsley set against the white fish.

2 tablespoons corn or peanut oil
1 large onion, thinly sliced
3 large potatoes, peeled and sliced ⅛ inch thick (use a mandoline)
3 cloves garlic, smashed and minced
3 cups homemade (page 82) or canned low-salt chicken broth
Salt and freshly ground black pepper to taste
2 bay leaves, crushed
2 whole cloves
2 pounds codfish fillets, cut into serving pieces
Extra virgin olive oil for drizzling
4 pinches grated lemon zest
4 pinches chopped fresh parsley

In a large skillet over medium-high heat, heat the oil until very hot but not smoking, then add the onion and sauté until it colors, about 5 minutes. Add the potatoes and garlic and stir well. Add the broth, generous pinches of salt and pepper, the bay leaves and cloves and bring to a boil.

Reduce the heat to low, cover tightly with an oiled square of aluminum foil, and cook 10 minutes.

Remove the cover and place the codfish on top of the simmering potatoes. Drizzle lightly with the olive oil and sprinkle with the lemon zest and half of the parsley. Replace the cover and cook 6 minutes. Turn, sprinkle the other side with the remaining parsley, and cook, covered, until firm, white, and shiny, another 6 minutes.

To serve, arrange the potato mixture in the center of four plates and top with the fish.

MAKES 4 SERVINGS

Quick Codfish

Morue à la Minute

This dish cooks quickly and has a wonderful fresh feeling. Leave the skin on the tomato for a rustic touch.

2 pounds codfish fillets
Salt and freshly ground black pepper to taste
All-purpose flour for dredging
2 tablespoons corn or peanut oil
8 large button mushroom caps, thinly sliced
1 leek, white and tender green parts, well washed and thinly sliced
1 large tomato, roughly chopped
3 tablespoons minced fresh parsley
1 teaspoon thinly sliced garlic
2 tablespoons extra virgin olive oil
4 lemon wedges for garnish

Sprinkle the fish with salt and pepper and dredge in the flour, tapping off any excess. In a large skillet over medium-high heat, heat the oil until very hot but not smoking, then cook the fish until golden brown and crusty, 5 to 8 minutes on each side.

Pour out most of the oil, return the pan to the heat, and add the mushrooms, leek, and tomato. Sprinkle with salt and pepper and sauté 5 minutes. Add the parsley and garlic and sauté another 5 minutes. Remove from the heat, drizzle with the olive oil, and mix well.

To serve, divide the fish among four plates and place a generous serving of vegetables beside it. Garnish with lemon wedges.

MAKES 4 SERVINGS

Codfish with Olives

Morue aux Olives

Here are two excellent recipes that I have developed using pan-fried codfish. The delicate fish cooks quickly, but it has enough texture for you to prepare it early in the day and combine it with its accompaniments or sauce just before serving.

This rough and rustic sauce has fantastic deep colors and a lot of earthy flavor. The ingredients are Provençal, but the interpretation is my own.

2 pounds codfish fillets
All-purpose flour for dredging
2 tablespoons corn or peanut oil
Salt and freshly ground black pepper to taste
4 lemon wedges for garnish
Sprigs fresh basil or Italian (flatleaf) parsley for garnish

For the sauce

2 tablespoons corn or peanut oil
1 large onion, thinly sliced
5 cloves garlic, thinly sliced
½ cup thinly sliced scallions, white and tender green parts
2 tablespoons minced fresh parsley
32 small black olives marinated in olive oil and herbs (from Provence,
    Greece, or Italy), pitted
1 large tomato, cut into ½-inch dice
Salt and freshly ground black pepper to taste

Dredge the fillets in the flour, tapping off any excess. In a large skillet over medium-high heat, heat the oil until very hot but not smoking and cook the codfish on the inner, rough side until golden, 5 to 7 minutes. Reduce the heat to low, turn the fish, sprinkle generously with salt and pepper, and cook slowly until firm, white, and shiny, another 5 to 10 minutes. Remove to a platter to allow the oil to run off, blot with paper towels, and set aside in a warm place.

In another large skillet over medium-high heat, heat the oil to very hot but not smoking, then add the onion and sauté until golden, about 5 minutes. Add the garlic and sauté another 3 minutes. Add the scallions, parsley, olives, and tomato and season with salt and pepper. Reduce the heat to low and cook until everything is softened, about 10 minutes.

To serve, divide the olive sauce among four plates, mounding it in the center. Place the fish over the sauce and garnish with the lemon wedges and basil.

MAKES 4 SERVINGS

Codfish with Cauliflower Puree

Morue à la Purée de Chou-fleur

Green parsley, golden brown croutons, and orange salmon caviar give color to the creamy cauliflower and light golden fish. To highlight the sweet taste of the cauliflower, don't season it with any salt after cooking. You may substitute salmon for the cod in this dish, if you prefer.

1 head cauliflower, broken into florets, stems discarded
8 small red potatoes, peeled, halved, and sliced ½ inch thick
¼ cup extra virgin olive oil
Generous pinch salt
¼ cup regular or low-fat milk
Pinch freshly grated nutmeg
2 pounds cod fillets

For the garnish

¼ cup corn or peanut oil
2 slices white bread, crusts trimmed and cut into ¼-inch dice
8 to 10 sprigs fresh parsley

1 tablespoon chopped fresh parsley

¼ cup salmon caviar (optional)

Place the cauliflower and potatoes in a large saucepan with water to cover, 2 tablespoons of the olive oil, and the salt. Bring to a boil over high heat, then reduce the heat to medium and simmer until the vegetables are soft, 30 to 40 minutes.

Drain the cauliflower and place it in a food processor. Add the milk and nutmeg and process to a puree.

In a large skillet over medium-high heat, heat the remaining olive oil until it is very hot, then cook the codfish on the inner, rough side until golden, 5 to 7 minutes. Reduce the heat to low, turn the fish, and cook slowly another 5 to 10 minutes. When firm, white, and shiny, drain, blot with paper towels, and set aside in a warm place.

To prepare the garnish, in a large skillet over medium-high heat, heat the oil until very hot but not smoking. Fry the bread cubes until browned, about 3 minutes. When the bread is almost done, add the parsely sprigs and immediately remove the pan from the heat. Drain the oil, blot the bread and parsley lightly with paper towels, and set aside.

To serve, divide the cauliflower puree among four plates, tipping and turning the plates to cover entirely with the puree. Top with the fish, and sprinkle the fish lightly with salt and pepper. Garnish equally with the bread cubes, fried parsley, chopped parsley, and salmon caviar.

MAKES 4 SERVINGS

Brandade of Cod

Brandade de Morue

Traditionally, salt cod is used in this chunky mixture, but I prefer my fresh version.

2 medium-size potatoes, peeled
Large pinch salt
3 tablespoons corn or peanut oil
1 medium-size onion, cut into small dice
2 pounds cod fillets, cut into small dice
2 tablespoons all-purpose flour
1 clove garlic, minced
2 cups heavy cream
Salt and freshly ground black pepper to taste
2 slices white bread, crusts removed and cut into ¼-inch cubes

Place the potatoes, salt, and water to cover in a large saucepan over medium-high heat. Bring to a boil and boil steadily until the potatoes are tender, 25 to 30 minutes. Drain the potatoes, cut into ½-inch cubes when cool enough to handle, and set aside.

In a large pot over medium-high heat, heat 1 tablespoon of the oil until very hot but not smoking, then add the onion and sauté until softened but not colored, 3 to 5 minutes. Add the fish and cook, stirring, 3 minutes. Add the flour and mix with a wooden spoon until the ingredients mass together in dry clumps. Add the garlic, cream, salt, and pepper and bring to a boil. Reduce the heat to medium and cook, stirring occasionally, 15 minutes.

Meanwhile, in a small skillet over medium-high heat, heat the remaining oil until it sizzles when a cube of bread is immersed in it. Sauté the bread cubes just until they brown, about 30 seconds, then drain well and set aside.

To serve, place the cod in the center of a plate and arrange potatoes on one side of it and croutons on the other. The fish and potatoes can be refrigerated up to 2 days and may be served hot or cold. Store the croutons at room temperature.

MAKES 4 TO 6 SERVINGS

Codfish Fillet Omelette Style

Filet de Morue en Omelette

Chop the fish by hand for this mock omelette—it takes a lot less time than cleaning up a food processor and the result is better. Turmeric adds natural yellow color and makes the fish pancake look like a real omelette, and generous pinches of pepper give personality to the finished dish. We often made this on the farm and served it with boiled red potatoes or a salad.

2 pounds codfish fillets, roughly chopped with a sharp knife
Salt and freshly ground black pepper to taste
1 heaping tablespoon minced shallots
1 tablespoon thinly sliced scallions, white and tender green parts
2 heaping tablespoons minced fresh parsley
1 tablespoon chopped fresh basil
4 cloves garlic, smashed and minced
1 tablespoon extra virgin olive oil
1 heaping teaspoon ground turmeric
2 large egg whites
2 tablespoons corn or peanut oil

Preheat the oven to 400°F. Place the fish in a large bowl and sprinkle with salt and pepper. Mix in the remaining ingredients except the corn oil.

In a large ovenproof skillet over medium-high heat, heat the corn oil to almost smoking, then pour in the fish mixture to make a large pancake. Flatten the mixture and cook 5 minutes; loosen with a spatula, invert onto a plate, and return to the pan to cook the other side another 5 minutes. Place in the oven until very crisp and golden, 5 to 10 minutes.

To serve, drain off the oil, invert the "omelette" onto a platter, and cut into four wedges. If it sticks to the pan, just remove it in chunks and reassemble it—a rustic appearance is fine. Season lightly with salt and generously with pepper.

MAKES 4 SERVINGS

Cod Fritters

Beignets de Morue

While the cod can be pureed in a food processor, the potatoes cannot, because their texture will suffer. They must be ground in a food grinder and then combined with the pureed fish (or do everything in the grinder). These fritters are crisp on the outside and meltingly smooth on the inside.

3 large potatoes, peeled and quartered
Large pinch salt
2 pounds codfish fillets, cut into 2-inch chunks
2 tablespoons extra virgin olive oil
2 large eggs
4 cloves garlic, smashed and minced
2 tablespoons minced fresh parsley
1 tablespoon minced fresh thyme or herb of your choice
2 tablespoons minced scallions, white and tender green parts
3 allspice berries, smashed
¼ teaspoon fennel seeds
⅛ teaspoon baking soda
Salt and freshly ground black pepper to taste
Corn or peanut oil for frying
2 cups bread crumbs made from plain white bread, crusts included
Lemon wedges for garnish

Place the potatoes, water to cover, and the salt in a medium-size saucepan over high heat and bring to a boil. Reduce the heat to medium and cook until tender, 15 to 20 minutes. Drain and set aside.

Place the cod in a food processor and process to a rough puree. Remove to a large bowl. Put the potatoes through a food grinder and combine with the cod. The amounts should be almost equal. (Or you can put the fish through the grinder first, and then the potatoes.) Add the olive oil, eggs, garlic, parsley, thyme, scallions, allspice, fennel, and baking soda and mix well. Season with generous pinches of salt and pepper.

Meanwhile, fill a large, high-sided saucepan or deep-fryer halfway with corn oil, place it over medium-high heat (or turn the deep-fryer to the medium setting), and heat to 375°F, or until a bit of beignet mixture sizzles on contact.

Pour the bread crumbs into a small pan or platter. For each beignet, take 1 generous tablespoon of the fish mixture, roll it in the bread crumbs, and flatten into a cake about 3 by 2 inches. Immediately deep-fry several cakes at once—making sure they do not touch—in the hot oil, turning until brown on all sides, about 5 minutes. Drain on paper towels and serve hot, garnished with the lemon wedges.

MAKES 12 BEIGNETS; 4 SERVINGS

Little Provençal Cod Fritters

Petits Acras de Morue Provençal

These simple fritters make a wonderful appetizer. Use only cod—no other fish cooks as fast and is as tender.

The oil shouldn't be so hot that the fritters burn. They should cook slowly and turn golden.

For the marinade

2 tablespoons extra virgin olive oil
1 teaspoon grated lemon zest
Salt and freshly ground pepper to taste
1 shallot, chopped
1 clove garlic, smashed and minced
1 pound cod fillet cut in 1-inch dice
1 tablespoon fresh lemon juice

For the garnish

2 medium tomatoes, juice and seeds squeezed out, skin peeled off, and
    finely chopped
1 clove garlic, smashed and minced, optional
1 tablespoon chopped basil
3 tablespoons extra virgin olive oil
1 tablespoon fresh lemon juice
Salt and freshly ground pepper

For the fritters

1 cup all-purpose flour
1 tablespoon baking soda

2 tablespoons extra virgin olive oil

3 tablespoons thinly sliced scallions, white and tender green parts

1 tablespoon chopped fresh rosemary

½ dried bay leaf

1 clove garlic, smashed and minced

1 cup regular or low-fat milk

1 large egg, lightly beaten

Salt and freshly ground black pepper to taste

6 tablespoons corn or peanut oil

Lemon wedges

In a large, nonreactive bowl, combine the marinade ingredients and the cod and allow to marinate, refrigerated, two hours or overnight. In a small bowl, combine the garnish ingredients and set aside.

In a large mixing bowl, combine the flour, baking soda, olive oil, scallions, rosemary, bay leaf, garlic, egg, and salt and pepper to taste. Add the milk and mix well. Add the marinated codfish, drained, and mix well.

Heat the oil to 375°F. Drop the batter by tablespoonsful and cook the fritters slowly, turning until golden on all sides, about 5 minutes. Do not crowd and do not let them burn. Drain on paper towels, sprinkle with salt and pepper, and serve hot with the tomato garnish and lemon wedges.

SERVES 6 TO 8 AS AN APPETIZER

Crab Cakes

Beignets de Crabe

On Sunday and holidays when I was young, my mother used to make this easy and delicious dish for the family. Years later, it became one of the favorites of Lady Marcia Harrison, the widow of Sir Rex Harrison, when I prepared it for her in New York.

You may substitute salt cod for the crabmeat, as is commonly done in Provence.

2 large potatoes, peeled and coarsely grated but not soaked (you need the starch)
2 cloves garlic, minced
Large pinches salt and freshly ground pepper
2 tablespoons minced fresh parsley
1 teaspoon chopped fresh basil
2 shallots, minced
1 large egg, lightly beaten
3 generous tablespoons lump crabmeat, cartilage removed, or an equal quantity of reconstituted salt cod
2 tablespoons corn or peanut oil

In a large mixing bowl, combine all the ingredients except the corn oil and mix well.

In a medium, flat skillet over medium-high heat, heat the oil until very hot but not smoking and add enough mixture to form a large pancake, or cook it by tablespoonsful to form small pancakes. Sauté until crisp and browned, 3 to 4 minutes on each side, and drain on paper towels.

MAKES 4 LARGE OR 12 SMALL CRAB CAKES, SERVING 4

Red Snapper Fillets with Prune Stuffing and Grape Sauce

Red Snapper aux Pruneaux et Sauce Verjus

Sweet bits of prune add a mysterious, fruity flavor to this stuffing and verjus vinegar, imported from France, permeates the piquant sauce. This is my creation, and the small amounts of butter and cream add to the luxurious texture of the dish.

1 tablespoon unsalted butter
2 tablespoons minced shallots
3 slices white bread, crusts removed and torn into small chunks
12 pitted prunes, cut into small dice
2 tablespoons minced fresh parsley
1 large egg
⅓ cup heavy cream
Salt and freshly ground black pepper to taste
4 thin red snapper fillets, about 6 ounces each

For the sauce

1 teaspoon verjus vinegar (available in specialty food stores)
½ cup (1 stick) unsalted butter, softened
Salt and freshly ground black pepper to taste
1 tablespoon minced fresh parsley or chives

Preheat the broiler. If you have a separate oven, preheat it to 400°F. In a small skillet over medium-high heat, melt the butter and sauté the shallots until softened but not colored, about 3 minutes, and set aside. Lightly butter a medium-size gratin dish.

In a medium-size bowl, combine the bread chunks, prunes, parsley, egg, cream, salt, and pepper. Mix well. Add the reserved shallots and mix well.

Heat a nonstick skillet over medium heat and sear the snapper fillets 1 minute on each side. Arrange them on the buttered gratin dish and mound the stuffing on top. Place the fish under the broiler just until the stuffing has browned, about 1 minute, then transfer to the oven and bake 5 minutes.

Meanwhile, in a small skillet over high heat, bring the vinegar to a boil and reduce by half. Whisk in the butter and continue whisking until incorporated. Add the salt, pepper, and parsley and mix well. To serve, place one stuffed fillet on each of four plates and pour the sauce around it.

MAKES 4 SERVINGS

Red Snapper with Tomato Fondue and Fresh Tomatoes

Red Snapper à la Fondue de Tomate Fraîche

This recipe is ideal for a dinner party, because all the components can be prepared ahead separately and then put together at the last minute. And it gives you flexibility in shopping as well, since you can substitute monkfish, striped bass, or any other firm-fleshed fish for the snapper. The luscious fresh tomatoes and the herbs provide a Provençal accent, both in looks and flavor.

2 pounds red snapper fillets, cut into quarters (see substitutes, above)
All-purpose flour for dredging
5 tablespoons corn or peanut oil
Salt and freshly ground black pepper to taste
1 large or 2 small tomatoes, sliced about ½ inch thick
2 cups Fresh Tomato Fondue (page 107)
1 cup homemade (page 82) or canned low-salt chicken broth
1 teaspoon minced fresh basil
½ teaspoon minced fresh thyme or rosemary
2 generous tablespoons minced fresh parsley

2 cloves garlic, smashed and minced
¼ teaspoon grated lemon zest

For the garnish

1 generous tablespoon minced fresh parsley
2 cloves garlic, smashed and minced
2 tablespoons extra virgin olive oil
Generous pinch freshly ground black pepper

Preheat the oven to 400°F. Lightly dredge the fillets in the flour, tapping off any excess. In a large skillet over medium-high heat, heat 2 tablespoons of the oil to very hot but not smoking, then cook the fish until golden, about 10 minutes on each side. Place the pan in the oven and cook the fish until it is the same color all the way through, another 10 minutes. When done, blot with paper towels, sprinkle with salt and pepper, and set aside in a warm spot.

Meanwhile, in a second large skillet over medium-high heat, heat the remaining 3 tablespoons of the oil to very hot but not smoking and sauté the tomato slices until colored, about 5 minutes on each side. Remove the tomatoes and place on a platter, so the oil can drain from them (they are too delicate to blot with paper towels).

Pour any remaining oil from the skillet and place the skillet over medium heat. Add the fondue, broth, basil, thyme, parsley, garlic, and lemon zest. Season with salt and pepper and simmer until reduced by about half, 10 to 15 minutes. The sauce should be soft, with soft chunks of tomatoes.

For the garnish, in a mixing bowl, combine the parsley, garlic, and olive oil. Season with a generous pinch of pepper. To serve, divide the sauce among four plates, placing it in a puddle in the center of each. Arrange the fish pieces over the sauce and top each piece with one or two tomato slices. Garnish with the parsley and garlic mixture.

MAKES 4 SERVINGS

Red Snapper with Sweet Garlic

Red Snapper à l'Ail Doux

I love sweet garlic—it has a really subtle flavor. Keep some in the refrigerator, in its syrup, and use it with various recipes. Garlic is one of the basic elements of Provençal cooking, and this is an imaginative way to present it.

For the garlic

1½ cups water
1 cup sugar
16 cloves garlic, unpeeled
2 tablespoons extra virgin olive oil
1 tablespoon minced fresh parsley
Freshly ground black pepper to taste

For the red snapper

Four 4-ounce red snapper fillets, about ¼ inch thick, cut on the diagonal
    from a large fillet (you can substitute halibut)
Salt and freshly ground black pepper to taste
½ cup all-purpose flour
2 tablespoons corn or peanut oil
4 sprigs fresh rosemary for garnish
4 lemon wedges for garnish

In a large, heavy saucepan over high heat, bring to a boil the water and sugar. Add the garlic, reduce the heat to low, and simmer until the garlic is soft, about 40 minutes. Remove the garlic from the syrup (discard the syrup) and reserve 4 cloves for garnish. Smash the remaining cloves to remove the skins and place the flesh in a mortar or small bowl. Combine the garlic with the olive oil, minced parsley, and a sprinkling of pepper and mix until creamy. Set aside.

Meanwhile, preheat the oven to 400°F. Season the fillets with salt and pepper and dredge in the flour, tapping off any excess.

In a large skillet over medium-high heat, heat the oil until very hot but not smoking. Add the fillets and cook until brown around the edges, about 1 minute. Turn the fillets and put the pan in the oven until the flesh of the fish is the same color all the way through, about 8 minutes.

Arrange the fish on individual plates or a serving platter. Spoon the garlic cream along the length of each fillet and garnish with a whole garlic clove, rosemary sprig, and lemon wedge.

MAKES 4 SERVINGS

Red Snapper with Zucchini and Anchovies

Red Snapper aux Courgettes et Anchois

We use anchovies a lot in Provence; here they do a good job of reinforcing the taste of fresh zucchini.

2 large zucchini, thinly sliced lengthwise on a mandoline
Four 4-ounce red snapper fillets, about ¼ inch thick, cut on the diagonal
    from a large fillet
Freshly ground black pepper to taste
6 cloves garlic, thinly sliced
12 oil-packed anchovy fillets
2 tablespoons minced fresh thyme
2 large eggs, lightly beaten
2 tablespoons corn or peanut oil
1 large onion, thinly sliced
1 large tomato, coarsely chopped
1 tablespoon minced fresh parsley
1 tablespoon red wine vinegar

Preheat the oven to 400°F. Fill a large saucepan halfway with water, bring to a boil over high heat, and blanch the zucchini 30 seconds. Immediately plunge into cold water to stop the cooking and drain on paper towels.

Season the fillets with pepper. Divide three of the garlic cloves, the anchovies, and 1 tablespoon of the thyme among the fillets, sprinkling them on both sides and pressing in slightly.

Dip the zucchini slices into the beaten eggs and wrap them around each fillet so that the fillet is enclosed in a zucchini package. Use about 6 slices per fillet. (You may prepare the recipe to this point and refrigerate up to 2 hours before cooking.)

In a large, heavy skillet over medium-high heat, heat the oil until it is very hot but not smoking. Add the zucchini-wrapped fillets and the onion and cook until brown on the bottom and around the edges, about 2 minutes. Turn and add the tomato and the remaining garlic. Place in the oven and cook until the flesh of the fish is the same color all the way through, 8 to 10 minutes.

Remove the fillets from the pan and drain on paper towels. Drain any excess oil from the tomato mixture and return the pan to high heat. Add the remaining thyme, the parsley, and vinegar, sprinkle with a little pepper, and allow to reduce 1 minute.

Arrange the fillets on four plates or on a serving platter and pour the sauce over them.

Makes 4 servings

Sardines with Spinach

Sardines aux Épinards

Sardines are one of the few fish you always buy whole, not filleted. Their shine will show you they are very fresh, and their eyes should seem almost alive. They need to look as if they are saying, "Buy me!" When not fresh, their skins are dry and their eyes are flat and dull. On the farm, we prepared sardines as simply as possible: we made a big fire and let the fish cook on the embers, seasoned with salt, pepper, and olive oil.

I always make sardines for lunch, not dinner, because of their strong flavor. Give yourself the day to digest them—some people find that they take a while.

I serve sardines with the head and tail attached, because I like the look of a fresh fish. This recipe of my mother's needs no sauce—the simple fish and vegetables are perfect together.

12 to 16 whole sardines
1 tablespoon extra virgin olive oil
3 shallots, minced
Salt and freshly ground black pepper to taste
Extra virgin olive oil for drizzling
2 tablespoons corn or peanut oil
½ large or 1 small onion, thinly sliced
3 cloves garlic, thinly sliced
1½ pounds spinach, well washed, tough stems removed, and leaves cut into
    chiffonade
1 tablespoon fresh thyme leaves
Juice of ½ lemon
Lemon halves for garnish
Minced fresh parsley for garnish

Preheat the broiler. Cut the sardines from the tail to the head, cutting deeply into the fish, and remove the bone structure and any flesh that clings to it. Set aside.

In a small skillet over medium-high heat, heat the olive oil, then sauté the shallots until softened but not colored, about 4 minutes. Sprinkle the inside of the fish with salt and pepper and stuff each with one quarter of the shallots.

Lightly oil an ovenproof platter large enough to hold the sardines in one layer and arrange the fish on the platter. Drizzle lightly with olive oil.

In a large skillet over medium heat, heat the corn oil and sauté the onion until just colored, about 5 minutes, adding the garlic midway through the cooking. Add the spinach and thyme and cook, stirring, until the spinach wilts and decreases in volume, about 1 minute. Remove it from the heat, season with salt and pepper, and add the lemon juice.

Place the sardines on their platter under the broiler and cook 3 to 5 minutes. The fish will soften and their skin will char and crack. Turn and cook on the other side until cooked through, 3 to 5 minutes.

To serve, place a mound of spinach in the center of four plates and top with the sardines. Garnish with the lemon wedges and parsley.

MAKES 4 SERVINGS

Marinated Sardines

Sardines Marinées

Sardines are very soft and easy to fillet, but if you prefer, you can ask your fish market to remove the bones for you. Although in Provence we eat the fillets nearly raw, an overnight marination, which "cooks" them somewhat, is more to American tastes. Serve the fish with a mixed salad, some country bread, and a nice glass of rosé.

Fillets from 12 whole sardines, cut off with a sharp knife, the top fin cut
    off and discarded, skin on (discard the rest of the fish)
Salt and freshly ground black pepper to taste
2½ tablespoons extra virgin olive oil
Juice of 2 lemons
1 clove garlic, very thinly sliced
1 shallot, very thinly sliced
1 plum tomato, thinly sliced
2 tablespoons minced fresh dill
1 tablespoon pink peppercorns or peppercorns of your choice
1 tablespoon minced fresh thyme
2 tablespoons minced fresh parsley
Mixed greens for garnish

Arrange the fillets flesh side up on a flat dish, season with salt and pepper, and drizzle with the olive oil and lemon juice. Sprinkle with the garlic, shallot, tomato, dill, peppercorns, thyme, and parsley.

Cover with plastic wrap and refrigerate at least 1 hour or overnight. Serve on a platter surrounded by mixed greens.

MAKES 4 SERVINGS

Sautéed Sardines

Sardines Sautées Provençales

I season these sardines generously with pepper, and you can follow my method, or just use a little bit. The finished dish will have a fresh look with its specks of red and green. Serve with Warm Potato Salad with Basil and Sweet Garlic (page 165).

12 whole sardines, cut open at the stomach, gutted, and well cleaned, but
    not boned
All-purpose flour for dredging
2½ tablespoons corn or peanut oil
Salt and freshly ground black pepper to taste
1 large tomato, coarsely chopped
3 tablespoons coarsely chopped fresh parsley
3 cloves garlic, coarsely chopped
¼ large red bell pepper, seeded and coarsely chopped
1 teaspoon coriander seeds, smashed
1 bay leaf, crushed
2 tablespoons extra virgin olive oil
Juice of ½ lemon

Dredge the sardines in flour, tapping off any excess. In a large skillet over medium-high heat, heat the oil until it just starts to smoke, then cook the sardines until golden brown, about 5 minutes on each side. The skin will split and a film of tiny bubbles will erupt at the top, indicating that they are done. Sprinkle the fish with just a touch of salt and a generous amount of pepper. Pour off most of the cooking oil.

Return the pan with the fish to medium-high heat. Add the tomato and cook until it is softened, 1 to 2 minutes. Add the parsley, garlic, bell pepper, coriander, and bay leaf and cook another 2 minutes. Add the olive oil and lemon juice, stir, and remove from the heat immediately—you don't want to cook the oil.

To serve, arrange fish in the center of four plates and spoon vegetables over.

MAKES 4 SERVINGS

Sardines in Court Bouillon

Sardines au Court Bouillon

Test the fish for doneness in the oven by pressing it with your finger. If the impression remains, the fish is done. This delicate dish can be eaten warm or cold.

2 tablespoons plus 1 teaspoon extra virgin olive oil
12 whole sardines, cut open at the stomach, gutted, and well cleaned, but not boned
Salt and freshly ground black pepper to taste
1 cup dry white wine
1 cup water
2 to 3 sprigs fresh thyme
2 bay leaves, crumbled
¼ large onion, thinly sliced and separated into rings
½ large tomato, roughly chopped
½ large carrot, thinly sliced
3 tablespoons coarsely chopped fresh parsley
2 cloves garlic, thinly sliced
½ lemon, cut into 2 wedges

Preheat the oven to 400°F. Oil a large ovenproof gratin pan with 1 teaspoon of the olive oil and arrange the fish in the pan in one layer. Sprinkle with salt and pepper and pour the wine and water over and around the fish. Sprinkle with the remaining olive oil, scatter the other ingredients over the fish, gently squeezing the lemon wedges.

Place the pan over high heat and bring to a boil. Lightly butter a square of aluminum foil slightly larger than the pan and cover the pan tightly with it. Place in the oven until the sardines are done, about 15 minutes.

To serve, place the fillets in the center of each of four soup bowls or a plate with high sides, surround with the vegetables, and pour some bouillon over all.

MAKES 4 SERVINGS

Roasted Monkfish

Rôti de Lotte

I remember sniffing the jar of cloves that sat on my mother's kitchen table and being reminded of the dentist. I didn't like cloves then, but now I love them, and they add their earthy, spicy perfume to many of my favorite dishes, such as this one. Serve this hearty, colorful fish with *Riz Camarguais* (page 190) and ratatouille (page 142).

4 monkfish fillets (about 2 pounds), slashed several times lengthwise and
    flattened at the cuts
Salt and freshly ground black pepper to taste
1 teaspoon finely chopped fresh basil
1 tablespoon minced fresh thyme
2 tablespoons minced shallots
4 whole cloves
All-purpose flour for dredging
2 tablespoons corn or peanut oil
6 to 8 shallots, halved
6 cloves garlic, halved if large, left whole if small
6 to 8 plum tomatoes, quartered lengthwise
1 stalk celery, cut into ½-inch slices (optional)
Sprigs fresh basil for garnish
Lemon wedges for garnish

Preheat the oven to 400°F. Sprinkle the fillets with the salt, pepper, basil, thyme, and minced shallots and place a clove on each fillet. Fold the fillets in half from top to bottom, enclosing the herbs, and fasten with a toothpick. Dredge in flour, tapping off any extra, and set aside.

In a large skillet over medium-high heat, heat the oil until very hot but not smoking and brown the fillets about 3 minutes on each side. Add the shallot halves and garlic and cook until just colored, about 1 minute, then add the tomatoes and celery. Immediately put the pan in the oven and cook until the fish and vegetables are a rich brown and the vegetables are slightly caramelized, 15 to 20 minutes.

To serve, divide the fillets among four dishes and remove the toothpicks. Surround the fish with the vegetables and garnish with the basil sprigs and lemon wedges.

MAKES 4 SERVINGS

Monkfish with Couscous

Couscous de Lotte

Monkfish is substantial in texture, yet neutral in flavor, and it can marry with all kinds of other textures and flavors. This couscous, combined with fish and vegetables, shows the North African influence on Provençal cooking. It is started the traditional way in a strainer over simmering broth to separate the grains of wheat, and then the semolina is combined with the simmering vegetables.

Sauté the monkfish in very hot oil, so the fish immediately crusts over and retains its moisture. It should be cooked until it is well done. You will need only half a bell pepper for this dish, but keep the other half. If you are cooking Provençal, you can always use half a pepper.

¼ cup corn or peanut oil
1 large onion, roughly diced
2 carrots, cut into sticks about 3 inches by ¼ inch
4 cloves garlic, smashed and peeled
2 sprigs fresh thyme
2 small bay leaves
3 to 4 sprigs fresh parsley, roughly chopped
5 to 7 cups homemade (page 82) or canned low-salt chicken broth
2 medium-size zucchini, quartered lengthwise and cut into 2-inch pieces
1 stalk celery, halved lengthwise and cut into 2-inch pieces
3 plum tomatoes, quartered lengthwise
½ large red or green bell pepper, seeded and cut into 2-inch chunks

2 whole cloves
Salt and freshly ground black pepper to taste
1½ cups couscous
2½ tablespoons extra virgin olive oil
2 pounds monkfish fillets, cut on the diagonal into slices ¼ to ½ inch thick
All-purpose flour for dredging
Sprigs fresh basil or parsley for garnish
Lemon wedges for garnish

In a large skillet over medium-high heat, heat 2 tablespoons of the corn oil until very hot but not smoking, then add the onion and sauté until colored, about 5 minutes. Add the carrots and garlic, stir well, and cook 1 minute. Add the thyme, bay leaves, and parsley and stir. Add 5 cups of the broth, stir, and bring to a boil. Reduce the heat to medium and simmer 10 minutes. Add the zucchini, celery, tomatoes, bell pepper, and cloves, season with generous pinches of salt and pepper, and bring to a boil. Reduce the heat to medium and cook another 5 minutes.

Pour the couscous into a large, flat, fine-mesh strainer the same diameter as the skillet and drizzle with the olive oil. Place over the simmering vegetables, cover tightly with a square of aluminum foil, and cook until tender, 15 to 20 minutes. Then spoon the couscous into the pan with the vegetables, stir well, and cook together 5 minutes. If the mixture seems too thick, add another 1 to 2 cups of broth.

Meanwhile, in a large skillet over medium-high heat, heat the remaining corn oil until it is very hot but not smoking. Dredge the fillets in flour, tapping off any excess, sprinkle with salt and pepper, and cook until browned and cooked through, about 5 minutes on each side (reduce the heat if the fish starts to burn).

To serve, mound the couscous and vegetables generously on each of four plates and top with the fillets. Garnish with the basil and lemon.

MAKES 4 SERVINGS

Monkfish in Cabbage Leaves

Paupiettes de Lotte

This dish smells like heaven. The *paupiette* stuffing is flecked with green herbs and has a mysterious underlying flavor of juniper. Serve with *Riz Camarguais* (page 190).

2 pounds monkfish fillets, skinned and cut into medium-size chunks
4 shallots, peeled
5 cloves garlic, peeled
2 large eggs
2 tablespoons minced scallions, white and tender green parts
2 tablespoons minced fresh parsley
1 teaspoon finely chopped fresh basil
1 whole clove, smashed
2 juniper berries, minced
3 slices white bread, crusts removed and torn into rough chunks
2 tablespoons corn or peanut oil
1 large onion, coarsely diced
8 large leaves green cabbage, wedge-shaped core removed, steamed over
     boiling water or parboiled in water to cover just until softened, then
     drained and refreshed in cold water
Salt and freshly ground black pepper to taste
2 cups homemade (page 82) or canned low-salt chicken broth

Preheat the oven to 400°F. In a food grinder with a medium blade, grind the fillets with the shallots and garlic.

In a large bowl, combine the ground fish mixture with the eggs, scallions, parsley, basil, clove, juniper berries, and bread. Mix well.

In a large ovenproof skillet or saucepot over medium-high heat, heat the oil until very hot but not smoking, then add the onion and sauté until golden, about 5 minutes.

Meanwhile, pat the cabbage leaves dry and arrange on a work surface. Place 2 tablespoons of the fish mixture in the center of each leaf and fold over the cabbage to enclose it in a little package. Arrange the paupiettes seam side down on top of the onion in the saucepot, sprinkle with salt and pepper, and pour in the broth. Bring to a boil, then cook in the oven until the cabbage is tender and the paupiettes are firm, about 30 minutes. Check after a few minutes and if they seem to be drying out, cover with a square of aluminum foil.

To serve, arrange two paupiettes in the center of four plates and top with the onions.

MAKES 4 SERVINGS

White Monkfish Stew

Blanquette de Lotte

A blanquette is usually made with cream, but you can substitute whole or skim milk, if you prefer. Serve this richly flavored stew with white rice.

2 pounds monkfish fillets

For the broth

1 leek, white and tender green parts, well washed and roughly chopped
½ large or 1 small carrot, roughly chopped
½ large or 1 small onion, roughly chopped
1 clove garlic, smashed and minced
2 cups dry white wine
4 cups hot water
1 bay leaf
1 teaspoon black peppercorns
2 allspice berries
1 whole clove
2 sprigs fresh parsley
1 plum tomato, quartered lengthwise

To finish the dish

½ teaspoon sea salt
2 tablespoons arrowroot dissolved in 2 tablespoons cold water
1 cup heavy cream
Chopped fresh parsley for garnish

Remove and reserve the filmy skin and dark-colored portions of the monkfish (put the point of a sharp knife just under the skin and cut through the length of the fish); if you have the fish market do this, ask for the bones and skin from the fish. Cut the fillets into 2-inch chunks and set aside.

Place the monkfish trimmings and the broth ingredients in a large, high-sided saucepan over medium-high heat. Bring to a boil, then lower the heat to medium and simmer 15 to 20 minutes, skimming off any scum as necessary.

Strain the broth into a large, heavy saucepan, discarding the fish trimmings and reserving the vegetables in the refrigerator (you may cut the vegetables into bite-size pieces, if you like). Add the fish chunks and sea salt to the broth. Place the pan over medium-high heat and bring to a boil. Reduce the heat to medium and simmer 10 to 15 minutes.

Strain the broth, reserving the fish in a warm place. Return the broth to the saucepan and bring to a gentle boil over medium heat. Add the arrowroot mixture slowly to the boiling stock, mixing well with a whisk (you will see the stock beginning to thicken). Add the heavy cream and boil until the sauce coats a wooden spoon, 2 to 3 minutes. Add the reserved vegetables and cook another 2 minutes, then add the fish and cook until firm and resilient, another 3 to 5 minutes.

Serve the fish in a soup bowl surrounded by sauce and vegetables and garnished with parsley.

MAKES 4 SERVINGS

Farm-Style Salmon in Individual Packets

(Steelhead)

This is good 2'04

(12 min per 1 inch thick)

Saumon en Papillote

❧

The individual packets should be opened at the table, so everyone can enjoy the burst of herbal aroma as the foil is cut. This is a full meal in itself, with fish and vegetables steamed together for each portion.

2 tablespoons corn or peanut oil
1 large onion, thinly sliced
1 large carrot, cut into 2-inch pieces, then into thin julienne sticks
4 cloves garlic, minced
1 large tomato, juice and seeds gently squeezed out and cut into 1-inch slices
1 medium-size leek, white and tender green parts, well washed, halved lengthwise, and cut into 1-inch slices
½ jalapeño pepper, minced
1 teaspoon minced fresh rosemary
1 teaspoon extra virgin olive oil
Salt and freshly ground black pepper to taste
Grated zest of 1 lemon
Eight 2-ounce salmon fillets, about ¼ inch thick, cut on the diagonal from a large fillet
Lemon wedges for garnish

In a large skillet over medium-high heat, heat the oil until very hot but not smoking, then add the onion and sauté until golden, about 5 minutes. Add the carrot and sauté until softened, 3 to 5 minutes. Add the garlic, tomato, leek, jalapeño, and rosemary. Sprinkle with the olive oil, salt, pepper, and lemon zest. Mix well, reduce the heat to low, and cook 5 to 8 minutes. Drain and cool or refrigerate until room temperature.

Preheat the oven to 400°F. Lightly oil four 12-inch lengths of aluminum foil and place 2 tablespoons of the vegetable mixture at one end of each. Top with 2 slices of the salmon, sprinkle with salt and pepper, then top with another 2 tablespoons of the vegetables. Fold the foil over the fish and seal the edges with a tight

½-inch fold, then a second fold. (You can refrigerate the papillotes up to 2 hours ahead at this point and bring to room temperature before baking.)

Place the papillotes in the oven and cook until they have puffed up, about 5 minutes. Place each packet on a plate and open at the table, scraping the fish and vegetables onto the plate. Garnish with the lemon wedges.

MAKES 4 SERVINGS

Salmon with Olive Paste

Saumon á la Tapenade

❧

In this dish, the salmon cooks quickly and is flavorful and juicy, while the tapenade crust adds the rich Provençal flavors of olives, garlic, and anchovies.

½ cup Tapenade (page 57)
1 large egg
1 teaspoon minced fresh thyme
Four 4-ounce salmon fillets, about ¼ inch thick, cut on the diagonal from a
    large fillet
4 teaspoons minced fresh parsley
Freshly ground black pepper to taste
4 lemon wedges for garnish

Preheat the broiler. If you have a separate oven, preheat it to 400°F.

In a small bowl, combine the tapenade, egg, and thyme. Season with pepper.

Arrange the salmon fillets on a lightly oiled or buttered baking pan. Spread each fillet with one quarter of the tapenade, then sprinkle with the parsley and pepper. Place the salmon under the broiler until browned, about 2 minutes. Then put into the 400°F oven until cooked through, 3 to 5 minutes. Serve garnished with the lemon wedges.

MAKES 4 SERVINGS

Bluefish in the Pot

Bluefish à l'Étouffé

Bluefish is not native to Provence, but it can be prepared very well in Provençal style. It is affordable and easy to find in most fish markets.

¼ cup corn or peanut oil
4 shallots, thinly sliced
4 cloves garlic, thinly sliced
1¼ pounds bluefish fillets, skinned and each fillet cut into 3 pieces
2 small heads Boston lettuce, 8 large outer leaves reserved and the heads quartered
2 medium-size tomatoes, roughly chopped
2 medium-size carrots, halved lengthwise and thinly sliced crosswise
8 fresh basil leaves, minced
⅔ cup dry white wine
Salt and freshly ground black pepper to taste
1½ tablespoons extra virgin olive oil
¼ cup water

In a medium-size saucepan over medium-high heat, heat the oil until very hot but not smoking, then add the shallots and garlic and sauté until softened, about 1 minute. Add the bluefish, lettuce quarters, tomatoes, carrots, basil, wine, salt, and pepper. Cook until the fish is golden on all sides, about 8 minutes.

Reduce the heat to low and add the olive oil and water. Cover closely with a piece of aluminum foil and cook until cooked through, firm, and juicy, 5 to 7 minutes.

To serve, arrange two of the reserved lettuce leaves on each plate and place the fish on top. Meanwhile, keep the vegetables cooking for another 1 to 2 minutes. Spoon the vegetables and juice over and around the fish.

MAKES 4 SERVINGS

Spicy Marinated Pan-Grilled Shrimp

Grillade des Crevettes

The marinade gives a strong Provençal flavor to this very simple dish. The shrimp are delicious served with plain white rice.

Grated zest of 1 lemon
2 tablespoons extra virgin olive oil
2 tablespoons minced scallions, white and tender green parts
1 cup diced fresh tomato
Pinch freshly grated nutmeg
2 tablespoons chopped fresh parsley
2 drops Worcestershire sauce
1 bay leaf, crumbled
Generous pinches salt and freshly ground black pepper
32 large shrimp, peeled and deveined
1 teaspoon corn or peanut oil
4 sprigs fresh Italian (flatleaf) parsley
4 lime wedges

In a large bowl, mix together the zest, olive oil, scallions, tomato, nutmeg, parsley, Worcestershire, bay leaf, salt, and pepper and pour over the shrimp. Cover with plastic wrap and refrigerate 4 to 6 hours or overnight.

In a large skillet over medium-high heat, heat the corn oil until very hot but not smoking. Remove the shrimp from the marinade, shaking off the excess, and cook until browned, about 3 minutes. Turn, add the marinade, and cook until browned, another 3 minutes. Serve the shrimp hot, topped with a little of the cooked marinade vegetables. Garnish each serving with a sprig of parsley and a wedge of lime.

MAKES 4 SERVINGS

Squid Salad

Suppion en Salade

This beautifully colored Provençal salad is simple to put together, but it can make your luncheon table very special.

½ lemon
1 sprig fresh rosemary or thyme
1 tablespoon sea salt
2 pounds cleaned squid (see note below)
2 tablespoons corn or peanut oil
2 small red onions, thinly sliced
½ red bell pepper, seeded and sliced into julienne strips
½ green bell pepper, seeded and sliced into julienne strips
2 plum tomatoes, cut into thin wedges
3 cloves garlic, peeled
6 to 8 black olives marinated in olive oil and herbs (from Provence,
    Greece, or Italy), pitted
1 bay leaf
2 tablespoons thin strips fresh basil leaves
Salt and freshly ground black pepper to taste
1 tablespoon minced fresh parsley
Grated zest of ½ lime

Fill a large saucepan halfway full with water, add the lemon, herbs, and sea salt, and bring to a boil over high heat. Add the squid and blanch 2 minutes. Drain, pat dry with paper towels, and cut into ½-inch rings.

In a large skillet over medium-high heat, heat the oil until very hot but not smoking and sauté the onions until softened and colored, about 4 minutes. Add the peppers, tomatoes, garlic, olives, squid, bay leaf, and basil. Season with salt and pepper, toss to mix, and sauté until squid is softened and cooked through, 5 minutes. Garnish with the parsley and lime zest and serve hot, warm, or cold.

MAKES 4 SERVINGS

NOTE: The fish market will clean the squid for you. If you clean them at home: first remove and discard the heads. Under cold running water, slip off the black, gelatinous covering with your fingers.

Light Stew of Snails with Spices

Ragoût d'Escargots aux Épices

Far simpler than my grandmother's recipe, this ragoût still captures the herbal flavors and aromas of our Christmas table.

2 tablespoons corn or peanut oil
1 red onion, thinly sliced
3 cloves garlic, minced
1 large tomato, juice and seeds gently squeezed out and cut into medium dice
Pinch ground cumin
Pinch curry powder
2 tablespoons minced scallions, white and tender green parts
3 tablespoons minced fresh parsley
½ teaspoon minced fresh rosemary
1 whole clove
1 tablespoon extra virgin olive oil
48 canned snails, drained (available in specialty food stores)

In a large skillet over medium-high heat, heat the oil until very hot but not smoking, then add the onion and sauté until softened and colored, about 5 minutes.

Add all the remaining ingredients, stir, and cook 10 minutes. Serve from a terracotta casserole and accompany with plain white rice.

MAKES 4 SERVINGS

6 oranges et piler la peau des 6 autres avec les

12 oranges. Après avoir bien pilé, passer le tout.

Mettre de sucre livre par livre et faire cuire

pendant 1 heure (3 livres de sucre pour 12 oranges).

Civet de Lièvre (Recette du Bugey)

Procurez-vous un lièvre, le coupez par morceaux

après l'avoir dépecé. Gardez avec soin le foie et

le sang. Mettez les morceaux dans une marmite

en fonte avec un notable morceau de beurre.

Hachez auparavant un morceau de lard consistant

avec 2 oignons piqués d'une échalotte. Ajoutez

laurier, sel et poivre. Il faut mettre le

tout au lièvre avec persil, thym, un peu

tout en même temps sur le feu et bien couvrir.

Au bout de quelque temps de cuisson, il y aura

l'eau dans la marmite. Une fois atteinte l'eau

évaporée, saupoudrez de farine et remuez un

tantinet; puis mouillez avec de bon vin rouge

un peu fort. Goûtez alors : si la sauce est

trop forte, ajoutez du bouillon gras ou maigre.

Sinon, on le fait entièrement au vin.

Laissez finir de cuire. Au moment de servir,

on ajoute le foie écrasé et mêlé au sang. Ne

plus laisser bouillir, et avant de verser dans le

plat mettre une bonne cuillerée d'huile d'olives.

Si la sauce était trop claire, une fois le

lièvre cuit, il faudrait ajouter du beurre manié

de farine, avant de mettre le foie à le sang, et

laisser cuire un moment.

Le lard et les oignons hachés doivent remplir

presque une assiette.

Il faut environ 3 heures de cuisson pour un

lièvre de grosseur ordinaire. Ce serait trop pour

un petit lièvre et pas assez pour un gros.

Si on veut conserver un lièvre, il vaut mieux

CHAPTER 6

Meats and Furred Game

If you haven't lived on a farm, it may be hard for you to understand that we were able to raise farm animals almost like pets and then, when the time came, kill them for food. That was life on a farm—it was our world.

We had a pink pig called Toutouille, who was like a member of the family. We bought her when she was little, but within two years, she grew huge and soon became very aggressive. She followed my grandmother everywhere, oinking loudly. She bit people who came to the farm, attacked our dogs, and ran after cars.

Toutouille was smart enough to open the gate of her pen with her snout and then run free, rolling in the mud, eating the flowers in the garden, and sometimes staying out all night. Eventually, she became too much trouble to us and too expensive to feed, and she had to be killed. This was a horrible event for me, and I hid in my room with a pillow over my ears.

Then my father made ham and sausage. He hung the ham in the attic until it was completely dry, going up every day to salt and pepper it, and the strong smell of cured meat permeated the upstairs of our house for months. Mother made pâté for the winter, as well as cooked pork preserved in fat. Toutouille was forgotten, but the ham was so good.

My grandfather Antoine was a fine hunter and he brought home rabbit, woodcock, partridge, and sometimes even wild boar. He never could persuade me to go with him because I always hated hunting, even as a child. One winter day, when I was very small, my father had taken me hunting and I had shot a little bird. When

I saw the beautiful creature fall from the sky and soak the fresh snow with its dark blood, I became ill. I was haunted by the event for a long time and I never again hunted.

But later in life, as a chef, I learned many traditional game recipes from Madame Borelli, who owned Auberge Borelli in Callas, a suburb of Aix-en-Provence. Her restaurant was located in a hunting region and she was well known for her spicy stews—civets—of hare, boar, and birds. Her secret was to add equal parts of chopped parsley and garlic when the stew was finished, just before serving. I include this special Provençal touch in many of my recipes.

Game aside, we didn't eat that much meat on the farm. It was something special for Sunday, or for a holiday or a celebration. When my father sold his crops at a very good price he always bought a steak for the family's dinner. His eyes were bigger than his stomach, and he bought so much, when he put it on the platter, it extended over the sides. I would ask, "How are we going to eat all that?" But my mother's rule was that when something was on the table, we had to finish it.

In the fall, when we cut and stored the hay, my mother would make pot-au-feu, leaving the fragrant stew to simmer for hours, while we all worked outside. This was the time of year the plane trees started to lose their leaves, making a yellow and white carpet under our feet, and hundreds of blackbirds sat on the electric lines, getting ready to fly off to a warmer place. The fennel plants dried slowly, releasing their sweet anise perfume, as we cut the grass all day. Before long, we could smell the hay around us everywhere. As soon as it dried in the fields, we had to put it in the barn—a little rain could be a disaster. This meant a lot of work for everyone, young and old, men and women, getting the heavy hay into the barn, as the blazing red sun finally set. Then the steaming pot-au-feu would be waiting for us in the kitchen. I can never smell freshly cut grass without thinking of that wonderful dish.

Beef Shoulder with Carrots

Boeuf aux Carottes

My grandmother Marguerite served this fragrant, rustic dish to the family on Sundays, when we had plenty of time to sit around the table and savor it. Make it a day ahead and it will be even better. The calves' feet are my addition—they give the sauce extra richness.

¼ cup corn or peanut oil
2 pounds beef shoulder, cut into 1-inch cubes
3 medium-size onions, thinly sliced
3 cloves garlic, minced
1 large tomato, roughly chopped
3 tablespoons all-purpose flour
2 whole cloves
3 cups dry red wine
3 cups veal stock (page 80) or canned low-sodium beef consomme
Bouquet garni made of 2 sprigs each fresh parsley, thyme, and basil and
    2 bay leaves, tied together with kitchen string
2 or 3 fresh sage leaves, roughly chopped
Salt and freshly ground black pepper to taste
6 large carrots, thickly sliced
Peel of ½ orange

For the calves' feet

2 calves' feet
2 large carrots, roughly chopped
1 large onion, roughly chopped
2 or 3 cloves garlic, roughly chopped
Bouquet garni made of 2 sprigs each fresh parsley, thyme, and basil and
    2 bay leaves, tied together with kitchen string
2 or 3 allspice berries, smashed
2 or 3 whole cloves

In a large skillet over medium-high heat, heat 2 tablespoons of the oil until very hot but not smoking, then add the beef and sauté until well browned, 10 to 15 minutes. Drain to remove the oil and set aside.

In a large pot over medium-high heat, heat the remaining 2 tablespoons of oil until very hot but not smoking, then add the onions and sauté until colored, about 5 minutes. Add the garlic, beef, tomato, and flour and mix with a wooden spoon until everything comes together in dry clumps. Add the cloves, wine, stock, bouquet garni, sage, salt, and pepper. Bring to a boil and reduce the heat to medium. Cook 45 minutes, skimming occasionally, then add the carrots.

Meanwhile, in a large pot over medium-high heat, combine the calves' feet and the remaining ingredients with water to cover and bring to a boil. Cook the calves' feet until tender, about 1 hour, drain, and cut the meat into 1-inch cubes. Discard the cooking liquid, which will have a lot of fat, and add the meat to the pot of beef. Cook another 35 minutes. Add the orange peel and cook 10 minutes. Season to taste and serve hot.

MAKES 6 SERVINGS

Provençal Boiled Beef

Pot-au-feu

Whenever my mother made pot-au-feu, that was a good day! In the cool weather of fall or winter, she would put a large kettle of meat and aromatic vegetables on the stove to boil gently for hours (the dish was also called *bouilli*, to boil). When it was time to eat, we started the meal with the bouillon strained from the meat, cooked with a little pasta. Then Mother put a large terra-cotta tureen containing the tender meat and vegetables in the middle of the table and surrounded it with bowls of mustard and pickles and a little pot of sea salt. With expectation and cool weather fueling our appetites, this was always a long, comfortable family meal.

Pot-au-feu is an easy recipe—put it on the stove and it cooks alone. Just give it enough time to cook, skim it occasionally, and enjoy the aroma. If there are any leftovers, use them to make my mother's *Boeuf Mironton* (recipe follows) or invent a cold beef salad with a mustard vinaigrette (use the vinaigrette in Cold Potato Salad Provençal, page 164), or a casserole of mashed potatoes, meat, and vegetables (for inspiration, see Provençal Mashed Potatoes with Vegetables, page 152).

For the initial boiling

3 pounds lean beef rump, shank, chuck, or brisket, cut into serving pieces
    (2 pounds will serve 4; 1 pound is added for leftovers)
2 large onions, peeled, 1 halved and 1 left whole and stuck with 4 cloves
2 bay leaves
2 tablespoons salt
1 tablespoon black peppercorns
Bouquet garni made of 2 sprigs each fresh parsley, thyme, and basil and
    2 bay leaves, tied together with kitchen string
4 medium-size carrots
4 medium-size leeks, white and tender green parts, well washed
3 cloves garlic, unpeeled and smashed
2 medium-size turnips, cut into quarters or halves
4 stalks celery (leaves optional)
1 large or 2 medium-size tomatoes, halved

For the final cooking

8 small red potatoes
2 large zucchini
1 small green cabbage, quartered
6 allspice berries
½ cup vermicelli or other small pasta (optional)
Dijon mustard for garnish
Cornichons for garnish

In a large soup pot over high heat, combine the meat, water to cover generously, the halved onion, bay leaves, salt, peppercorns, and bouquet garni and bring to a boil. Add the remaining ingredients for the first boiling, reduce the heat to medium, and boil slowly, uncovered, 3½ hours, skimming off any scum that develops every hour or so.

After 3½ hours, add the remaining ingredients except the vermicelli and garnishes and cook until the vegetables are tender, 30 to 45 minutes. Strain out most of the broth and discard the bouquet garni. Reserve the meat and vegetables with a little hot broth in the pot, to keep them hot.

If you are serving the vermicelli, bring the broth to a boil in a large pot, add the vermicelli, and cook according to package instructions. Add a few vegetables to the broth, mash slightly, and serve with the vermicelli in soup bowls, as a first course.

Transfer the meat and remaining vegetables to a serving platter or tureen, moisten with a little broth, and serve accompanied by mustard and cornichons.

MAKES 4 SERVINGS, PLUS LEFTOVERS

Recycled Beef Farm Style

Boeuf Mironton

This delicious informal dish is simply reheated boiled beef and vegetables, sautéed with a few savory extra ingredients. Amounts will vary, depending upon your leftovers.

2 tablespoons corn or peanut oil
1 large onion, thinly sliced
Leftover meat and vegetables from Pot-au-feu (page 240), sliced
    ¼ to ½ inch thick (amounts will vary)
2 tablespoons minced scallions, white and tender green parts
2 tablespoons minced fresh parsley
4 cloves garlic, smashed and peeled
6 to 12 cornichons, cut into ¼-inch slices
Salt and freshly ground black pepper to taste

In a large skillet over medium-high heat, heat the oil until hot but not smoking, then add the onion and sauté until colored, about 5 minutes. Add the meat and sauté 5 minutes. Add the vegetables and sauté 5 minutes. Add the remaining ingredients, season with salt and pepper, and sauté until heated through, about 2 minutes.

SERVINGS WILL VARY, DEPENDING UPON AMOUNTS USED

Filet Mignon with Anchovy Sauce

Filet Mignon aux Anchois

Steak with *anchoïade* is a southern combination and this is my interpretation, using tender filet mignon. In my mother's kitchen we always stirred the simmering anchovy sauce with a stalk of celery, and when the sauce was cooked, the delicious stalk was a bonus for the cook.

1 tablespoon minced fresh thyme
3 cloves garlic, smashed and minced
12 oil-packed anchovy fillets
3 tablespoons extra virgin olive oil
4 stalks celery, 3 finely diced and 1 left whole
1 small bay leaf
2 tablespoons red wine vinegar
Freshly ground black pepper to taste
2 tablespoons finely chopped fresh parsley
2 tablespoons corn or peanut oil
4 filet mignon steaks, about 1 inch thick

In a small bowl, mix together the thyme, garlic, anchovies, and olive oil. Add the diced celery, bay leaf, and vinegar, season generously with pepper, and mix well. Place the mixture in a small saucepan over medium-high heat and cook until warm. Reduce the heat to very low and cook slowly, stirring vigorously with the remaining celery stalk, until the anchovies have melted, 10 to 15 minutes. Remove from the heat and stir in the chopped parsley.

In a large skillet over medium-high heat, heat the oil until very hot but not smoking, then add the steaks and brown on both sides, cooking until done to taste.

To serve, top each steak with the anchovy sauce.

MAKES 4 SERVINGS

VARIATION: You may broil the steaks in a preheated broiler or grill them over a wood or charcoal fire instead of pan-cooking them.

Steak with Quick Green Peppercorn Sauce

Steak au Poivre Sauce à la Minute

People often are afraid to tackle a peppercorn sauce, but this elegant sauce is so fast and easy, anyone can do it successfully. A dollop of heavy cream is optional— it makes the sauce more elegant than rustic. Serve with Saint-Rémy-Style Potatoes (page 150) for an echo of Provence.

4 shell steaks, 8 to 10 ounces each
Salt and freshly ground black pepper to taste
2 tablespoons corn or peanut oil
1 medium-size onion, cut into large dice
2 cloves garlic, smashed and minced
¼ cup port wine
¼ cup cognac
1 tablespoon brine-packed green peppercorns, drained
1 tablespoon pink peppercorns (optional)
1 cup veal stock (page 80) or canned low-sodium beef consomme
1 tablespoon minced fresh thyme
¼ cup heavy cream (optional)

Season the steaks with salt and pepper. In a large skillet over medium-high heat, heat the oil until very hot but not smoking, then add the steaks and cook until brown and crusty, about 2 minutes on each side. Remove from the pan and set aside.

Add the onion to the pan and sauté until brown, about 6 minutes. Add the garlic and sauté 2 minutes. Remove the pan from the heat, add the port and cognac, and, if you wish, ignite the liquor using a long match or by shaking the pan over a gas flame. If you include this step, be very careful that the flames do not touch you (especially your hair) and your clothing. When the flame dies down, return the pan to medium-high heat and add the peppercorns and stock. Reduce by half, scraping up any brown deposits from the bottom of the pan, and sprinkle with the thyme.

Add the cream and reduce the mixture to a glaze, shaking the pan as it cooks. Serve each steak with some of the pepper sauce spooned over.

Makes 4 servings

VARIATION: You may broil the steaks in a preheated broiler or grill them over a wood or charcoal fire instead of pan-cooking them.

Boiled Lamb

"Lou Bouilli" d'Agneau

This traditional farm dish provides two courses: serve the soup first and then follow it with the meat. The meat will be tender and flavorful and the soaked beans will be perfectly cooked as they boil (hence the name bouilli) along with the stew. For a rustic touch, don't tie the herb sprigs together for the bouquet garni, just throw them into the pot. In Provence the pepper you use would be a *piment fort*; here a jalapeño is the perfect substitute.

2 lamb shanks, about 1 pound each, most of the fat removed
1 pound lamb bones
1 pound dried navy beans, picked over, then soaked overnight in water to
    cover and drained
3 large carrots, halved lengthwise, then cut into 2-inch slices
1 large onion, cut into rough chunks
3 leeks, white and tender green parts, well washed
1 stalk celery, leaves removed
2 large tomatoes, each cut into 4 to 8 wedges
4 cloves garlic, peeled
1 jalapeño pepper, halved lengthwise
2 tablespoons sea salt

Bouquet garni made of 2 sprigs each fresh parsley, thyme, and basil and
    2 bay leaves, tied together with kitchen string
6 allspice berries, crushed
3 whole cloves
2 bay leaves
2 tablespoons extra virgin olive oil
2 to 3 sprigs fresh parsley
2 medium-size zucchini, cut into 3-inch sections, then quartered lengthwise
Salt and freshly ground black pepper to taste
Sprigs fresh parsley for garnish
Dijon mustard for garnish

Put the lamb, bones, beans, and all the vegetables in a large kettle and add hot water to cover. Place over medium-high heat and add the garlic, jalapeño, sea salt, bouquet garni, allspice, cloves, bay leaves, olive oil, and parsley sprigs. Bring to a boil and cook 45 minutes. Add the zucchini and cook until the zucchini and lamb are tender, an additional 15 minutes. The stew should boil vigorously throughout.

To serve, divide into two courses. First spoon the broth, with some of the beans and vegetables, into soup bowls. Second, serve the meat on separate plates accompanied by the remaining beans and vegetables, with parsley and mustard as garnish.

MAKES 4 SERVINGS

Lamb Chops Provençal

Côtes d'Agneau Provençales

Use your own homemade crumbs from fresh bread to dredge these chops. Don't toast them, because you don't want a dark coating on the lamb. The breading keeps the chops juicy and crisp, and pounding them thin before cooking allows them to cook in no time at all.

2 heaping tablespoons minced fresh thyme
2 heaping tablespoons minced fresh basil
2 heaping tablespoons minced fresh parsley
12 lamb chops cut from the rack, all fat removed and flattened to ½-inch thickness
Salt and freshly ground black pepper to taste
2 large eggs, lightly beaten
2 cups fine bread crumbs made from fresh bread, crusts included
2 tablespoons corn or peanut oil
Lemon wedges or halves for garnish

Combine the minced herbs. Sprinkle the chops lightly with salt and generously with pepper. Dip them in the beaten eggs and dredge on both sides in the minced herbs, pressing down so the herbs adhere. Dredge the chops in the crumbs.

In a large skillet over medium-high heat, heat the oil until moderately hot, then add the chops. Reduce the heat to medium and cook until crusty and brown, about 3 minutes, turn, and repeat on the other side. Regulate the heat as you cook, so that the crumbs do not burn. When done, the lamb should be pink in the center. Serve with lemon wedges.

MAKES 4 SERVINGS

Rack of Lamb Farm Style

Carré d'Agneau comme à la Ferme

Lamb was so plentiful in the south that even on the farm, we sometimes used a luxury cut of meat like the rack, but we prepared it in a rustic style. The garlic and shallots that surround it aren't peeled—their skin gives the dish a hearty taste and it is edible. Serve with *Riz Camarguais* (page 190) and Baked Zucchini (page 179).

    1 rack of lamb (8 ribs), trimmed of all fat
    Salt and freshly ground black pepper to taste
    10 cloves garlic, 2 cloves cut into 4 slivers each, the rest left unpeeled
    2 tablespoons corn or peanut oil
    2 large shallots, unpeeled and halved
    1 large carrot, cut into rough chunks
    1 sprig fresh thyme
    1 sprig fresh rosemary
    2 bay leaves
    1 medium-size tomato, cut into 8 wedges
    ¼ large green bell pepper, seeded and coarsely chopped (optional)
    ¼ large red bell pepper, seeded and coarsely chopped (optional)

Preheat the oven to 400°F. Sprinkle the lamb lightly with salt and generously with pepper. Cut 8 deep slits through the meat on both sides and insert the garlic slivers.

In a large kettle over medium-high heat, heat the oil until very hot but not smoking and sear the lamb until very brown, about 5 minutes per side. At the same time, add the remaining ingredients. Put the lamb in the oven and roast until done to taste, 30 to 45 minutes.

To serve, carve the lamb into individual chops. Place 2 chops on each dish and surround with the roasted vegetables.

MAKES 4 SERVINGS

Lamb Neck Stew

Petit Fricaut de Cou d'Agneau

Lamb neck is a bony cut of meat, so you need about 1 pound for each serving. The beans add healthful fiber as well as flavor to this farm dish.

3 tablespoons corn or peanut oil
4 pounds lamb neck, cut into large chunks
1 large onion, quartered, then thinly sliced
4 cloves garlic, smashed and peeled
2 large tomatoes, thickly sliced
2 tablespoons prepared tomato puree
1½ tablespoons all-purpose flour
½ pound dried navy beans, soaked overnight and cooked 40 minutes according to package instructions with 1 carrot, 1 onion, and 1 stalk celery, all quartered, added to the water
Sprigs fresh parsley for garnish

In a large skillet over medium-high heat, heat 1 tablespoon of the oil until very hot but not smoking and sauté the lamb until brown, 5 to 8 minutes on each side. Drain and set aside.

Meanwhile, in a large kettle over medium-high heat, heat the remaining 2 tablespoons of oil until very hot but not smoking, then add the onion and sauté until colored, about 5 minutes. Add the garlic, tomatoes, and lamb. Add the tomato puree and flour and stir well with a wooden spoon. Add the beans and cook, uncovered, until the lamb is tender, about 1 hour, keeping the stew at a medium boil.

To serve, arrange the meat in soup bowls or high-sided plates and spoon the beans and vegetables over it. Garnish with the parsley.

MAKES 4 SERVINGS

VARIATION: Instead of using dried beans, you may add 4 cups canned navy beans, drained, to the stew for the last 10 minutes of cooking.

Lamb Stew Marie-Thérèse

Ragoût d'Agneau Marie-Thérèse

My mother adds dried orange peel to this dish and it is easy to dry your own in the kitchen (see page 19), but you can substitute fresh.

When she was young, Mother's Christmas presents were modest and her favorite was a fresh orange. It was so special to her that she loved the flavor and used it in cooking whenever she could.

After you brown the lamb, pour off the oil and discard it, so that any rendered lamb fat will be discarded as well. I like to cook the stew at a medium boil for 45 minutes to 1 hour, but in the old days, we put the stew pot in a warm corner of the stove and let it cook slowly for hours. Try it either way.

¼ cup corn or peanut oil
1 large onion, halved and thinly sliced
6 cloves garlic, smashed and peeled
4 lamb shoulder chops, cut into quarters
8 to 10 small red potatoes, halved
¼ cup prepared tomato puree
1 heaping tablespoon all-purpose flour
6 cups water
Salt and freshly ground black pepper to taste
Two 2-inch strips dried or fresh orange peel
Sprig fresh parsley
2 bay leaves
3 whole cloves

In a large saucepan over medium-high heat, heat 2 tablespoons of the oil until very hot but not smoking, then add the onion and sauté until colored, 5 minutes. Add the garlic and sauté until softened, about 2 minutes.

In another large skillet over medium-high heat, heat the remaining 2 tablespoons of oil until very hot but not smoking, then add the lamb and cook until browned, 2 to 3 minutes on each side. Drain the lamb, discarding the cooking oil, and place over the onions. Add the potatoes, tomato puree, and flour and stir well with a wooden spoon. Add the water and season with salt and generously with pepper. Add the peel, parsley, bay leaves, and cloves and stir well. Cook at a medium boil until the lamb is tender, 45 minutes to 1 hour. Or cook the old-fashioned way over low heat. Serve the meat on a plate surrounded by the vegetables and gravy.

MAKES 4 SERVINGS

Spicy Pork Stew

Civet de Porc

This is a satisfying, spicy country stew my mother made in the winter. It is delicious served with Creamy Mashed Potatoes with Olive Oil and Garlic (see page 151) or Provençal Mashed Potatoes with Vegetables (page 152). I like to add some freshly minced garlic and parsley during the final few minutes of cooking—it makes the stew outstanding.

¼ cup corn or peanut oil
2 pounds pork rump, cut into 1-inch cubes
1 large onion, thinly sliced
1 large carrot, cut into thirds crosswise and then into thin sticks
6 cloves garlic, smashed and peeled
2 leeks, white and tender green parts, well washed, cut into 1-inch lengths, and halved lengthwise
1 stalk celery, cut into 2-inch lengths
2 medium-size tomatoes, cut into thin wedges
1 large or 2 small bay leaves
2 whole cloves
3 tablespoons all-purpose flour
3 cups dry red wine
Salt and freshly ground black pepper to taste

Pinch dried thyme
Pinch freshly grated nutmeg
Pinch ground cumin
One 3-inch strip orange peel
3 to 4 cups homemade (page 82) or canned low-salt chicken broth or
    water
1 beef or chicken bouillon cube (optional)

To finish the stew

2 cloves garlic, smashed and minced
2 tablespoons minced fresh parsley

In a large skillet over medium-high heat, heat 2 tablespoons of the oil until very hot but not smoking and sauté the pork until browned on all sides, 5 to 8 minutes. Drain and set aside, discarding the oil.

In the same skillet over medium-high heat, heat the remaining oil until very hot but not smoking and sauté the onion until colored, about 4 minutes. Add the carrot, garlic, leeks, celery, and tomatoes and mix well. Add the drained meat, bay leaf, and cloves, mix well, and cook 5 minutes.

Add the flour and cook, stirring, until the ingredients come together in dry clumps, about 3 minutes. Add the wine, generous pinches of salt and pepper, the thyme, nutmeg, cumin, and peel and mix. Add broth to cover (or water mixed with the bouillon cube) and mix well. Bring to a boil, reduce the heat to medium, and cook, stirring occasionally, until the meat is tender and cooked through, about 1 hour. Stir in the minced garlic and parsley 5 minutes before cooking is completed.

MAKES 6 SERVINGS

Provençal Pork Chops

Côtes de Porc Provençale

This is a colorful, hearty dish that can be made in just a short amount of time. Start a pan of Sautéed Potatoes (page 157) when the chops are almost done, and serve the meat and potatoes together.

2 pounds center-cut loin pork chops
Salt and freshly ground black pepper to taste
2 tablespoons corn or peanut oil
1 medium-size onion, thinly sliced
1 cup diced fresh tomato
8 cornichons, thinly sliced
4 cloves garlic, thinly sliced
½ cup chopped scallions, white and tender green parts
12 black olives marinated in olive oil and herbs (from Provence, Greece, or
    Italy), pitted
1 bay leaf, slightly crumbled
One 3-inch strip orange peel
1 generous teaspoon chopped fresh basil
Few drops Worcestershire sauce
½ cup dry white wine
1 tablespoon plus 1 generous teaspoon minced fresh parsley

Preheat the oven to 350°F. Sprinkle the chops with salt and pepper on both sides. In a large skillet over medium-high heat, heat the oil until very hot but not smoking and cook the chops until brown, about 5 minutes on each side. Add the onion, mix well, and cook until the onion is well colored, about 5 minutes. Add the remaining ingredients, except for 1 tablespoon of the parsley, sprinkle with salt and pepper, and mix well. Place in the oven until the chops are cooked through, 25 to 30 minutes.

Remove the pork chops to serving plates. Place the pan over medium-high heat and reduce the vegetable mixture by half. Sprinkle with the remaining parsley, spoon the mixture generously over the pork chops, and serve.

MAKES 4 SERVINGS

Rabbit Braised in Mustard

Lapin à la Moutarde

In the south of France, rabbits are raised for food on every small farm. In this dish, a variation of my mother's recipe for rabbit roasted with mustard, the meat cooks in a golden, aromatic sauce that gives it spicy flavor. Serve it with a simple pasta and Spinach Gratin (page 168).

¼ cup corn or peanut oil
One 2½- to 3-pound rabbit, cut into serving pieces
1 large onion, thinly sliced
4 cloves garlic, smashed and peeled
½ cup Dijon mustard
3 cups veal stock (page 80), or homemade (page 82) or canned low-salt
   chicken broth
1 cup water
Salt and freshly ground black pepper to taste
1 plum tomato, quartered
1 bay leaf

In a large skillet over medium-high heat, heat 2 tablespoons of the oil until very hot but not smoking, then cook the rabbit until very brown, at least 5 minutes on each side.

In a large saucepan over medium-high heat, heat the remaining oil until very hot but not smoking and sauté the onion until soft but not colored, about 4 minutes. Add the garlic and cook another 5 minutes.

When the rabbit is browned, drain it and add it to the onion, still over medium-high heat. Add the mustard, stock, and water. Add a generous pinch of salt and pepper and mix well. Add the tomato and bay leaf and bring to a boil. Reduce the heat to low, cover, and cook 45 minutes. Remove the cover and cook until the rabbit is tender, another 45 minutes.

MAKES 4 SERVINGS

Rich Rabbit Stew

Civet de Lapin

We looked forward to my grandfather Antoine's catch of wild rabbits, which my grandmother cooked in this hunter's stew. Today, we prepare a civet with domestic rabbit, but if you have a hunter in your family, try it with wild game. Serve it in a rustic terra-cotta casserole, along with pasta or potatoes.

Cloves have a very strong flavor and too many can ruin your dish, so be moderate.

¼ cup corn or peanut oil
One 2½- to 3-pound wild or domestic rabbit, cut into serving pieces
2 large onions, thinly sliced
2 large carrots, quartered and cut into 3-inch pieces
5 cloves garlic, smashed and peeled
1 large tomato, cut into eighths
2 tablespoons all-purpose flour
Bouquet garni made of 2 sprigs each fresh parsley, thyme, and basil and
  2 bay leaves, tied together with kitchen string
1 bay leaf
¼ cup prepared tomato puree
5 cups dry red wine
¼ cup dry sherry
4 cups veal stock (page 80), or homemade (page 82) or canned low-salt
  chicken broth

2 whole cloves
Salt and freshly ground black pepper to taste
½ teaspoon each minced garlic and fresh parsley, combined

In a large skillet over medium-high heat, heat 2 tablespoons of the oil until very hot but not smoking, then cook the rabbit until very brown, at least 5 minutes on each side.

In another large saucepan over medium-high heat, heat the 2 remaining tablespoons of oil until very hot but not smoking, then add the onions and sauté until softened and lightly colored, about 5 minutes. When they are almost brown, add the carrots and garlic and stir well. After 5 minutes, when the carrots start to color, add the tomato. Stir well. You will see that the sauce already has a lot of body.

When the rabbit is golden, drain it and add to the onions. Add the flour and stir until dry clumps are formed and the flour disappears. Add the bouquet garni and bay leaf. Add the tomato puree, wine, and sherry and stir well. Add the broth and stir. Add the cloves and season generously with salt and pepper. Reduce the heat to low and cook, uncovered, until the rabbit is tender, about 1½ hours, stirring occasionally. Just before serving, stir in the garlic and parsley.

MAKES 4 SERVINGS

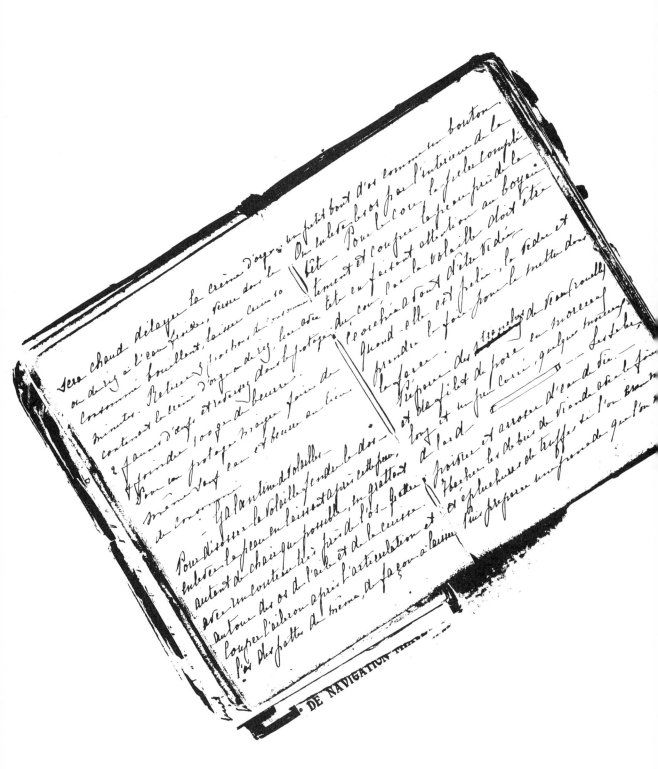

CHAPTER 7

Poultry and Feathered Game

❧

The year I was five, almost at the end of the summer, there was an old woman at the market in Saint-Étienne-du-Gres selling white geese. I said to my father, "Oh, I would love to have a little goose," and he answered, "Okay, I will buy one for you." So a little goose became my pet and I named her Zeze, because she hissed "zeze" all the time. She was a sweet little bird, but over the years, she became very big and very nasty too, pinching people with her beak—this seems to be what happened with all our pets on the farm. Zeze thought she was a dog, and whenever people came to visit us, she chased after them, making a lot of noise. But she loved my mother, and I remember some winter days when I came back from school, Mother would be sitting in her chair with Zeze on her lap! Time passed, I left for my apprenticeship, and while I was away from home, my father died. I never bothered to ask about the goose. But one day I returned home and asked "Where is Zeze?" My mother looked away and just said, "Well . . ." They hadn't told me, but Zeze had finished in the pot.

Another farm character was my grandmother Marie's hen, Gigue. She was allowed the run of the place and the other animals seemed to know they had to leave her alone (everyone was a little afraid of my grandmother, even the animals). At that time, we grew our own grapes and made wine, and Gigue, always underfoot, would eat the fragrant grape skins that fell to the ground after the wine had been pressed. Having been fermented, these contained enough alcohol to intoxicate the poor hen. Our tipsy Gigue would reel around the farm and then fall over in a drunken sleep.

We raised ducks, chickens, and guinea hens for their eggs and their meat, letting them out of their pens at times to scratch under the trees and eat the wild thyme and rosemary. Although we didn't raise turkeys, we understood very well the French saying, "You are stupid as a turkey," and I'll give you an illustration of what that meant. On his farm, my uncle had a big pen full of turkeys. Whenever he wanted to cook one, he would stand at the fence and make clucking noises. The male turkeys—never the females—would trot right over to him, and he would pick out his dinner. The turkeys never learned.

Sunday night on the farm was time for our chicken dinner, and we often had chicken for the holidays, too. Even if you can't get free-range, herb-fed birds like the ones we had, you can duplicate our delicious dishes by cooking them Provençal style, with garlic, herbs, and potatoes. I have included many chicken recipes in this chapter, quite a few straight from my mother's kitchen and the others representing my variations on her themes.

We don't celebrate Thanksgiving in France, but it is a holiday so much like our French feasts that it has become very important to me. Several years ago my mother had a stroke and was in the hospital for six months. Miraculously, she came out with no handicaps, so I had something to be especially thankful for. On Thanksgiving, when she was recovering, I contacted City-Meals-on-Wheels and went to a senior citizens' center in Queens, where I cooked Thanksgiving dinner for four hundred people. I just wanted to do something special for them. It is so good when you can make four hundred people happy—it was the best present I had in my life. They asked for my mother's address and sent her a thank-you letter, which made her feel wonderful. Now I do this every Thanksgiving. In Provence we believed it was our duty to do something for the poor, and that applies very well to life here, too.

11/12/95

Old-Fashioned Roast Chicken

Poulet Cuit à l'Ancienne

❧

On Sundays, my mother would go to the coop and pick out a chicken for dinner. The chicken would be killed and then roasted immediately with herbs, potatoes, and garlic. The house smelled so wonderful, with all those good things cooking together.

2 tablespoons sour cream
1 teaspoon chopped fresh basil
1 teaspoon chopped fresh parsley
1 clove garlic, smashed and minced
Salt and freshly ground black pepper to taste
One 3½-pound chicken, wing tips removed
¼ cup corn or peanut oil
10 small red potatoes, halved

Preheat the oven to 400°F. In a small bowl, combine the sour cream, basil, parsley, and garlic. Sprinkle salt and pepper in the cavity of the chicken and rub the cavity with the sour cream mixture. Season the chicken with salt and pepper, and truss.

In a saucepan just large enough to hold the chicken, over medium-high heat, heat the oil until very hot but not smoking and brown the chicken on all sides, starting with the breast and turning with tongs.

When the chicken is browned, roast in the oven for 15 minutes, basting several times with the pan juices. Season the potatoes lightly with salt and add them to the pan. Continue roasting and basting until the juices run clear, 40 to 60 minutes longer.

MAKES 4 SERVINGS

Chicken with Curds

Poulet a Fleur de Lait

This dish itself is not Provençal, but it is made up of Provençal elements. We use curds in Provence instead of cream, and they are really simple to make. The finished dish is beautiful, with its red, green, and golden colors.

2 quarts whole milk
Juice of 2 lemons
4 chicken breast halves, skinned and boned
Grated zest of ½ lemon
Salt and freshly ground black pepper to taste
2 tablespoons corn or peanut oil
1 large onion, thinly sliced and separated into rings
3 cloves garlic, thinly sliced
1 large ripe tomato, roughly chopped
6 fresh basil leaves, roughly chopped

In a large saucepan over high heat, bring the milk to a rolling full boil, then pour in the lemon juice. The curds—fleur de lait, or flowers of the milk—will begin to separate from the whey. Continue boiling until the curds are completely separate, then pour into a strainer and discard the whey.

Season the chicken breasts with salt, pepper, and the lemon zest. In a large skillet over high heat, heat the oil until very hot but not smoking, add the onion, and sauté. When it begins to brown, about 5 minutes, add the garlic and chicken breasts. Cook 10 minutes, turn the breasts over, and add the tomato and basil. Reduce the heat to low and cook slowly until the chicken is cooked all the way through, 10 to 15 minutes. To serve, mound some fleur de lait in the middle of four plates, top with the chicken, then spoon the sauce on top.

MAKES 4 SERVINGS

Chicken with Eggplant

Blanc de Poulet aux Aubergines

This recipe can be quickly put together with fresh Provençal ingredients such as eggplant, garlic, tomatoes, and herbs. Any leftover eggplant can be served hot or cold.

When you cook vegetables in oil, as in this recipe, you can save the oil and recycle it for another recipe, as we did in my mother's kitchen. Strain the oil through a sieve lined with paper towels before saving it.

    5 to 6 tablespoons corn or peanut oil
    2 medium to large eggplant, peeled and sliced ½ inch thick
    2 medium-size red onions, cut in half and each half thinly sliced
    4 chicken breast halves, skinned and boned
    1 medium-size tomato, peeled, seeded, and finely chopped
    4 cloves garlic, thinly sliced
    1 teaspoon minced fresh thyme
    Pinch ground cumin (optional)

In a large skillet over high heat, heat 3 tablespoons of the oil until very hot but not smoking, then add the eggplant and sauté until golden, about 5 minutes on each side (add another tablespoon of oil, if needed). Drain on paper towels, salt and pepper lightly, set aside, and keep warm.

In another large skillet over high heat, heat 2 tablespoons of the oil until very hot but not smoking, add the onions and sauté until softened but not colored, 3 to 5 minutes, and season with salt and pepper.

Season the chicken with salt and pepper and place it in the pan. Cook over high heat until browned, about 10 minutes on each side. Add the tomato, garlic, thyme, and cumin and cook another 5 minutes.

To serve, mound the eggplant in the center of four plates. Slice each chicken breast ½ inch thick, arrange over the eggplant, and spoon the onion mixture on top.

MAKES 4 SERVINGS

Chicken Florentine

Poulet Florentine

This may seem like a rich dish, but it is easily adapted to lighter diets. You can prepare the béchamel with skim milk instead of whole, and poach the chicken instead of sautéing it. The dish will still be creamy, with the flavors of fresh spinach and onion.

Don't worry about lumps in the béchamel. When you add the cold milk to the hot ingredients, all the lumps will disappear. The reverse also is true: for cold ingredients, you need to add hot milk.

For the béchamel

2 tablespoons unsalted butter
2 tablespoons all-purpose flour
3 cups cold milk, regular or low-fat
Pinch salt
Pinch freshly grated nutmeg
Few drops Tabasco sauce
1 large egg, lightly beaten

For the chicken

4 chicken breast halves, skinned and boned
Salt and freshly ground black pepper to taste
Grated zest of ½ lemon
2 tablespoons corn or peanut oil
1 large onion, chopped roughly into medium dice
24 large leaves spinach, tough stems removed, well washed, and drained
3 generous pinches grated Swiss cheese
3 tablespoons plain bread crumbs

In a medium-size saucepan over high heat, melt the butter for the béchamel. Add the flour, milk, salt, nutmeg, and Tabasco and whisk until the mixture begins to thicken. Cook, whisking constantly, until the sauce is well cooked and about as thick as pancake batter, 10 to 15 minutes. Set aside and keep warm.

Flatten the chicken breasts with the palm of your hand and season on both sides with salt, pepper, and lemon zest. In a large skillet over high heat, heat the oil until very hot but not smoking and cook the chicken, turning, until browned and crisp on all sides, 15 to 20 minutes. When the chicken is almost completely cooked, add the onion and sauté until golden, about 5 minutes.

Remove the chicken from the pan and keep it warm. Add the spinach to the pan with the onion and sauté 5 to 8 minutes.

Meanwhile, preheat the oven to 400°F and preheat the broiler. Beat the egg into the sauce. Lightly oil a large gratin dish. Arrange the chicken breasts in the gratin dish. Cover with the spinach-and-onion mixture and spoon the sauce over all. Sprinkle the cheese and bread crumbs over the top and bake 15 minutes. Place under the broiler just until browned.

Makes 5 servings

TO POACH THE CHICKEN: Fill a medium-size saucepan half full of water, or use 1 cup dry white wine and water. Add 2 teaspoons sea salt (or 1 chicken bouillon cube), 1 onion, roughly sliced, 1 carrot, roughly sliced, 1 clove garlic, peeled, 2 whole cloves, and a small sprig of fresh thyme or ½ teaspoon dried thyme. Bring to a boil over high heat, reduce the heat to medium, and cook the chicken, covered, 20 minutes. Drain and proceed with the recipe.

Chicken with Red Pepper Puree

Poulet à la Purée de Poivrons Rouges

I like to add some grated lemon zest when I sauté chicken for a lively citrus flavor. This quickly prepared dish combines a sweet red puree of peppers with crunchy sautéed potatoes and juicy chicken.

6 tablespoons corn or peanut oil
2 medium-size red onions, cut in half and then thinly sliced
3 large bell peppers of assorted colors, seeded and cut into ¾-inch slices
¼ cup peeled, seeded, and chopped fresh tomatoes
3 cups homemade (page 82) or canned low-salt chicken broth
Pinch sugar
1 bay leaf
1 tablespoon tomato puree
Few drops Tabasco sauce
4 cloves garlic, smashed and minced
1 tablespoon minced fresh thyme
Salt and freshly ground black pepper to taste
Pinch grated lemon zest
4 chicken breast halves, skinned and boned
6 small red potatoes, sliced ⅛ inch thick
2 tablespoons minced fresh parsley
1 teaspoon minced fresh rosemary

In a large skillet over high heat, heat 2 tablespoons of the oil until very hot but not smoking, add the onions and sauté until golden, about 5 minutes. Add the bell peppers and tomatoes and sauté until tender, 5 to 10 minutes.

Add the chicken broth, sugar, bay leaf, tomato puree, Tabasco, garlic, thyme, salt, pepper, and lemon zest to the pan, reduce the heat to medium, and cook until the sauce is reduced by about half. Remove the bay leaf and discard.

Place the pepper mixture in a food processor and process into a slightly textured puree. Set aside and keep warm.

Rinse and dry the skillet and return it to medium-high heat. Heat 2 tablespoons of the oil until very hot but not smoking and brown the chicken breasts until golden on all sides, about 15 minutes. Set aside, keeping warm.

In another large skillet over medium-high heat, heat the remaining 2 tablespoons of oil, then add the potatoes and sauté until golden, 10 to 15 minutes. Drain and combine with the chopped parsley.

To serve, spoon the pepper puree onto four plates, completely covering the bottom. Arrange the potatoes on top in several mounds, top with the browned chicken breast, and sprinkle with the rosemary.

Makes 4 servings

Chicken with Broccoli

Poulet aux Brocolis

A sweet puree of broccoli and leeks provides the base for the sautéed chicken and the dish is garnished with barely cooked, crunchy broccoli florets. This has a fresh-from-the-farm taste.

Pinch sea salt
4 stalks broccoli, stems peeled and cut into 1-inch lengths, florets cut into
    small bunches and reserved for garnish
2 medium-size potatoes, peeled and cut into 1-inch dice
3 cloves garlic, smashed and minced
1 medium-size onion, roughly cut
1 stalk celery, roughly cut
1 medium-size leek, white and tender green parts, well washed
2 tablespoons corn or peanut oil
4 chicken breast halves, skinned and boned
Salt and freshly ground black pepper to taste
½ teaspoon grated lemon zest
Croutons made from 2 slices white bread (page 121) for garnish

Fill a large saucepan half full of water, add the sea salt, and bring to a boil over high heat. Add the broccoli stems and the other vegetables, reduce the heat to medium, and simmer until tender, about 20 minutes. Drain, reserving a few tablespoons of the cooking water, place the vegetables and water in a food processor, and process to a puree. Reserve and keep warm.

In a large skillet over high heat, heat the oil until very hot but not smoking. Season the chicken breasts with salt, pepper, and lemon zest and brown in the hot oil until golden and crisp on all sides, 15 to 20 minutes.

Meanwhile, bring a large saucepan half full with water to a boil over high heat and cook the broccoli florets 30 seconds to 1 minute. Drain and rinse with cold water to stop the cooking.

To serve, spoon the broccoli puree into four plates, covering the bottom. Top with one portion of chicken and one quarter of the florets and croutons.

MAKES 4 SERVINGS

Chicken with Fennel

Poulet aux Fenouil

Anise is a common flavor in Provence, present in crisp fennel as well as in our favorite drink, pastis. You will also find many desserts delicately flavored with the licorice-like anise.

I prefer this chicken generously seasoned with pepper, but you can cook it without pepper, or even without salt, if you prefer.

¼ cup corn or peanut oil
2 medium-size fennel bulbs, sliced ⅛ inch thick (slice the fennel as you
    would an onion; start from the bottom, slicing at a slight angle)
Salt and freshly ground black pepper to taste
1 tablespoon sugar
Juice of 1 lemon
4 chicken breast halves, skinned and boned

Grated zest of ½ lemon
Sprigs of fennel leaves for garnish
4 lemon quarters for garnish

In a large skillet over high heat, heat 2 tablespoons of the oil until very hot but not smoking, then add the fennel. Sprinkle with salt and a generous amount of pepper and toss it in the hot oil. Add the sugar and sauté until golden, 5 to 8 minutes. Add the lemon juice, reduce the heat to low, and cook slowly until the fennel is tender, about 10 more minutes. I like to keep it a little bit al dente, but if you like it softer, cook it longer.

Season the chicken breasts with salt, pepper, and the lemon zest. In a second large skillet over high heat, heat the remaining oil until very hot but not smoking and brown the chicken until crisp on all sides, about 10 minutes.

When the fennel is glossy and caramelized, drain it in a strainer (don't drain it on paper towels, or it will lose its crispness and shine). Place a mound of fennel in the center of each of four plates, top with a portion of chicken breast, and garnish with fennel leaves and a lemon wedge.

MAKES 4 SERVINGS

Provençal Chicken

Poulet à la Provençale

This is easy to do for a party, if you prepare the vegetables ahead and the chicken at the last minute, and then combine the two. The dish has beautiful colors and flavors.

  5 tablespoons corn or peanut oil
  2 medium-size carrots, cut into ½-inch cubes
  1 large or 2 small zucchini, cut into ½-inch cubes
  ¼ medium-size green bell pepper, seeded and cut into ½-inch pieces
  2 medium-size leeks, white and tender green parts, well washed, quartered
        lengthwise, and cut into ½-inch sections
  3 plum tomatoes, cut into ½-inch cubes
  Salt and freshly ground black pepper to taste
  4 cloves garlic, smashed and minced
  1 teaspoon chopped fresh basil
  ¼ teaspoon minced fresh tarragon
  ½ teaspoon minced fresh thyme
  1 large onion, thinly sliced
  1 cup homemade (page 82) or canned low-salt chicken broth
  4 chicken breast halves, skinned and boned

In a large saucepan over medium-high heat, heat 2 tablespoons of the oil until very hot but not smoking and sauté the carrots until they begin to soften and color, 3 to 5 minutes. Add the zucchini, pepper, and leeks, reduce the heat to medium, and cook about 3 minutes. Add the tomatoes and cook another 5 to 7 minutes. Season with salt and pepper. Just before the vegetables are done, add the garlic and herbs and mix well. The vegetables should be shiny, soft, and lightly colored. Pour into a strainer and drain off all the oil.

Meanwhile, in a large saucepan over medium-high heat, heat another 2 table-spoons of the oil until very hot but not smoking and sauté the onion until golden, about 5 minutes. Add the chicken broth and mix well.

In a large skillet over medium-high heat, heat the remaining 1 tablespoon of oil until very hot but not smoking and sauté the chicken breasts until brown and cooked through, 3 to 4 minutes on each side. Season with salt and pepper.

Over medium heat, pour the vegetables into the pot with the onion and combine. Place the chicken over the vegetables and heat until the flavors combine slightly, about 3 minutes. To serve, slice each breast thinly and fan out on individual plates. Heap the vegetable mixture around and over the chicken.

MAKES 4 SERVINGS

Little Bundles of Chicken with Steamed Leeks

Paupiettes de Poulet et Poireau à la Vapeur

Bay leaf adds a wonderful taste to the chicken, but you must add only a little, or it can ruin your dish. The delicate leeks make a very nice contrast to the hearty stuffed chicken.

6 chicken breast halves, skinned and boned, with the smaller flap on the
    underside of the breast removed and reserved
3 cloves garlic, peeled
2 tablespoons chopped fresh parsley
2 tablespoons thinly sliced scallions, white and tender green parts
1 teaspoon roughly chopped fresh basil
1 small or ½ large bay leaf
2 slices white bread
1 large egg, lightly beaten
Salt and freshly ground black pepper to taste
2 tablespoons corn or peanut oil
2 teaspoons extra virgin olive oil
4 leeks, white and tender green parts, well washed and sliced into ¼-inch
    rounds
4 lemon wedges for garnish
Sprigs fresh parsley for garnish

Place 2 breast halves plus the small flaps of all 6 breasts, the garlic, parsley, scallions, basil, bay leaf, bread, egg, and a large pinch each of salt and pepper in a food processor. Process to a thick puree.

Very carefully, with a sharp knife, slice each breast horizontally into two thin cutlets. Place 1 tablespoon of the puree in the center of each cutlet and roll the chicken to enclose the filling. Sprinkle with salt and pepper and set aside.

In a large skillet over high heat, heat the oil until it is very hot but not smoking. Brown the paupiettes on both sides, then reduce the heat to medium, cover the pan, and cook 15 minutes.

Meanwhile, fill a large saucepan halfway with water, bring to a boil over high heat, and add the olive oil. Add the leeks and cook until al dente, 5 to 8 minutes, and drain.

To serve, mound the leeks in the center of each of four plates and sprinkle with salt, pepper, and olive oil. Place one paupiette on either side of each mound and garnish with the lemon and parsley.

MAKES 4 SERVINGS

Herb-Breaded Chicken Breasts

Blanc de Volaille Pané aux Herbes

The herbed breading, fragrant with scallions, parsley, basil, and thyme, turns simple sautéed chicken cutlets into something heavenly. Crisp potato cubes are the perfect accompaniment.

¼ cup corn or peanut oil
2 large potatoes, peeled and cut into large dice
1 cup fresh bread crumbs made from white bread (supermarket bread is fine)
2 tablespoons minced scallions, white and tender green parts
2 tablespoons minced fresh parsley
8 to 10 fresh basil leaves, minced
1 tablespoon minced fresh thyme
4 chicken breast halves, skinned, boned, and halved horizontally to form 8
    thin scallops
Salt and freshly ground black pepper to taste
Grated zest of ½ lemon
2 large eggs, lightly beaten
4 lemon wedges for garnish

In a large skillet over high heat, heat 2 tablespoons of the oil until very hot but not smoking, add the diced potatoes, and sauté until golden brown on all sides, about 15 minutes. Set aside, keeping warm.

In a large, flat dish, mix the crumbs, scallions, parsley, basil, and thyme.

Sprinkle the chicken scallops with salt, pepper, and lemon zest. Dip them in the beaten eggs, then roll generously in the crumbs, pressing to make the crumbs adhere.

In a large skillet over medium-high heat, heat the remaining 2 tablespoons of oil until very hot but not smoking and cook the chicken until golden, about 5 minutes on each side. Serve with the potatoes and lemon wedges.

MAKES 4 SERVINGS

Chicken Breasts with Chicken Livers

Blanc de Poulet au Foies de Volaille

This is a wonderful combination of tastes and textures, with a rich, bubbling sweet-and-sour sauce. Chicken livers are inexpensive, but they add an elegant note. This is delicious served with Creamy Mashed Potatoes with Olive Oil and Garlic (page 151).

4 chicken breast halves, skinned and boned
Salt and freshly ground black pepper to taste
Grated zest of 1 lemon
2 tablespoons corn or peanut oil
6 chicken livers, trimmed and halved
4 shallots, minced
2 cloves garlic, finely minced
2 tablespoons chopped fresh parsley
1 teaspoon chopped fresh thyme
2 tablespoons red wine vinegar
1 teaspoon honey
1 tablespoon homemade (page 82) or canned low-salt chicken broth

Season the chicken breasts with salt, pepper, and lemon zest. In a large skillet over medium-high heat, heat the oil until very hot but not smoking and brown the chicken on both sides, then cook until cooked through, about 15 minutes. Remove the chicken from the pan and keep warm.

Add the livers, along with the shallots, garlic, parsley, and thyme. Sauté about 10 minutes, shaking the pan to combine the livers and vegetables. When the livers are almost cooked through, add the vinegar and reduce it completely down. Add the honey, broth, salt, and pepper, and cook just until the sauce bubbles. To serve, divide the chicken and livers among four plates and top with just a touch of the sauce.

MAKES 4 SERVINGS

Chicken Breasts with Caramel and Orange

Blanc de Poulet au Caramélisé à l'Orange

I always like a little taste of sweet with everything. In this interesting recipe, a combination of orange and bay leaf seasons the breast of chicken and the caramel sauce is flavored with fresh orange. Since this has a rich flavor, you need something simple with it, like plain white rice.

4 chicken breast halves, skinned, boned, and flattened to about ¼-inch thickness
Salt and freshly ground black pepper to taste
1 orange, zest grated and the orange cut in half and seeded
1 teaspoon crushed bay leaf
2 tablespoons corn or peanut oil
¼ cup sugar
1½ tablespoons hot or cold water
Sprigs fresh parsley for garnish

Sprinkle the chicken breasts with salt, pepper, the orange zest, and bay leaf. In a large skillet over medium-high heat, heat the oil until very hot but not smoking and quickly brown the chicken on both sides, then cook until it is cooked through, about 15 minutes.

Meanwhile, in a medium-size, high-sided saucepan over medium-high heat, bring the sugar and water to a boil and stir once to mix. When the mixture starts to color, reduce the heat to low and cook until it is a golden, bubbling syrup, about 10 minutes in all. Remove the pan from the heat and carefully squeeze the orange juice into it. This will reduce the heat of the caramel and stop its cooking. Return to medium heat until it thickens slightly, about 3 minutes, then remove from the heat.

When the chicken is cooked, dip it in the warm caramel sauce on both sides and place it in the sauce. Place the pan over medium heat and cook the chicken in the sauce 1 minute on each side. Garnish with the parsley and serve with plain steamed rice.

M AKES 4 SERVINGS

Doormat of Chicken

Paillasson de Poulet

Here is an outstanding dish that looks rustic but tastes elegant. The chicken cake is crisp and juicy and the strong, fresh taste of herbs prevail. You can make this "doormat" with your own freshly ground chicken, or you can buy 1½ pounds of ground chicken or turkey in the supermarket—just be sure it is very fresh.

> 1½ pounds skinless, boneless chicken breasts or 1½ pounds ground
>   chicken or turkey
> 3 chicken livers, trimmed
> 4 cloves garlic, peeled
> 5 shallots, peeled
> 3 to 4 sprigs fresh thyme
> 2 slices white bread
> Salt and freshly ground black pepper to taste
> 2 tablespoons minced fresh parsley
> Pinch grated lemon zest
> 2 large eggs, lightly beaten
> 3 tablespoons corn or peanut oil
> 6 small red potatoes, peeled and sliced ½ to ¼ inch thick, for garnish
> ½ medium-size onion, sliced ½ to ¼ inch thick, for garnish
> 1 cup Brown Chicken Stock (see page 83)
> Sprig fresh rosemary for garnish

Preheat the oven to 375° F. In a food grinder (don't do this in a food processor; you won't get the right texture), grind together the chicken, chicken livers, garlic, shallots, thyme, and bread. Remove to a large bowl, add the salt, pepper, parsley, lemon zest, and eggs, and mix well.

In a large skillet over medium-high heat, heat 1 tablespoon of the oil until very hot but not smoking and add the chicken mixture, speading it to fill the pan. Sprinkle with salt and pepper and cook until brown, about 2 minutes. Invert the pancake on a plate, season, and return to the pan to brown the other side, about 2 minutes.

Place the pan in the oven and bake until cooked through but still soft and moist, about 25 minutes. If the pancake is overcooked, it will harden.

Meanwhile, in a large skillet over medium-high heat, heat the remaining 2 tablespoons of oil until very hot but not smoking, add the potatoes, and sauté until brown and cooked through, 20 to 30 minutes. About 5 minutes before they are finished, add the onion and sauté until golden. Drain the potatoes and onions in a strainer and set aside.

To serve, place the pancake on a plate, pour the warm stock over it, and garnish with the fried potatoes and onions and a sprig of rosemary. Cut into four wedges.

MAKES 4 SERVINGS

Quick Chicken Pie

Tourte de Poulet Minute

My mother often made this simple chicken pie for dinner. It is light and fresh-tasting, and nothing at all like the gravy-soaked pies you may have eaten before.

2 pounds skinless, boneless chicken breasts, cut into 1-inch cubes
6 shallots, roughly chopped
6 cloves garlic, thinly sliced
2 tablespoons extra virgin olive oil
Salt and freshly ground black pepper to taste
1 bay leaf
2 tablespoons minced scallions, white and tender green parts
1 teaspoon minced fresh basil
½ cup diced tomato
2 tablespoons minced fresh parsley
1 sheet frozen puff pastry, thawed
Egg wash made with 1 large egg yolk lightly beaten with 2 tablespoons
    warm water

In a large bowl, combine the chicken, shallots, garlic, oil, salt, pepper, bay leaf, scallions, basil, tomato, and parsley, cover with plastic wrap, and refrigerate 1 hour.

Preheat the oven to 400°F. Lightly oil a 6-inch tart pan with a removable bottom. Roll out the pastry to half its original thickness and fit it into the pan. Pour in the chicken mixture, top with the remaining rolled-out pastry, and crimp to close tightly. Decorate with pastry strips in a lattice pattern, if you like. Brush the top crust with the egg wash and bake until brown and firm, 30 to 40 minutes.

MAKES 4 SERVINGS

Chicken and Mashed Potato Casserole

Poulet Parmentier

This casserole of mashed potatoes is given texture and body by pureed chicken, and fresh flavor by Provençal herbs. Serve it with just a salad for a light lunch or dinner.

4 chicken breast halves, skinned and boned
3 shallots, roughly chopped
3 cloves garlic, peeled
1 tablespoon chopped fresh thyme
Salt and freshly ground black pepper to taste
1 tablespoon chopped scallions, white and tender green parts
1 generous tablespoon minced fresh parsley
2 large eggs
2 tablespoons extra virgin olive oil
3 large potatoes, peeled, quartered, cut into ½-inch slices, and boiled for
    30 minutes in salted water to cover
¼ cup plain bread crumbs

In a food processor, combine all the ingredients except the potatoes and bread crumbs and pulse to a coarse puree. Then add the potatoes and process to a fine puree.

Butter a medium-size gratin dish or 10-inch-square casserole and pour in the chicken puree. Sprinkle with the bread crumbs and bake until golden and firm, about 20 minutes.

MAKES 4 SERVINGS

Easygoing Chicken Curry

Cari de Poulet Pas de Chi-chi

This curry is made with a minimum of fuss and is served simply with plain white rice. The chunks of chicken and vegetables and the finishing touch of minced garlic and parsley establish it as Provençal fare, but the burnished hot-and-sweet sauce clearly is exotic.

3 tablespoons corn or peanut oil
1 large onion, cut in half and then into ¼-inch chunks
4 cloves garlic, smashed and minced
3 plum tomatoes, cut into 4 lengthwise slices and then halved crosswise
1 large carrot, cut into lengthwise quarters and then ½-inch chunks
2 leeks, white and tender green parts, well washed and sliced ¼ inch thick
    crosswise
2 tablespoons raisins
1 large red-skinned apple, cored and cut into ½-inch chunks
2 sprigs fresh thyme
1 tablespoon chopped fresh parsley
1 teaspoon grated orange zest
Salt and freshly ground black pepper to taste
One 2½- to 3-pound chicken, disjointed and each breast half cut into 3
    chunks and each thigh into 2 pieces
3 tablespoons curry powder
2 large tablespoons all-purpose flour
4 cups homemade (page 82) or canned low-salt chicken broth

To complete the dish

1 large or 2 small cloves garlic, smashed and minced
2 tablespoons minced fresh parsley

In a large saucepan over medium-high heat, heat 1 tablespoon of the oil until very hot but not smoking and sauté the onion until soft but not colored, 4 to 5 minutes. Add the garlic and cook 30 seconds. Then add the tomatoes, carrot, leeks, raisins, apple, thyme, parsley, and orange zest and mix well. Season with salt and pepper.

In another large saucepan over medium-high heat, heat the remaining 2 tablespoons oil until very hot but not smoking and brown the chicken until golden on all sides, about 15 minutes. Add the curry powder and flour and mix together with the chicken. The dry ingredients should coat the chicken. Add the broth, raise the heat to high, and bring to a boil. Then reduce the heat to low, cover, and cook until the chicken is tender and the sauce is shiny, 30 to 40 minutes.

To finish the dish, mince the garlic and parsley together and add to the pot. Mix well for a few seconds and serve with plain white rice.

MAKES 4 SERVINGS

Caramelized Chicken Wings

Ailes de Poulet Caramélisées

These wings make a spicy sweet appetizer or lunch dish. Poaching them beforehand ensures that they are fully cooked before they are flavored with the caramelized sauce.

16 chicken wings
2 tablespoons sea salt
2 tablespoons corn or peanut oil
6 tablespoons prepared tomato puree
2 tablespoons sugar
¼ teaspoon Tabasco sauce
⅛ teaspoon grated orange zest
⅛ teaspoon grated lemon zest
2 cloves garlic, smashed and minced
Pinch minced fresh rosemary
1 cup homemade (page 82) or canned low-salt chicken broth
Salt and freshly ground black pepper to taste

In a large saucepan over medium-high heat, poach the chicken wings in boiling water to cover with the salt for 15 to 20 minutes. Drain the wings and dry well.

In a large skillet over high heat, heat the oil until very hot but not smoking and brown the chicken wings well on all sides, 6 to 10 minutes. Drain off the oil, reduce the heat to medium-high, and add the remaining ingredients. Reduce the sauce to a glaze and serve the wings and sauce on individual plates.

MAKES 4 LUNCH OR 6 TO 8 APPETIZER SERVINGS

Provençal Chicken and Seafood Stew

Paella Provençale

Once everything is combined, you don't have to watch this dish—just let it simmer until it has finished cooking. You can prepare it equally well with rabbit instead of chicken, or with a combination of chicken and rabbit.

2 tablespoons corn or peanut oil
One 2½- to 3-pound frying chicken, cut into 8 pieces
1 large red onion, cut in half and each half thinly sliced
6 cloves garlic, smashed and minced
3 tablespoons peeled, seeded, and chopped fresh tomato
Salt and freshly ground black pepper to taste
1 cup long-grain rice, rinsed
6 to 8 cups homemade (page 82) or canned low-salt chicken broth
1 pound squid, cleaned (page 235) and both bodies and tentacles sliced ½ inch thick
2 pounds mussels, soaked in several changes of water, scrubbed, de-bearded, and drained
8 to 10 medium-size shrimp, shelled and deveined
¼ teaspoon saffron threads
3 tablespoons minced fresh parsley
2 tablespoons chopped scallions, white and tender green parts
1 teaspoon chopped fresh basil
2 tablespoons extra virgin olive oil

In a large saucepan over high heat, heat the oil until very hot but not smoking and cook the chicken legs and thighs, turning, until brown, about 15 minutes. When they are almost completely browned, add the breasts and wings, and brown all the parts thoroughly, cooking for a total of about 25 minutes.

Add the onion and sauté until softened but not colored, about 5 minutes. Reduce the heat to medium and add one third of the garlic, the tomato, salt, and pepper. Mix well and cook, stirring, until all the vegetables are soft, about 10 minutes. Add the rice and chicken broth to cover and simmer until the rice is tender, 30 to 40 minutes. Add the squid, mussels, and shrimp to the pot and simmer another 15 minutes.

In a small bowl, combine the saffron, parsley, scallions, basil, the remaining garlic, and the olive oil. Add the mixture to the simmering paella and cook 10 minutes. Season with salt and pepper and serve on individual plates, or from a large serving platter.

MAKES 4 SERVINGS

Rich Chicken Stew

Poulet en Daube

Perfect for guests, this orange-red fragrant stew is a complete meal in itself. You can prepare it a day ahead of time and it will improve as it waits. You can even freeze it and reheat it before serving.

One 2½- to 3-pound chicken or 2½ pounds chicken parts
¼ cup peanut or corn oil
1 large onion, sliced ¼ inch thick
5 to 6 cloves garlic, smashed and minced
2 large tomatoes, roughly chopped into ⅛-inch dice
2 leeks, white and tender green parts, well washed and cut into 2-inch slices
1 stalk celery, cut into 1-inch slices
8 to 10 medium-size button mushrooms, caps only
4 to 6 carrots, cut into 1-inch slices
⅛ teaspoon freshly grated nutmeg
2 bay leaves, partially crumbled
3 whole cloves
Two 2-inch strips orange peel
2 tablespoons tomato paste
2 generous tablespoons all-purpose flour

2 cups dry red wine

3 cups water

Brown Chicken Stock (page 83) as needed

1 bunch fresh basil, stems included

Salt and freshly ground black pepper to taste

2 medium-size zucchini, quartered lengthwise and cut into 3-inch sticks

8 small red potatoes

If using a whole chicken, cut it up as follows: separate the thighs from the legs, cut each breast in half and then cut each half into three pieces, and remove the wing tips and discard; reserve the carcass for stock or broth.

In a large skillet over medium-high heat, heat 2 tablespoons of the oil until very hot but not smoking and cook the chicken pieces, turning, until the skin is brown and crisp, about 10 minutes.

While the chicken is browning, over medium-high heat, heat the remaining 2 tablespoons of oil until very hot but not smoking in a large, high-sided saucepan, add the onion, and sauté until golden, about 5 minutes. Add the garlic, tomatoes, leeks, and celery and continue to cook another 5 minutes.

Add the mushrooms and carrots and cook until softened, 5 to 10 minutes. Drain the chicken and add it to the pot. Add the nutmeg, bay leaves, cloves, and orange peel and mix well. Add the tomato paste and flour and mix well with a wooden spoon until the ingredients hold together in large clumps. Add the wine, water, and chicken stock to cover, add the basil, season generously with salt and pepper, and bring to a boil. Add the zucchini and potatoes, reduce the heat to medium-low, and simmer slowly until the potatoes are tender, about 30 minutes. Stir from time to time.

MAKES 4 SERVINGS

Light Chicken Stew

Ragoût de Poulet Léger

For a light dinner, this stew is perfect, and it will use up the dark meat of the chicken if you have cooked the breasts for another meal. The blast of fresh parsley and garlic in the final minutes of cooking lends a special Provençal touch. You can prepare this dish the morning or even the day before serving.

1 tablespoon corn or peanut oil
4 chicken legs and thighs, skin and fat removed
1 large onion, roughly chopped
4 cloves garlic, smashed and peeled
1 cup prepared tomato puree
1 tablespoon minced fresh thyme
3 cups homemade (page 82) or canned low-salt chicken broth
3 large carrots, cut into 3-inch slices and then into ½-inch sticks
4 small purple or red potatoes, peeled and halved
2 medium-size zucchini, quartered lengthwise
2 leeks, white and tender green parts, well washed and cut in half lengthwise and crosswise
1 stalk celery, quartered lengthwise (optional)
2 bay leaves
2 whole cloves
2 drops Worcestershire sauce
About 1-inch square lemon peel
About 1-inch square orange peel
Salt and freshly ground black pepper to taste
¼ cup finely chopped fresh parsley
2 cloves garlic, smashed and minced
Chopped fresh parsley for garnish

In a large saucepot over medium-high heat, heat the oil until very hot but not smoking and sauté the chicken, onion, and garlic until brown, about 15 minutes.

Add the tomato puree and stir. Add the remaining ingredients, except the chopped parsley, minced garlic, and garnish and bring to a boil. Reduce the heat to medium, cover, and simmer 45 minutes to 1 hour.

When the chicken is cooked through, add the parsley and garlic and simmer 2 minutes. To serve, garnish with chopped parsley.

MAKES 4 SERVINGS

Chicken with Sauce Poulette

Poulet à la Sauce Poulette

We grow and eat a lot of rice in the south of France and one way we serve it is in this typical farm dish, with the flavorful chicken stew spooned over plain rice, in large soup bowls. Use both the chicken and the broth from Country Chicken Soup to make the dish. Fresh thyme is imperative—you can find it all year long at greengrocers, so there is no excuse for using dried.

1 to 2 cups homemade (page 82) or canned low-salt chicken broth
1 tablespoon minced shallots
1 teaspoon minced fresh thyme
1 teaspoon arrowroot
2 tablespoons water
Pinch freshly ground black pepper (optional)
One 2½- to 3-pound chicken, cooked for Country Chicken Soup (page 84),
    cut into 4 portions, and skin removed
¾ cup cooked white rice
4 sprigs fresh thyme for garnish

In a large saucepan over medium-high heat, bring the broth to a boil with the shallots and thyme. Reduce the heat to medium and and simmer 10 minutes.

Mix the arrowroot and water and add to the broth. Simmer another 10 minutes, to cook away the arrowroot taste. Season with pepper.

To serve, place 3 tablespoons cooked rice in bottom of each of four soup bowls. Place one quarter of the chicken on top and pour the sauce around the rice. Garnish each bowl with a sprig of fresh thyme.

MAKES 4 SERVINGS

Warm Chicken Salad

Salade Tiède de Poulet

This is a welcome change from the ordinary cold chicken salad. Serve the chicken and vegetables hot from the pan, rather than at room temperature.

For the dressing

1 tablespoon Dijon mustard
1 tablespoon red wine vinegar
Salt and freshly ground black pepper to taste
3 tablespoons extra virgin olive oil

For the chicken salad

3 tablespoons corn or peanut oil
4 chicken breast halves, skinned and boned
Salt and freshly ground black pepper to taste
1 large carrot, cut into julienne sticks
1 large zucchini, cut into julienne sticks
2 leeks, white and tender green parts, well washed and cut into julienne
    sticks
2 stalks asparagus, cut into 1-inch slices, blanched in boiling water for 1
    minute, and drained (optional)
¼ pound fresh green beans, cut into 1-inch slices, blanched in boiling
    water for 1 minute, and drained (optional)

2 fresh sage leaves
1 tablespoon minced fresh thyme
1 tablespoon finely chopped fresh parsley
1 tablespoon finely chopped shallots
1 clove garlic, smashed and minced
Lettuce leaves for lining the plates
Chopped fresh parsley for garnish

Combine all the dressing ingredients with a spoon or fork until the consistency of mayonnaise. Set aside.

In a large skillet over medium-high heat, heat 1 tablespoon of the oil until very hot but not smoking. Season the chicken with salt and pepper, then cook, turning, until browned and crisp on all sides, about 15 minutes.

Meanwhile, in a second large skillet over high heat, heat the remaining oil and add the julienned and blanched vegetables. Sauté about 10 minutes, then add the sage, thyme, parsley, and shallots. Cook until the vegetables have softened and colored, another 5 to 10 minutes, then add the garlic and cook 30 seconds more. Drain in a strainer and mound in the center of four lettuce-lined plates.

When the chicken is cooked, slice each breast on the diagonal into about 6 slices and arrange, in petal-like fashion, over the vegetables. Spoon dressing to taste over the chicken and garnish with chopped parsley.

MAKES 4 SERVINGS

Cold Chicken Salad

Salade de Poulet Froide

This salad, with its hints of curry and cumin, is lovely with simple mixed greens and a thick slice of country bread. It is a good way to use chunks of leftover chicken, whether roasted or poached.

When you season, remember that the other spices in the salad heighten the taste of salt, so use salt sparingly.

One 2½- to 3-pound chicken, roasted or poached and cooled
1 large tomato, peeled, seeded, and cut into ½-inch dice
1 stalk celery, sliced into 4 lengthwise strips and the strips sliced ¼ inch thick
1 tablespoon capers, drained and minced, or substitute chopped sweet pickles
½ teaspoon celery seeds
Pinch ground cumin
Pinch curry powder
Pinch paprika
1 teaspoon chopped fresh basil
2 cloves garlic, smashed and minced
Juice of 1 lemon
1 generous teaspoon chopped fresh parsley
Salt and freshly ground black pepper to taste
Sprigs fresh parsley for garnish

Cut the meat off the chicken in large chunks and remove the skin, then cut the meat into bite-size pieces.

Combine the remaining ingredients, except the parsley for garnish. Place in a serving bowl and garnish with the parsley.

MAKES 4 SERVINGS

Turkey Wings in the Style of Aunt Thérèse

Ailes de Dindes comme Tante Thérèse

I like to spotlight those often-ignored turkey wings, which carry a surprising amount of tasty meat. Prepared with a hearty stuffing, as my aunt used to do, they are delicious with *Riz Camarguais* (page 190) and Candied Carrots Provençal (page 134).

4 large turkey wings, fat removed, long bone removed and reserved (with a
    small, sharp knife, open both halves of the wing, cutting along the
    bones, to make pockets for stuffing)
Salt and freshly ground black pepper to taste
3 tablespoons corn or peanut oil
1 large onion, quartered and thickly sliced
1 large carrot, thickly sliced
6 cloves garlic, peeled

For the stuffing

2 slices white bread, crusts removed and torn into rough chunks
6 button mushrooms, caps only, cut into thin dice
2 shallots, minced
1 clove garlic, smashed and minced
1 large egg, lightly beaten
¼ cup heavy cream
1 tablespoon minced fresh parsley
1 tablespoon minced scallions, white and tender green parts
1 teaspoon minced fresh thyme
Generous pinches salt and freshly ground black pepper

To complete the dish

3 tablespoons dry white wine, plus extra for deglazing
2 tablespoons water

Preheat the oven to 400°F. Sprinkle the wings with salt and pepper. In a large, heavy skillet over medium-high heat, heat 2 tablespoons of the oil until very hot but not smoking and cook the wings until brown, about 5 minutes on each side.

In a large ovenproof saucepot over medium-high heat, heat the remaining oil until very hot but not smoking and sauté the onion, carrot, and garlic until they soften and begin to color, about 5 minutes.

In a medium-size bowl, combine the bread, mushrooms, shallots, and garlic. Add the egg and cream and mix well. Add the parsley, scallions, and thyme. Season with salt and pepper.

Add the wings skin side down to the saucepot with the vegetables. Spread the stuffing over the top of the wings and into the pockets, pressing down a little. Strew the reserved bones and pour the wine around everything. Reduce the heat to medium-low, cover the pot, and cook 10 to 15 minutes. Then add the water, cover, and bake 1 hour. When you remove the wings from the pot, drain the fat and deglaze the pot with a little white wine. Pour the sauce over the wings and serve.

MAKES 4 SERVINGS

Turkey Breast Roasted Like a Leg of Lamb

Ailes de Dindes Rôties comme un Gigot

This is a crisp-skinned turkey roast with a rich, dark sauce. Slice it on an angle, like lamb, and serve it with the cooking vegetables and a little sauce, along with Baked Eggplant (page 138) and Country Casserole (page 159). It carries the flavor of Provence in every garlic-laden bite. It is important to brown the turkey well, so the roast will be crisp and colorful.

1 turkey breast, about 3 pounds
3 cloves garlic, slivered
2 whole cloves
Salt and freshly ground black pepper to taste
2 tablespoons corn or peanut oil
1 large onion, quartered
1 large carrot, thickly sliced
1 unpeeled head of garlic, halved crosswise
Bouquet garni made of 1 sprig each fresh rosemary, sage, and thyme and 2
  bay leaves, tied together with kitchen string
½ cup water or homemade (page 82) or canned low-salt chicken broth

Preheat the oven to 400°F. Pierce the turkey breast in several spots on the skin side and insert the garlic slivers. Insert one clove near the middle and one near the end of the breast. Sprinkle with salt and pepper.

In large saucepan over medium-high heat, heat the oil until very hot but not smoking and brown the turkey breast skin side down, 8 to 10 minutes. Turn and brown 8 to 10 minutes on the other side. Add the onion, carrot, garlic, and bouquet garni. Cook 5 minutes, then put in the oven for 20 minutes. Add the water and bake until browned, shiny, and firm, another 20 minutes. To serve, slice the roast thinly and moisten with a few tablespoons of the sauce.

MAKES 4 TO 6 SERVINGS

Roast Turkey

Dinde Rôtie

If your turkey is frozen, defrost it completely. Fresh or frozen, clean the cavity well with a paper towel before roasting. Stuff it immediately before cooking—never let a stuffed uncooked bird wait, even in the refrigerator, because it will become a breeding ground for bacteria.

> 1 turkey, 10 to 15 pounds, cleaned
> Salt and freshly ground black pepper to taste
> ¼ cup extra virgin olive oil
> 2 medium-size carrots, peeled
> 2 medium-size onions, unpeeled, halved crosswise
> 10 shallots, unpeeled
> 2 heads garlic, unpeeled, halved crosswise
> 2 stalks celery
> 2 to 3 leeks, white and tender green parts, well washed and halved
>   lengthwise
> Bouquet garni made of 2 to 3 sprigs each fresh thyme and parsley, 1 sprig
>   fresh basil, 1 bay leaf, 2 cloves, and 3 allspice berries, tied together in a
>   small cheesecloth bag
> 1½ to 2 cups dry white wine, homemade (page 82) or canned low-salt
>   chicken broth, or water

Turn the oven to 500°F. Sprinkle the cavity of the turkey with salt and pepper, stuff it, if desired, place it in a heavy roasting pan, and pour the olive oil around it. Roast until brown on all sides, about 15 minutes.

Reduce the temperature to 375°F and continue roasting 1½ hours, basting frequently with the oil and juices. Scatter the remaining ingredients except the wine around the turkey and roast another 1½ hours, basting (for a larger turkey, add 30 minutes extra roasting time for every five pounds). The turkey is done when you can pierce it with a knife and the juices run clear.

Remove the turkey and vegetables (which will be caramelized) and allow the turkey to rest about 15 minutes before carving. Skim the fat and deglaze the pan with the wine over high heat, scraping up any brown particles from the bottom of the pan. Serve this sauce with the turkey and vegetables.

Makes 8 to 10 servings

Stuffing with Ground Turkey

Farce à la Chair de Dinde

This tasty stuffing can be doubled for a larger turkey.

    1 tablespoon corn or peanut oil
    5 or 6 shallots, minced
    3 cloves garlic, smashed and chopped
    6 slices white bread, crusts removed and torn into rough chunks
    2 large eggs, lightly beaten
    1 pound ground turkey
    2 generous tablespoons sour cream
    2 tablespoons minced scallions, white and tender green parts
    1 large tomato, halved, juice and seeds gently squeezed out, and roughly
        chopped
    6 mushroom caps, chopped
    Salt and freshly ground black pepper to taste
    1 tablespoon unsalted butter
    ¼ cup homemade (page 82) or canned low-salt chicken broth (optional)

In large skillet over medium-high heat, heat the oil until very hot but not smoking and sauté the shallots and garlic until softened but not colored, about 4 minutes.

In a large bowl, combine the bread, shallots, and garlic. Add the eggs and turkey and mix well. Add the remaining ingredients (except the chicken broth) one at a time, mixing well after each addition. Lightly pack the mixture into the cavity of the turkey and roast. Or mix the chicken broth into the stuffing and spoon the mixture into a lightly oiled ovenproof pan or casserole large enough to accommodate it. Bake with the turkey for the last 30 minutes, covering it with aluminum foil if it gets too brown.

Wild Rice and Fresh Cranberry Stuffing

Farce de Riz Sauvage et aux Airelles

This beautiful red and brown stuffing is a combination of Provençal ingredients and American style. It is a good idea to put a lot of pepper in the wild rice.

    2 tablespoons corn or peanut oil
    1 large onion, minced
    2½ cups raw wild rice, cooked according to package directions
    3 cloves garlic, smashed and peeled
    One 12-ounce package fresh cranberries, picked over
    Salt and freshly ground black pepper to taste
    1 tablespoon cognac
    2 tablespoons unsalted butter
    2 to 3 tablespoons sour cream
    1 teaspoon minced fresh rosemary
    ¼ cup homemade (page 82) or canned low-salt chicken broth (optional)

In a large skillet over medium-high heat, heat the oil until very hot but not smoking and sauté the onion until lightly colored, about 5 minutes. Add the cooked rice, garlic, and cranberries and stir well. Add generous pinches of salt and pepper. Add the cognac, reduce the heat to medium, and cook, stirring, 5 minutes. Add the butter, sour cream, and rosemary and cook another 5 minutes.

Remove from the heat and allow to cool before stuffing the turkey. Or mix the chicken broth into the stuffing and spoon the mixture into a lightly oiled ovenproof pan or casserole large enough to accommodate it. Bake with the turkey for the last 30 minutes, covering it with aluminum foil if it gets too brown.

Spicy Apple Stuffing

Farce aux Pommes Épicées

This stuffing is quite loose when it is hot, but it becomes compact as it cooks. After you roast your turkey, deglaze the pan with cider to add to the wonderful apple flavor of the stuffing.

2 tablespoons corn or peanut oil
1 large onion, thinly sliced
6 Rome Beauty apples, 3 peeled and 3 unpeeled, sliced ¼ inch thick
6 to 8 allspice berries, smashed
2 whole cloves, smashed
¼ teaspoon freshly grated nutmeg
¼ teaspoon ground cinnamon
½ teaspoon minced fresh thyme
2 bay leaves, crumbled
2 cloves garlic, smashed and peeled
2 tablespoons chopped fresh parsley
Leaves from ½ bunch celery, coarsely chopped
Salt and freshly ground black pepper to taste
2 tablespoons unsalted butter
9 slices white bread, crusts removed and torn into coarse chunks
2 cups unsweetened applesauce (your own or good-quality storebought)
⅔ cup unsweetened apple juice
3 tablespoons applejack or other apple-flavored liqueur
3 large eggs, lightly beaten
¼ cup homemade (page 82) or canned low-salt chicken broth (optional)

In a large skillet over medium-high heat, heat the oil until very hot but not smoking and sauté the onion until lightly colored, about 5 minutes. Add the apples and stir well. Add the spices, thyme, bay leaves, garlic, parsley, and celery leaves and stir well. Season generously with salt and pepper. Reduce the heat to medium. Add the butter and cook, stirring, 10 minutes.

Place the bread chunks in a large bowl, add the applesauce, and mix well. Add the apple juice, applejack, and eggs and season generously with salt and pepper. Add the apple mixture and mix well. Allow to cool in the refrigerator before using to stuff the turkey. Or mix the chicken broth into the stuffing and spoon the mixture into a lightly oiled ovenproof pan or casserole large enough to accommodate it. Bake with the turkey for the last 30 minutes, covering with aluminum foil if it gets too brown.

MAKES ENOUGH STUFFING FOR ONE 15- TO 20-POUND TURKEY

Provençal Dreams Turkey Stuffing

Farce aux Rêves Provençals

The colorful, aromatic vegetables in this stuffing bring dreams of Provence. Since the carrots take the longest to cook, start them first and when they color, add the other vegetables. This is really a ratatouille turned into a stuffing. You could serve it alone, as a luncheon dish, if you like.

2 medium-size carrots
2 medium-size zucchini
1 medium-size eggplant, peeled
2 stalks celery, including leaves
3 leeks, white and tender green parts, well washed
1 medium-size green bell pepper, seeded
1 medium-size red bell pepper, seeded
½ cup plus 3 tablespoons extra virgin olive oil
Salt and freshly ground black pepper to taste
3 tablespoons minced garlic
2 bay leaves, crumbled
1 teaspoon minced fresh thyme
1 teaspoon minced fresh rosemary
1 teaspoon minced fresh sage

3 tablespoons minced fresh parsley
½ teaspoon fennel seeds
3 tablespoons minced scallions, white and tender green parts
6 slices white bread, crusts removed and torn into rough chunks
2 large eggs, lightly beaten
1 tablespoon unsalted butter
½ cup finely chopped shallots
¼ cup homemade (page 82) or canned low-salt chicken broth

Cut all of the vegetables into ½-inch dice, keeping the carrots separate.

In a large skillet over medium-high heat, heat ½ cup of the olive oil until very hot but not smoking and sauté the carrots until they color, about 5 minutes. Add the remaining diced vegetables, season generously with salt and pepper, and sauté until cooked through, about 8 minutes. Add the garlic, herbs, fennel seeds, and scallions, mix well, and cook another 2 minutes. Allow the mixture to cool 15 minutes at room temperature.

In a large bowl, combine the bread, eggs, and the remaining olive oil.

In a small, heavy saucepan over medium-high heat, melt the butter and sauté the shallots until softened but not colored, about 3 minutes. Add this to the bread mixture and mix well. Add the vegetables and mix well. Allow to cool, refrigerated, before stuffing the turkey. Or mix the chicken broth with the stuffing and spoon the mixture into a lightly oiled ovenproof pan or casserole large enough to accommodate it. Bake with the turkey for the last 30 minutes, covering it with aluminum foil if it gets too brown.

MAKES ENOUGH STUFFING FOR ONE 15- TO 20-POUND TURKEY

Roast Duck

Canard Rôti

This is the simplest way to prepare duck: roast it until crisp, and then combine it with a fruit or vegetable and herb garnish. Following the basic roasting instructions, I present two garnishes, one savory and one sweet, that speak of Provence.

Salt and freshly ground black pepper to taste
One 4- to 5-pound duck, washed well in water and thoroughly dried
1 sprig fresh thyme, rosemary, or sage

Preheat the oven to 400°F. Sprinkle salt and pepper inside and over the duck and place the herb in its cavity. Roast on a rack in a roasting pan, turning once, until well done and crisp, about 1½ hours. As fat accumulates in the pan, drain it off.

Cut the duck into quarters and serve hot with one of the following garnishes.

MAKES 2 TO 3 SERVINGS

Duck with Artichokes and Olives

Canard aux Artichauts et Olives

This chunky garnish is spicy and herbaceous.

For the artichoke hearts

1 lemon, halved
1 tablespoon sea salt
2 large artichokes

To complete the dish

2 tablespoons corn or peanut oil
1 medium-size onion, thinly sliced
3 cloves garlic, thinly sliced
2 plum tomatoes, cut into thin wedges
12 green olives marinated in olive oil and herbs (from Provence, Greece, or Italy), pitted
12 black olives marinated in olive oil and herbs (from Provence, Greece, or Italy), pitted
½ teaspoon minced fresh thyme
Salt and freshly ground black pepper to taste
1 cup homemade (page 82) or canned low-salt chicken broth
Two 4- to 5-pound ducks, roasted (page 300) and cut into quarters

To cook the artichokes, fill a large pot half full of water and add the lemon halves (first squeeze their juice into the water) and salt. Bring to a boil over high heat, add the artichokes, reduce the heat to medium, and cook until soft and cooked through, 45 minutes to 1 hour. When cool enough to handle, remove the leaves and choke and slice the heart thinly. Set aside.

In a large saucepan over medium-high heat, heat the oil until very hot but not smoking and sauté the onion until golden, about 4 minutes. Add the garlic, tomatoes, artichoke hearts, olives, thyme, salt, and pepper and mix well. Cook until the artichokes have colored and softened, about 5 minutes.

Add the broth, bring to a boil, and cook until the liquid is almost completely reduced. The vegetables will be glossy. Spoon the vegetable mixture generously over each portion of roasted duck.

Makes 4 to 6 servings

Duck with Figs

Canard aux Figues

Sweet figs, cooked with wine and sugar, contrast with the crisp roasted duck.

  10 ripe figs
  2 cups dry red wine
  ¾ cup sugar
  1 roasted duck (page 300)

In a small saucepan over medium-high heat, combine the figs, wine, and sugar and bring to a boil. Boil until thick and bubbly, about 30 minutes. The juices should not caramelize. Spoon the sauce generously over each portion of the duck.

MAKES 2 TO 3 SERVINGS

Cornish Hens in a Casserole

Coquelet en Cocotte

These Cornish hens require very little attention as they simmer with vegetables and herbs until they become tender and juicy. When they are done, create a delicious sauce by reducing their aromatic, vegetable-enriched cooking juices with a little wine and water—this is the simplest and the best sauce you can make. If you prefer a larger bird, you can prepare a chicken in the same way.

  4 small or 2 large Cornish hens, trussed
  Salt and freshly ground black pepper to taste
  4 generous tablespoons sour cream, or enough to stuff the birds
  2 to 4 small bunches fresh thyme or herb of choice for stuffing the birds

1 tablespoon corn or peanut oil

1 medium-size carrot, sliced into quarters lengthwise and then roughly cut into 2-inch slices

1 large onion, cut in half and each half cut into quarters

4 cloves garlic, peeled

Small bunch fresh sage

Small bunches fresh rosemary, thyme, or other herb of choice (optional)

2 tablespoons dry white wine

¼ cup water

Season the hens inside and out with salt and pepper and stuff with the sour cream and herbs. In a large, heavy saucepan or casserole over medium-high heat, heat the oil until very hot but not smoking and brown the hens well on all sides, about 20 minutes. Place the hens in a strainer to drain off any excess oil and return to the pot.

Add the remaining ingredients, except the wine and water, and season with salt and pepper. Reduce the heat to medium, cover, and cook until the juices run clear when you pierce the hens with a knife, 45 minutes to 1 hour, turning occasionally and basting with the sauce.

Remove the hens from the pot and set aside. Raise the heat to high, add the wine and water to the pot, and reduce by half. To serve, cut the hens in half and place half a large hen or both halves of a small hen on each individual plate. Pour the sauce over the hens.

MAKES 4 SERVINGS

Cornish Hens with Artichokes

Coquelet aux Artichauts

In Provence, even when you eat simply, it is important to eat well and to taste each individual ingredient. That's how it is in this dish, where the Cornish hens emerge from the oven surrounded by enticing heaps of artichokes, carrots, onions, and garlic.

> Salt and freshly ground black pepper to taste
> 2 large Cornish hens
> 2 tablespoons corn or peanut oil
> 8 fresh baby artichokes, cooked 30 minutes in boiling salted water, outer
>   leaves discarded, and cut into quarters (or use frozen)
> 1 large red onion, cut in half and then sliced into ¼-inch slices
> 1 large carrot, cut into quarters lengthwise and then into ½-inch crosswise
>   slices
> 4 cloves garlic, quartered
> 1 medium-size tomato, cut in half and then into rough dice
> 2 sprigs fresh thyme
> 1 bay leaf

Preheat the oven to 400°F. Sprinkle a pinch each of salt and pepper inside the hens.

In a large saucepan over medium-high heat, heat the oil until very hot but not smoking and brown the hens on all sides until crisp and golden, about 30 minutes. Place in the oven and cook 15 minutes, uncovered.

Reduce the heat to 350°F and strew the vegetables around the hens. Sprinkle with salt, pepper, thyme, and bay leaf and cook 40 minutes. To serve, place half a hen on each plate and garnish with the mixed vegetables.

MAKES 4 SERVINGS

Fillet of Guinea Hen Breast with Wild Mushrooms

Filet de Pintade aux Champignons

Here is a romantic, festive meal for two, with a rustic feeling. Make it in the fall when the variety of wild mushrooms is available—you can smell the forest as the mushrooms cook.

2 pounds mixed fresh wild mushrooms, such as oyster, chanterelle, shiitake, or porcini
2 guinea hen breast halves, skinned and boned
Salt and freshly ground black pepper to taste
2 tablespoons corn or peanut oil
4 cloves garlic, smashed and minced
2 shallots, minced
2 tablespoons minced fresh parsley
Several sprigs fresh herbs of choice for garnish (optional)

Clean the mushrooms well in three or four changes of water and remove the stems. Halve the caps if they are large. Blanch in boiling water for 30 seconds and quickly remove. Drain and dry well.

Sprinkle the guinea hen breasts with the salt and pepper. In a small skillet over medium-high heat, heat 1 tablespoon of the oil until very hot but not smoking and cook the breast halves until brown, 5 to 8 minutes each side. One minute before the cooking is finished, add 2 tablespoons of the minced garlic.

In a second small pan over medium-high heat, heat the remaining oil until very hot but not smoking and sauté the mushroom caps until browned, about 10 minutes. Add the remaining garlic, the shallots, parsley, salt, and pepper and cook another 5 minutes.

To serve, mound the mushrooms in the center of each plate. Slice the guinea hen breast on the diagonal and arrange over the mushrooms. Garnish with the fresh herbs.

MAKES 2 SERVINGS

Hunter's Stew of Guinea Hen

Salmis de Pintade

This classic game stew, a specialty of my grandmother Marguerite, is an example of *cuisine mitonnée,* food that is slowly simmered. As it cooks, a wonderful herbal aroma wafts through the kitchen. When it is finished, the sauce is a deep gold and all the vegetables are tender, but separate. Serve the salmis in a deep casserole accompanied by Farm-Style Tomatoes Provençal (page 172) and rice or pasta.

Guinea hens are available at many butcher shops and supermarkets. However, if you can't find them, substitute free-range chicken.

¼ cup corn or peanut oil
1 large onion, thinly sliced
Legs, thighs, wings, breasts, and quartered carcass of 1 guinea hen
2 large carrots, halved crosswise and then cut into thin wedges
1 stalk celery, cut into 2-inch lengths
4 cloves garlic, smashed and peeled
2 medium-size tomatoes, halved, juice and seeds gently squeezed out, and
    roughly diced
Salt and freshly ground black pepper to taste
3 generous tablespoons all-purpose flour
2 cups Brown Chicken Stock (page 83)
2 tablespoons cognac
¼ cup port
¾ cup dry red wine, preferably a Burgundy
1 bay leaf, slightly crumbled
2 whole cloves
1 teaspoon dried herbes de Provence (page 26)

In a large saucepot, heat 2 tablespoons of the oil until very hot but not smoking and sauté the onion until golden, about 5 minutes.

In large, heavy skillet, heat the remaining oil until very hot but not smoking and sauté the hen pieces until light brown and crisp, about 5 minutes on each side.

Drain and add to the onion. Add the carrots, celery, garlic, and tomatoes to the pan with the hen and onion and stir well. Sprinkle generously with salt and pepper. Add the flour and stir with a wooden spoon until everything clings together in dry clumps. Add the stock, cognac, port, and wine and stir well. Add the bay leaf, cloves, and herbs and stir. Cover, reduce the heat to low, and cook slowly 1 hour, stirring occasionally.

Ladle individual servings into soup bowls or high-rimmed plates.

MAKES 4 SERVINGS

Roasted Pheasant in the Style
of My Grandfather Antoine

Faisan Rôti comme Mon Grand-père Antoine

Here is my grandfather Antoine's way with roasted pheasant—he was a cook as well as a hunter. When I was a child, I followed him around the kitchen as he made this dish and at the end he let me clean out the pot with a crust of country bread. I scooped up all the caramelized vegetables left on the bottom, mopped up the little puddles of rich sauce, and made quite a meal for myself. To this day, I love snacking on the morsels stuck to the bottom of a pot.

Pheasants are available at specialty markets or butchers specializing in game. You can substitute chicken, but that will make this a different dish.

Salt and freshly ground black pepper to taste
One 2- to 2½-pound pheasant, cleaned
Sprigs fresh thyme and oregano to taste
2 bay leaves
2 cloves garlic, peeled
2 tablespoons corn or peanut oil
1 large onion, roughly chopped
2 large carrots, halved lengthwise and each half quartered crosswise
5 cloves garlic, smashed and peeled
1 small head green cabbage, cored and cut into eighths
4 red potatoes, cut in half
2 leeks, white part only, well washed and halved lengthwise
4 to 6 juniper berries, smashed
6 to 8 sprigs fresh thyme
1 tablespoon extra virgin olive oil
Water or homemade (page 82) or canned low-salt chicken broth as needed

Preheat the oven to 400°F. Sprinkle salt and pepper in the pheasant's cavity and lightly stuff with the herbs, one of the bay leaves, and the garlic cloves.

In a large ovenproof skillet over medium-high heat, heat the oil until very hot but not smoking and cook the pheasant until brown, 5 to 10 minutes on each side. Add the onion and carrots and cook until softened and colored, about 5 minutes. Add the smashed garlic, cabbage, potatoes, and leeks and mix. Add the juniper berries, thyme, and the remaining bay leaf and drizzle with the olive oil. Mix well and sprinkle with salt and pepper. Cover and bake until cooked through, 1 hour to 1 hour 15 minutes, lifting the cover to stir every 20 minutes. If the pot seems dry, add water as needed.

MAKES 4 SERVINGS

Pheasant with Apple and Lemon

Faisan aux Pommes et Citron

This light dish has a country look and a "grandmother" feeling. Served in a deep bowl, it presents a beautiful combination of fruit and fowl and makes a romantic dinner.

¼ cup corn or peanut oil
1 large onion, thinly sliced
One 2- to 2½-pound pheasant, cleaned, cut into serving pieces, and the carcass cut in half
3 large Rome Beauty apples, cored, quartered, and then cut into ¾-inch slices (Rome Beauty is a good variety that won't break up in cooking)
1 tablespoon julienned lemon peel
1 tablespoon raisins
1 bay leaf
1 whole clove
Salt and freshly ground black pepper to taste
¼ cup unsweetened applesauce
1 cup Brown Chicken Stock (page 83) or homemade (page 82) or canned low-salt chicken broth

In a heavy saucepan over medium-high heat, heat 2 tablespoons of the oil until very hot but not smoking and sauté the onion until golden, about 5 minutes. In another skillet over medium-high heat, heat the remaining oil until very hot but not smoking and cook the pheasant pieces until very brown, about 5 minutes on each side.

Drain the pheasant, add it to the saucepan with the onion, and discard the browning fat. Add the apples and lemon peel and cook until the apples have softened slightly, about 5 minutes. Add the remaining ingredients, cover, and cook 20 minutes. Reduce the heat to medium, uncover, and cook until the juices run clear when the pheasant is pierced with a knife, another 40 to 45 minutes.

MAKES 4 SERVINGS

Quail with Lentils

Caille aux Lentilles

The combination of crisp little quail and simmered lentils is very delicate. If you want a stew feeling, you can put the quail in the pot with the lentils and let them cook together for a few minutes. But if you want to keep the tastes separate and the texture of the quail crisp, combine them only on the serving plate. You can also prepare these lentils as a side dish for chicken.

Quail are available—with bones or boneless—in many butcher shops. If you can't find them, substitute another small game bird.

For the lentils

½ pound dried green lentils (imported from France)
Small bunch fresh thyme
1 bay leaf
½ large carrot
½ large onion
1 teaspoon sea salt

2 tablespoons corn or peanut oil
2 large onions, thinly sliced
3 cloves garlic, smashed and peeled
2 cups Brown Chicken Stock (page 83), or homemade (page 82) or canned
    low-salt chicken broth
1 teaspoon minced fresh basil
Salt and freshly ground black pepper to taste

For the quail

8 quail, boneless or not, as you prefer
Salt and freshly ground black pepper to taste
8 bay leaves
4 cloves garlic, halved
2 tablespoons corn or peanut oil
½ cup chopped fresh rosemary for garnish
8 teaspoons grated lemon zest for garnish

In a large saucepan over medium-high heat, simmer the lentils with twice their volume of water, the thyme, bay leaf, carrot, onion, and salt until the lentils are soft but still firm, about 45 minutes. Drain and rinse the lentils.

In a large, heavy saucepan over medium-high heat, heat the oil until very hot but not smoking and sauté the sliced onion until soft and lightly colored, about 5 minutes. Add the smashed garlic and cook 2 minutes. Stir in the cooked lentils and stock. Add the basil and a pinch of salt and pepper, reduce the heat to low, and cook 20 minutes.

While the lentils are cooking, preheat the oven to 400°F. Sprinkle the cavity of each quail with a pinch of salt and pepper and stuff with 1 bay leaf and ½ clove garlic. In a large ovenproof skillet, heat the 2 tablespoons of oil until very hot but not smoking and cook the quail until nicely browned, about 10 minutes on each side. Place them in the oven for 10 to 15 minutes if boneless; 5 minutes longer if they have bones. The quail are done when their juices run clear when pierced with a knife.

To serve, arrange 2 quail on a bed of lentils and onions. Sprinkle with the rosemary and zest.

MAKES 4 SERVINGS

Quail with Cabbage

Petite Potée de Caille

As this dish comes out of the oven, it fills the kitchen with heavenly aromas. Enjoy it on a cold day, served on a table set in front of the fireplace.

¼ cup corn or peanut oil
1 large onion, thinly sliced
4 cloves garlic, smashed and peeled
1 small head green cabbage, cored and cut into eighths
1 stalk celery, thinly sliced
2 medium-size red potatoes, quartered and cut into 1-inch slices
4 or 5 juniper berries, smashed
1 or 2 slices bacon (optional)
½ cup dry white wine
4 cups water
Salt and freshly ground black pepper to taste
8 boneless quail (available in many butcher shops)
Sprigs fresh thyme for garnish

In a large, heavy ovenproof pot over medium-high heat, heat 2 tablespoons of the oil until very hot but not smoking and sauté the onion until it colors, about 5 minutes. Add the garlic and sauté 2 minutes. Add the cabbage, celery, potatoes, juniper berries, and bacon and mix well. Add the wine, water, and generous pinches of salt and pepper.

Preheat the oven to 400°F. Sprinkle the cavity of each quail with salt and pepper. In a heavy skillet over medium-high heat, heat the remaining oil until very hot but not smoking and cook the quail until nicely browned, about 10 minutes on each side. Add the quail to the vegetables, cover the pot with a piece of buttered aluminum foil, and bake until the juices run clear when the quail are pierced with a knife, about 1 hour.

For each serving, place 2 quail on a bed of the cabbage, put the potatoes on the side, and garnish with a sprig of thyme.

MAKES 4 SERVINGS

Boneless Quail Stuffed with Vegetables

Alouettes sans Têtes

Like many of the recipes I prepare, this dish is influenced by my mother, but I do my own interpretation—that's where the touch of lime comes in.

For the stuffing

1 large carrot
2 leeks, white part only, well washed
1 large zucchini
2 tablespoons corn or peanut oil
1 teaspoon minced fresh thyme
Salt and freshly ground black pepper to taste
4 shallots, minced
2 cloves garlic, minced
Grated zest of ½ lime
1 whole clove

To complete the dish

Salt and freshly ground black pepper to taste
8 boneless quail (available in many butcher shops)
¼ cup corn or peanut oil
½ large carrot, quartered lengthwise and cut into chunks
4 shallots, halved
2 cloves garlic, peeled
2 bay leaves
Small bunch fresh thyme
1 teaspoon all-purpose flour
½ cup dry white wine
4 cups water

⅓ teaspoon chopped garlic
⅓ teaspoon chopped fresh basil
⅓ teaspoon chopped fresh parsley

Cut the carrot, leeks, and zucchini into 1-inch julienne sticks.

In a large skillet over medium-high heat, heat the oil until very hot but not smoking and add the carrot, leeks, zucchini, thyme, and a pinch of salt and pepper. Sauté until softened and colored, 5 to 8 minutes. Add the minced shallots and garlic and cook another 5 minutes. Add the lime zest and clove. Drain the vegetables and refrigerate until cool enough to handle.

Sprinkle the cavity of each quail with salt and pepper and stuff with 2 tablespoons of the cooled cooked vegetables. Truss each with a single toothpick threaded through the wing, leg, other leg, and other wing, to make a plump little package

Preheat the oven to 400°F. In a large ovenproof skillet over medium-high heat, heat 2 tablespoons of the oil until very hot but not smoking and add the quail, breast side down. Cook until browned, about 5 minutes on each side, then add the carrot, shallots, garlic, bay leaves, and thyme. Put in the oven and roast 10 minutes.

Meanwhile, in a large skillet over medium-high heat, heat the remaining 2 tablespoons of oil. Remove the carrot, shallots, and garlic and add them to the skillet. Turn the quail and allow them to roast another 10 to 15 minutes. Sprinkle the flour over the vegetables and cook, mixing well. When the vegetables cling together in dry clumps, add the wine and water. Bring the mixture to a boil and reduce until thickened. At the last minute, add the chopped garlic, basil, and parsley, mix well, and sprinkle with salt and pepper.

To serve, remove the toothpicks from the quail and place on individual plates, topped with the vegetables.

MAKES 4 SERVINGS

Provençal Partridge

Perdreau Provençal

There used to be a lot of partridges in Provence, but now they are harder to find. This recipe stirs up wonderful memories of my grandfather Antoine, who kept our kitchen supplied with game. Partridge is available at specialty grocery stores and butcher shops. You can substitute another small game.

Salt and freshly ground black pepper to taste
2 partridges, cleaned
2 tablespoons corn or peanut oil
6 shallots, unpeeled
8 cloves garlic, unpeeled
1 carrot, quartered lengthwise and cut into 3-inch lengths
2 plum tomatoes, quartered lengthwise
3 sprigs fresh rosemary
Pinch sugar
1 cup plus 3 tablespoons water

Sprinkle salt and pepper in the birds' cavities. In a large skillet over medium-high heat, heat the oil until very hot but not smoking and cook the partridges until brown, about 3 minutes on each side. Add the remaining ingredients, except the sugar and water, cover the pot, and cook about 15 minutes for medium rare, about 25 minutes for medium, and 40 to 45 minutes for well done. Remove partridges from the pan and set aside.

Reduce the heat to low, sprinkle the vegetables with the sugar, cover, and continue cooking until soft and candied, about 40 minutes. In the middle of the cooking, add 3 tablespoons of the water and stir up the crust from the bottom of the pan.

Carve the partridges into serving portions and arrange over the candied vegetables on individual plates (the shallot and garlic skins are edible). Deglaze the pot with the remaining 1 cup water and pour this simple sauce over the birds.

MAKES 2 SERVINGS

Casserole of Pigeons

Pigeons en Cocotte

This is the kind of dish you could find in the best restaurant in the world, yet anyone can make it at home. The secret is to get the pigeons very brown—be patient. A pinch of sugar cooked with the vegetables caramelizes them and enhances their color and woodsy aroma. The finished dish is beautiful, with each vegetable golden and separate.

Pigeons are available at specialty grocery and butcher shops. You can substitute another small game bird.

4 pigeons, cleaned
Salt and freshly ground black pepper to taste
4 small bunches fresh rosemary
4 bay leaves
2 whole cloves, smashed
2 tablespoons corn or peanut oil
1 large carrot, cut in half lengthwise and then into 2-inch slices
1 stalk celery, cut into 2-inch slices
20 shallots, halved
12 cloves garlic, peeled
¼ teaspoon sugar
3 plum tomatoes, halved
Bouquet garni of 2 sprigs each fresh basil and parsley and 1 scallion, tied
    together with kitchen string

Sprinkle the cavities of the pigeons with a pinch of pepper and salt, then stuff each with the rosemary, 1 bay leaf, and ½ smashed clove.

In a large saucepot big enough for all the pigeons, over medium-high heat, heat the oil until very hot but not smoking and cook the pigeons until very brown, 8 to 10 minutes on each side. Add the carrot and celery and cook until colored and softened, 5 to 10 minutes. Add the shallots, garlic, and sugar and cook until caramelized. Add the tomatoes and the bouquet garni. For very rare pigeons, cook 5 to 6 minutes on each side after browning. For medium rare, cook 8 minutes on each side; for medium, cook 10 to 12 minutes on each side; for well done, 15 to 20 minutes on each side (I prefer them medium—just a little pink in the middle).

To serve, cut the pigeons in half and cut off the wing tips. Carve into leg, thigh, and breast quarters and arrange the vegetables on top.

MAKES 4 SERVINGS

Pigeons Hunter Style

Pigeons Façon Braconnier

My father's cousin Marius loved hunting and when he shot pigeons, my mother often prepared them hunter style (*Braconnier* means illegal hunter), simmered with fresh plum tomatoes and tomato puree. Serve this dish with some plain white rice.

2 tablespoons corn or peanut oil
2 pigeons, cut in half and flattened, with the rib bones and wing tips
    removed
2 large onions, thinly sliced
4 cloves garlic, thinly sliced
2 small or 1 large bay leaf
10 to 12 plum tomatoes, quartered
1 whole clove, smashed
½ cup tomato puree
1 cup brown chicken or veal stock (page 83 or 80)
1 cup water
Salt and freshly ground black pepper to taste
Pinch freshly grated nutmeg
2 fresh basil leaves, finely chopped (optional)

In a heavy large pot over medium-high heat, heat the oil until very hot but not smoking and cook the pigeons until very brown and crisp on one side, about 8 minutes. Turn them over, add the onions, and cook until the onions color, about 5 minutes. Add the garlic and bay leaves and cook until the onions are quite brown and the pigeons have browned on the second side, about 3 minutes more. Add the tomatoes and clove and stir well. Add the tomato puree, stock, and water. Add a generous pinch of salt and pepper, the nutmeg, and basil. Bring to a boil, cover, and reduce the heat to low. Cook until the juices run clear when the pigeons are pierced with a knife, about 45 minutes.

MAKES 4 SERVINGS

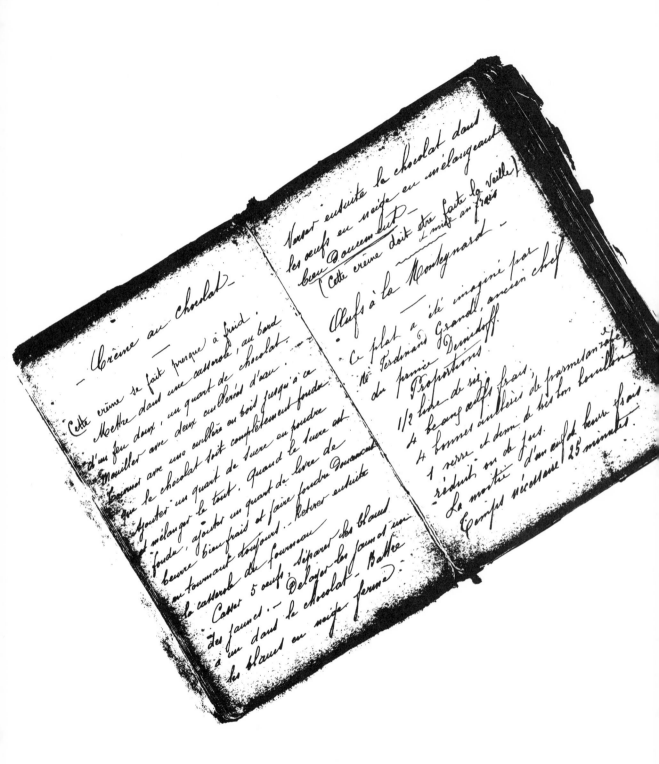

— Crème au chocolat —

Cette crème se fait presque à froid.
Mettre dans une casserole, au bord
d'un feu doux, un quart de chocolat.
Mouiller avec deux cuillerées d'eau.
Tourner avec une cuillère en bois jusqu'à ce
que le chocolat soit complètement fondu.
Ajouter un quart de sucre en poudre
et mélanger le tout. Quand le sucre est
fondu, ajouter un quart de livre de
beurre bien frais et faire fondre doucement
en tournant toujours. Retirer ensuite
la casserole du fourneau.
Casser 5 œufs, séparer les blancs
des jaunes. — Délayer les jaunes
à un dans le chocolat. Battre
les blancs en neige ferme.

Versant ensuite le chocolat dans
les œufs en neige en mélangeant
bien doucement.
(Cette crème doit être faite la veille)
(Cette crème doit être mise au frais)

Œufs à la Montagnard —
Ce plat a été imaginé par
Mr Ferdinand Grandt, ancien chef
de prince Demidoff.
Proportions
1/2 livre de riz
4 beaux œufs frais,
4 bonnes cuillerées de parmesan râpé
1 verre et demi de très bon bouillon
réduit ou de jus.
La moitié d'un œuf par leur frais
(Temps nécessaire 25 minutes)

CHAPTER 8

Desserts and Breads

Christmas in Provence was cold, but dry and clear, with the fragrance of pine and cypress replacing the summer smells of lavender and thyme. The fierce mistral of January and February was yet to come and we rarely had snow in December, although in those few winters when we did, Christmas seemed even more mystical and extraordinary. On the Sunday before the holiday, my sister and I would climb the hill behind our house to find a small pine tree, moss, and holly. All around the trees grew masses of dense green moss that looked as if it was full of stars, and when we picked it, we smelled the humus and the secret smell of the hill. It was more difficult to pick the holly, which grew in rocky and inaccessible places, but we finally managed to fill our big basket.

We dragged everything home, set up the tree in one corner of the living room, and then climbed the stairs to the attic and the dusty boxes where the beautifully dressed terra-cotta dolls that peopled our crèche—the *santons*—slept. There were so many, each different from the other and each a meticulously crafted work of art. We gently unwrapped the fisherman, in his red cap, blue pants, red sash, and striped shirt, with a net draped over his shoulders and a basket of silvery fish over his arm; the white-haired woman dressed in a brown printed skirt and shawl, carrying a bundle of straw; the shepherd in a long brown cloak, sheepskin vest, and wide-brimmed black hat; the baker, carrying a flat basket of eggs, dressed all in white with a towel folded over his arm; the farm woman, with her long shawl, white lace cap, and long printed skirt, carrying a basket of goat cheeses; the fishmonger, with a scale and balances hung from the waist of her printed skirt, carrying a basket of tiny sardines.

On a table beside the tree, we built our crèche. We covered shoeboxes with paper painted to look like rocks, spread the twinkling moss around them, and arranged the holly as backdrop. Mother carefully set all the *santons* in their traditional places on the road to the stable and around the manger. Only the manger itself remained empty until late Christmas Eve, when we would place the Christ Child doll in his cradle.

So many of our beliefs, in the south, are based on food. In the Christmas celebration, good luck, bountiful harvest, and good health are all bound up with religion and tradition, and everything comes together at the table. Our Christmas table was decorated with the bouquet of wheat we children called *Sante barbe*, or Santa's beard. Early each December, my mother would plant grains of wheat in some cotton spread over the bottom of a wide soup bowl, water them, and set them in a warm place near a sunny window until they grew into *lou blad de Calendo*, the wheat of Christmas. We believed that the thicker and taller this wheat grew, the better our harvest would be in the coming year. As we said in the ancient Provençal language: *Quand lou blad ven ben, tout ven ben!* (When the wheat is fine, everything is fine!)

By Christmas Eve, the grains had grown into a tall sheaf that we tied with a bright red ribbon and placed in the center of the table. When the holiday ended, we scattered the sacred wheat in the fields or burned it in the fireplace.

Our favorite tradition was the Thirteen Desserts, the grand finale to Christmas dinner. To insure good luck for the coming year, my mother was careful to serve all thirteen—this is very important to everyone in Saint-Rémy, the heart of Provence. There weren't thirteen cakes and pastries, as many people think; our desserts on Christmas Eve were simple, as they were all year round. We had fresh and dried fruit, such as pears, apples, grapes, melon, oranges, tangerines, figs, and dates— the choice varied each year. We also had almonds, walnuts, nougat, and chocolate candy, which concealed a lucky coin. The dessert table always held a bûche de Noël, an apple tart, cookies, and a sweet fougasse, made with orange flower water and sugar. Of course, we couldn't eat everything, but we tried to taste all the desserts, passing them back and forth to everyone.

The traditional Christmas Eve meal was served on a large table set up in the living room. Mother covered it with an antique ivory embroidered cloth and placed Sante barbe in the center and gleaming silver candlesticks at either end. Each place was set with treasured Provençal dishes and silverware (not necessarily matching) and worn but still elegant linen napkins, with their red monograms faded gently into the smooth fabric. (The monograms didn't match, either, since they represented several generations.) The fireplace blazed with the yule log we had sprinkled with wine blessed for Christmas, while chestnuts roasted around it and candles twinkled in the crèche. Although we never put candles on our tree, the room was full of warm light.

The meal was simple but grand. An appetizer of snails and fragrant herbal broth in a generous terra-cotta casserole was followed by my mother's special contribution, glistening poached cod surrounded by a mountain of carrots, leeks, potatoes, and fennel and accompanied by garlic mayonnaise—aïoli. Then, of course, came the Thirteen Desserts.

After dinner we attended midnight mass in Les-Baux-de-Provence, a beautiful medieval village carved out of white limestone, high in the Alpilles north of Saint-Rémy. This mountaintop fortress is full of legends. It was the home of ancient rulers of Provence who claimed to be descendants of Balthazar, king of Babylon, and its emblem is a six-pointed star inscribed with the phrase *Au Hazard Balthazar* (roughly translated, "Beware of Balthazar"). We traveled a high, winding road to reach the summit, glowing in the moonlight, where mass was celebrated in an eleventh-century chapel and everyone joined in singing ancient carols. I especially loved the live crèche, with real farm animals and people dressed like characters in the Christmas story.

When we returned, we gathered around our own crèche and tenderly placed the Christ Child doll in its manger, while we sang beautiful Provençal carols and prayed for a happy year.

The day after Christmas we relaxed from all the celebrating with a dinner at my grandmother Marguerite's house that I always dreaded, because it included the aunt, uncle, and cousins who were the bane of my young life. Everyone knew that my mother was a saint and her sister, my aunt Andrea, was a devil—and her children were devils, too. That day never passed fast enough for me.

Our next feast was January 6, when we celebrated the Epiphany. My mother prepared *la galette des Rois*, a big brioche with candied fruit around the top, and a little *fève* (bean) baked inside. (Some baked an almond *pithiviers*, instead of brioche.) Whoever was served the slice of cake with the bean was crowned king— but had to pay for the cake next year! This was a wonderful holiday, where neighbors visited house to house, sharing a bottle of sweet wine and some fruit and cake.

Apart from the holidays, we didn't fuss very much over desserts. Most of the time we had an overflowing basket of ripe fruit and berries on the table to end our meals. We served everything in season and never considered canned substitutes for fresh fruit, which was so plentiful that we could smell the ripening raspberries, strawberries, melons, apricots, and peaches everywhere we went. My grandmother told me that before she had a refrigerator, when the fall came, she enclosed the last opulent fruits in clay, wrapped them in hay, and stored them in the hayloft. The hay gave a very good flavor to the fruit and at the same time—I think by a kind of chemistry—the fruit stayed juicy and delicious all winter.

To accompany the fruit, my mother would make a creamy custard, or sometimes cookies or a simple cake. Provençal cakes—I call them Grandma Cakes—are natural and down to earth. They don't require much in the way of ingredients or experience, yet they always come out fluffy and rich, with a taste you can never find in complicated recipes. They are so simple to prepare, but they are intensely flavored with orange flower water, fruit, honey, or herbs.

In a few of the recipes that follow, I have used butter, which isn't typically Provençal, but I find that sometimes it just can't be escaped. However, plenty of baked desserts call for oil, among them Grandma's Apple Spice Cake, Easy Cherry Cake, Pound Cake with Lavender and Apple, and Anise Cake.

The breads I include in this chapter are my own, but they are based on the ingredients and the techniques common in Provence. Fougasse, a chewy, herbal flat loaf, especially is typical of the south of France.

My Mother's Baked Apples

Pommes Marie-Thérèse

Fresh rosemary sprigs and honey spooned into the hollowed cores of these apples fill the kitchen with the sweet smells of a midsummer orchard. If you can get Provençal lavender honey, the result will be even better. As simple as this is, it is my favorite dessert.

  1 tablespoon extra virgin olive oil
  4 large Rome Beauty or Golden Delicious apples, cored, leaving a slightly
      wider opening at the top
  4 sprigs fresh rosemary
  ¼ cup honey
  4 whole cloves
  4 small circles orange peel
  ¼ cup sugar
  2 teaspoons extra virgin olive oil
  ½ cup boiling water

Preheat the oven to 400°F. Grease a gratin pan large enough to accommodate the apples and arrange the apples in it.

In the core of each apple place a sprig of rosemary, 1 tablespoon of the honey, and 1 clove. Place a circle of the orange peel over the top and sprinkle the top with 1 tablespoon of sugar and ½ teaspoon of the olive oil. Pour the boiling water around the apples.

Place the pan over medium-high heat and bring the liquid to a rolling boil, then place the pan in the oven and bake until the apples are cooked through and the skin is slightly seared and split, 30 to 40 minutes.

Remove the apples from the pan. Place the pan over medium-high heat and reduce the accumulated juices to a syrup. To serve, pour a little syrup over each apple.

MAKES 4 SERVINGS

Baked Custard

Flan Fermier

This creamy custard was my mother's specialty. She served it simply, with some ripe berries spooned alongside.

For the caramel

1 cup sugar
⅓ cup water

For the custard

6 large eggs
1 cup sugar
3 cups whole milk
1 tablespoon orange flower water (available in specialty food stores)
Grated zest of 1 orange

Preheat the oven to 375°F.

In a small, heavy saucepan over medium-high heat, bring the sugar and water to a boil. Reduce the heat to medium and simmer until thick and golden, about 10 minutes. Pour into an 8-cup fluted flan mold and rotate the mold to cover the bottom and part of the sides with the caramel.

Meanwhile, in a large mixing bowl, lightly beat together the eggs and sugar. In a medium-size, heavy saucepan over medium-high heat, bring the milk to a boil. Slowly whisk the boiling milk into the egg mixture, combining well. Add the orange flower water and zest. Pour into the prepared mold and set the mold in a larger pan half filled with hot water. Bake until set, 30 to 40 minutes (the custard will quiver, even when set). Refrigerate at least 1 hour and unmold onto a serving plate.

MAKES 6 SERVINGS

Rice Pudding with Prunes and Pears

Gâteau de Riz aux Prunes et Poires Sèches

More elegant than the usual rice pudding, this creamy dessert is still very simple to prepare.

½ cup roughly chopped pitted prunes
½ cup roughly chopped dried pears
1 cup raw long-grain rice
3 cups water
4 cups regular or low-fat milk
1 vanilla bean, split
1 cup plus 2 teaspoons sugar
6 large eggs

Preheat the oven to 400°F. Lightly butter a 2-quart baking dish, sprinkle it with sugar, and set aside. Combine the dried fruits and set aside.

In a large saucepan over medium-high heat, combine the rice and water and bring to a boil. Reduce the heat to medium and simmer 10 minutes. Drain and rinse the rice under cold running water and return it to the saucepan.

Add the milk and vanilla bean and simmer until the rice is tender, about 45 minutes. Remove from the heat, remove the vanilla bean, and whisk in 1 cup of the sugar. Whisk in the eggs, adding them one by one and whisking until each is incorporated.

Place a layer of fruit over the bottom of the prepared mold and pour in half the rice mixture. Top with another layer of fruit and the remaining rice. Arrange the remaining fruit over the top and sprinkle with the remaining sugar (when the mold is inverted, the bottom will be caramelized).

Place the mold in a larger pan half filled with hot water and bake until firm and golden but still moist, about 35 minutes. Cool or refrigerate in the mold and then invert onto a serving platter. Serve cold.

MAKES 6 TO 8 SERVINGS

Potatoes with Sweet Milk Grandmother Marguerite

Pommes de Terre Douce Marguerite

This is a dessert from my grandmother's notebook that she made for us when we were sick. It has no butter or eggs, but it tastes like a custard.

8 medium-size red potatoes, peeled and quartered
4 cups regular or low-fat milk
1 cup sugar
1 vanilla bean, split lengthwise
Pinch freshly grated nutmeg
Two 1-inch squares lemon or orange peel

In a large saucepan over medium-high heat, combine all the ingredients and bring to a boil. Reduce the heat to low and cook slowly until somewhat thickened, 20 to 30 minutes.

Discard the vanilla bean and peel and pour the contents of the saucepan into a large bowl. Whisk very well until pureed, cover, and refrigerate. Serve cold, as you would a pudding or custard.

MAKES 4 SERVINGS

Peach Bread Pudding

Pain Perdu aux Pêches

Serve this for dessert with a fruit or custard sauce, then serve the leftovers the next day for breakfast. This pudding takes advantage of sweet peaches at the height of their season. Like all my mother's desserts, it is simple and rustic.

2 tablespoons corn or peanut oil
4 large peaches, peeled, pitted, and sliced ½ inch thick
1 cup sugar
2½ cups regular or low-fat milk
5 large eggs, lightly beaten
Grated zest of 1 orange
Six ½-inch thick slices country bread, crusts on (you can substitute supermarket white or whole-wheat)
2 cups Light Custard Sauce (page 355)

Preheat the oven to 375°F. Lightly butter a porcelain or Pyrex 11- by 8-inch (7-cup) baking dish.

In a large skillet over medium-high heat, heat the oil until very hot but not smoking. Cook the peaches and ½ cup of the sugar until the sugar has formed a bubbling, golden syrup and the peaches have caramelized, 5 to 10 minutes.

In a large bowl, combine the milk, eggs, the remaining sugar, and the orange zest. Cut the bread slices in half and add them, mixing well and mashing the bread until it has disintegrated and the mixture is creamy.

Pour the egg mixture into the baking dish. Drain the peaches and scatter them over the top, pushing them down into the batter. Bake until golden and somewhat firm (it will remain a little soft), 40 minutes. Serve cold with the sauce on the side.

MAKES 8 TO 10 SERVINGS

Almond and Hazelnut Soufflés

Soufflés Macaron

Don't be afraid to try your hand at soufflés. My grandmother made them all the time, and they are really not difficult. I find that individual soufflés are quicker and come out better than large ones. This dessert rises high and golden and tastes like a combination of macaroons and clouds.

1 generous tablespoon unsalted butter, softened
2 tablespoons all-purpose flour
3 tablespoons finely ground almonds
2 tablespoons finely ground hazelnuts
½ cup sugar
1½ cups cold regular or low-fat milk
1 tablespoon pure almond extract
4 large egg yolks
5 large egg whites

Preheat the oven to 400°F. Butter and sugar eight individual soufflé molds (¾ cup each).

In a medium-size saucepan over medium-high heat, melt the butter, swirling the pan. Remove from the heat and add the flour, whisking until combined. Add the almonds, hazelnuts, 6 tablespoons of the sugar, and the milk, place the pan over medium heat, and cook, whisking, until well combined and thick, about 4 minutes. Add the almond extract and egg yolks and whisk 1 minute.

Pour the mixture into a large bowl and cool to room temperature in a basin of ice water or refrigerate (this can be refrigerated, covered, up to 3 days).

In the bowl of an electric mixer or using a hand mixer and a large bowl, beat the egg whites until thick. Add the remaining sugar and continue beating until firm peaks form. Fold the beaten whites into the cooled egg-yolk mixture and fill the soufflé molds. Leave the tops rough. Run a moistened finger around the inner rim of each mold, to the depth of about ¼ inch, making a space between the mixture and the mold. Bake until risen, firm on top, and golden, about 10 minutes. Serve immediately.

MAKES 8 TO 10 INDIVIDUAL SOUFFLÉS

Pound Cake with Lavender and Apple

Gâteau à la Lavande et Pommes

This is a lovely cake to bring to friends as a present when they have invited you to dinner. It couldn't be simpler to prepare, yet the gentle fragrance of lavender makes it subtle and inviting.

3 large eggs
1 cup sugar
1 cup all-purpose flour
⅛ teaspoon baking powder
⅔ cup corn or peanut oil or melted unsalted butter or margarine
½ large Rome Beauty or Golden Delicious apple, peeled, cored, quartered, and cut into 1-inch slices
½ teaspoon grated lemon zest
2 tablespoons unsprayed dried lavender flowers (available in specialty food stores)
2 tablespoons pear liqueur or kirsch

Preheat the oven to 375°F. Butter and sugar a 6-inch round, 3-inch-high kugelhopf mold or a round mold of similar size.

In a large bowl, combine the eggs, sugar, flour, baking powder, and oil. Add the apple, zest, lavender, and liqueur. Mix well and pour into the prepared mold. Bake until golden and firm, about 30 minutes. Unmold warm and cool on a rack.

MAKES 6 SERVINGS

Grandma Cake with Apples and Rosemary

Gâteau de Grand-mère aux Pommes et Romarin

Fruit and herbs often are combined in the Provençal kitchen, and here fresh rosemary adds a light herbal undertone that enhances the apples. This simple, satisfying cake can be mixed together in one bowl in minutes.

3 tablespoons unsalted butter, softened
1 cup plus 1 tablespoon sugar
4 large eggs
1 cup sifted all-purpose flour
½ teaspoon baking powder
1 large Rome Beauty or Golden Delicious apple, peeled, cored, and cut
    into ¼-inch dice
1 teaspoon minced fresh rosemary
½ teaspoon pure orange extract

Preheat the oven to 400°F. Lightly brush a 5-cup kugelhopf mold or a round mold of similar size with 1 tablespoon of the softened butter and coat with 1 tablespoon of the sugar. In a large bowl, whisk together the eggs and remaining sugar until smooth. Add the flour and baking powder and whisk until blended. Add the remaining softened butter, the apple, rosemary, and orange extract and mix until well blended.

Pour the batter into the prepared mold and bake until brown and puffy, about 30 minutes. Unmold warm and cool on a rack.

MAKES 6 TO 8 SERVINGS

Grandma's Apple Spice Cake

Gâteau de Grand-mère aux Pommes et Épices

This cake takes me back to my grandmother's kitchen, with its pottery jars of fragrant cloves, allspice, and nutmeg. Like many Provençal cakes, this one contains olive oil rather than butter.

    4 large eggs, lightly beaten
    1 cup all-purpose flour
    ½ teaspoon baking powder
    2 tablespoons honey
    ¼ cup firmly packed dark brown sugar
    3 tablespoons extra virgin olive oil
    Grated zest of 1 orange
    1 whole clove, smashed
    2 allspice berries, smashed
    Pinch freshly grated nutmeg
    2 large Rome Beauty or Golden Delicious apples, cored, halved, and sliced
        1 inch thick

Preheat the oven to 400°F. Brush an 8-inch cake pan with a little butter or oil and coat with sugar. Set aside.

In a large bowl, combine the beaten eggs, flour, and baking powder and whisk until smooth. Add the honey, brown sugar, and olive oil and mix well. Add the orange zest, clove, allspice, and nutmeg and pour into the prepared pan. Arrange the apple slices in the batter skin side up, like the spokes of a wheel. Bake until brown and firm, 30 to 40 minutes. Turn out of the mold and let cool to room temperature.

MAKES ONE 8-INCH CAKE; 6 TO 8 SERVINGS

Apricot Semolina Cake

Gâteau d'Abricot au Couscous

This simple pudding cake has the chewiness of couscous and the tart flavor of apricots. Serve it with fresh fruit in season.

2 cups instant couscous
1 cup sugar
3 cups regular or low-fat milk
3 large eggs, lightly beaten
8 fresh apricots, halved, pitted, and each half cut into 3 or 4 strips
2 tablespoons maraschino liqueur or to taste (you can substitute kirsch or
    rum, or 1 tablespoon pure orange or lemon extract)
3 cups Light Custard Sauce (page 355) for garnish
Fresh mint leaves for garnish

Preheat the oven to 375°F. Lightly butter and sugar an 8- to 9-inch-diameter metal mixing bowl.

In a large saucepan, combine the couscous, sugar, and milk. Place over medium-high heat and bring to a boil, whisking continually. Allow to boil, whisking, until thickened, about 1 minute. Remove from the heat.

Add the eggs, apricots, and liqueur and whisk to combine. Pour the batter into the prepared bowl and place in a shallow roasting pan half filled with boiling water. Bake until firm and light brown, about 20 minutes.

Refrigerate until cool. To serve, unmold onto a serving platter and garnish with the custard sauce and mint leaves.

MAKES 6 TO 8 SERVINGS

Easy Cherry Cake

Clafoutis aux Cerises

When I was a little boy, my uncle Jacques had a big cherry tree just on the border of the hill, near our house. Each May I would check every day to see if the cherries were ripe, and when they were, I would climb the tree and eat as many as I could, clambering from branch to branch. Then, with my mouth suspiciously red, I would go home and say to my mother, "I think Uncle Jacques's cherries are ripe. May I pick some?" She always said yes, and then made me a special cherry clafouti.

    2 pounds ripe sweet or sour cherries, pitted
    ¾ cup sugar
    1 cup all-purpose flour
    ⅛ teaspoon baking powder
    2 large eggs, lightly beaten
    ¼ cup corn or peanut oil
    1½ cups whole milk
    2 tablespoons kirsch or other cherry-flavored liqueur

Preheat the oven to 375°F. Lightly butter and sugar an 8-inch round baking dish. Arrange the cherries over the bottom.

In a large bowl, combine the remaining ingredients and whisk together into a light batter. Pour over the cherries and bake until lightly browned and puffy (it will sink slightly as it cools), 30 to 40 minutes. Serve warm or at room temperature from the pan.

MAKES 6 TO 8 SERVINGS

Chocolate, Honey, and Nut Cake

Gâteau au Miel, Chocolat, et Noix

Honey enhances the chocolate, giving deep, rich flavor to this simple cake.

8 ounces semisweet chocolate, broken into rough chunks
1 cup whole milk
3 tablespoons unsalted butter, softened
½ cup sugar
5 large eggs
2 cups all-purpose flour
1 teaspoon baking powder
¾ cup lavender or plain honey
½ cup pignoli (pine nuts) or chopped walnuts
Grated zest of 1 orange

Preheat the oven to 375°F. Butter and sugar an 8-inch round, 3-inch-high cake pan with a detachable bottom.

In a small, heavy saucepan over medium heat, combine the chocolate, milk, butter, and sugar. Cook, stirring, until the chocolate begins to melt, about 1 minute. Remove from the heat and stir until smooth.

Pour the chocolate mixture into a large bowl. Add the eggs and whisk together. Sift the flour and baking powder over the bowl and mix well. Add the honey, pignoli, and zest and mix well.

Pour the batter into the prepared cake pan and bake until firm, 35 to 40 minutes. Unmold warm and cool on a rack. Serve cold.

MAKES ONE 8-INCH CAKE; 6 TO 8 SERVINGS

Warm Chocolate Cakes with Prune Lekvar

Gâteaux Chocolat Chaud à la Purée de Pruneaux

Lekvar—prune preserves—takes the place of butter in these little cakes and gives them a velvety texture.

I love the flavor of prunes because they remind me of my grandmother's kitchen. She always had a jar of them soaking in eau de vie, becoming plump and fragrant for her desserts.

8 ounces semisweet chocolate, melted in a bowl over simmering water
½ cup plus 2 tablespoons sugar
Grated zest of ½ orange
1 large egg
1 large egg yolk
3 tablespoons prune lekvar
½ cup all-purpose flour
¼ teaspoon baking powder
4 large egg whites

Preheat the oven to 350°F. Brush six heart-shaped cake molds (3½-inch diameter) with softened butter and set aside.

Combine the melted chocolate, ½ cup of the sugar, the orange zest, egg, and yolk and mix well. Add the lekvar and mix. Combine the flour and baking powder, sift it over the top of the mixture, and mix well.

In the bowl of an electric mixer or with a hand mixer in a large bowl, beat the egg whites until nearly stiff peaks form. Add the remaining 2 tablespoons sugar and beat until stiff. Fold them into the chocolate mixture, combining well but taking care not to break down the beaten whites.

Spoon the mixture into the prepared molds and bake until firm on top and somewhat soft in the middle, about 20 minutes. Invert the cakes onto a serving tray and serve warm.

MAKES 6 CAKES

Walnut Cake

Gâteau de Noix

My grandmother Marguerite's large walnut tree provided unripe nuts for green walnut wine and ripe ones for this moist, nut-flavored cake. She pulverized the nuts with a mortar and pestle, but it is a much easier job today, with a food processor. You may serve the cake with some melted chocolate, if you like.

¼ cup sugar
2 cups walnut meats, plus 12 walnut halves, for garnish
3 tablespoons ground hazelnuts
3 slices white bread, torn into rough chunks
2 tablespoons Frangelico (you may substitute almond extract)
3 large eggs
3 tablespoons extra virgin olive oil
½ teaspoon baking soda
⅛ teaspoon baking powder

Preheat the oven to 400°F. In a food processor, combine the sugar, walnut meats, ground hazelnuts, bread, and Frangelico and process into a chunky batter.

Stop the machine. Add the eggs, olive oil, and baking soda and pulse until the mixture becomes a thick puree.

Butter and sugar a small gratin dish and pour in the batter. Garnish the top with the walnut halves. Bake until firm, about 30 minutes. Cool in the baking dish and serve without unmolding.

MAKES 4 TO 6 SERVINGS

Anise Cake

Gâteau à l'Anis

This easy-to-prepare cake offers the mysterious flavor and aroma of anise, one of our favorite Provençal accents. It needs no frosting, because it emerges from the mold with a crisp sugar crust.

   3 large eggs, lightly beaten
   2 cups all-purpose flour
   1 cup sugar
   1 tablespoon baking soda
   ¼ teaspoon baking powder
   ¼ cup extra virgin olive oil
   2 teaspoons pure anise extract
   ⅓ teaspoon pastis or other anise-flavored liqueur

Preheat the oven to 375°F. Butter and sugar five 4-inch savarin molds, one 10-inch savarin mold, or other similar-sized molds.

In a large bowl, combine all the ingredients except the pastis, and mix well into a thick, smooth batter. Pour the batter into the molds, filling them halfway. Bake until golden and firm, about 35 minutes. Unmold onto a serving platter and drizzle with the pastis. Serve cold.

MAKES 5 SERVINGS

Almond Pithiviers

La Galette des Rois

January 6, the Feast of the Epiphany, is an occasion for people to visit each other and enjoy some wine and a *galette des Rois,* which may be an almond pithiviers, like this one, or a brioche studded with candied fruit. Either cake is baked with a bean (*fève*) hidden inside, and decorated with a crown. Whoever finds the bean is crowned king or queen and pays for next year's galette.

This tart is sold in every bakery in Provence. It is very easy to make at home with frozen puff pastry.

1 cup pulverized blanched almonds
¾ cup sugar
2 large eggs
2 slices white bread (supermarket white is fine), crusts removed and torn
    into large chunks
½ cup regular or low-fat milk
⅛ teaspoon pure almond extract
2 sheets frozen puff pastry, thawed
1 large egg yolk
1 tablespoon water

Preheat the oven to 350°F. In a large bowl, combine the pulverized almonds, sugar, whole eggs, bread, milk, and almond extract and mix well.

Using a dinner plate as a pattern, cut two circles about 10 inches in diameter from the sheets of puff pastry. Place one pastry circle on a buttered baking sheet and prick it all over with a fork. Spoon the filling on top, mounding it slightly, and leaving a 1-inch border all around. In a small bowl, mix the egg yolk with the water and brush the uncovered pastry border with this egg wash.

Fit the second pastry circle over the filling and press down with a fork around the edges to seal. Brush the top layer with the egg wash. Starting from the center of the tart, with a sharp knife, cut curving "spokes" out to the edge, making sure that the top pastry layer is cut through. Place a small ball of dough in the center and decorate the pie with pastry cutouts as desired. After decorating, brush again with the egg wash. Bake until risen, golden, firm, and cooked through, about 1 hour. Serve cold.

MAKES 6 SERVINGS

Pignoli Tart

Tarte aux Pignons de Pin

When you fit the puff pastry into the tart shell, leave a generous overhang, then crimp the extra pastry firmly around the rim. That way when the pastry retracts as it bakes, it still will hold firmly to the edges of the shell. Always bake the unfilled crust first, so it will be crisp when you pour in the filling.

1 sheet frozen puff pastry, thawed and rolled thin
1 cup pulverized blanched almonds
Grated zest of 1 orange
1 cup sugar
1 tablespoon orange flower water (available in specialty food stores)
1 tablespoon pure almond extract
2 tablespoons honey
2 large eggs
2 tablespoons extra virgin olive oil
¾ cup pignoli (pine nuts)

Preheat the oven to 400°F. Arrange the pastry snugly in a lightly buttered 8-inch tart pan with a removable bottom, doubling the pastry over the rim and crimping it securely. Cover the pastry with a square of buttered aluminum foil and fill with rice, dry beans, or pie weights. Bake 10 minutes; remove the foil and rice and continue baking until very dry and golden, 10 to 15 minutes more. Allow to cool.

Meanwhile, in a large bowl, combine the almonds, orange zest, sugar, orange flower water, almond extract, and honey and mix well with a wooden spoon. Add the eggs and mix well—the batter will be smooth and fairly thick. Add the olive oil and ½ cup of the pignoli and mix well.

Pour the mixture into the cooled tart shell and sprinkle with the remaining ¼ cup pignoli. Bake until golden and firm, about 25 minutes. Remove the ring's sides while the tart is warm. The bottom can remain. Serve cold.

MAKES ONE 8-INCH TART; 6 TO 8 SERVINGS

Lemon Tart with Lavender Flowers

Tarte au Citron et Fleur de Lavande

This isn't a mile-high pie in the American style, rather the meringue is spread in a thin, rough layer over the lemon custard. Lavender flowers add an unmistakable echo of Provence.

6 large eggs, lightly beaten
1 cup plus 3 tablespoons granulated sugar
Grated zest of ½ lemon
Juice of 6 lemons
1 cup (2 sticks) unsalted butter
3 tablespoons unsprayed dried lavender flowers (available in specialty food shops)
1 sheet frozen puff pastry, thawed, rolled thin and fitted into a 9½- or 10-inch tart mold with a removable bottom (or use a prepared pie shell), and baked until brown and crisp in a 375°F oven
3 large egg whites
2 tablespoons confectioners' sugar

Preheat the oven to 375°F.

In a large bowl, lightly beat the eggs, ½ cup of the sugar, and the lemon zest. All the sugar need not be dissolved.

In a medium-size saucepan over medium heat, heat the lemon juice, ½ cup of the sugar, and the butter until most of the butter has melted. Pour the hot butter very slowly into the egg mixture, whisking continually. Pour the mixture back into the saucepan and place over medium heat. Cook, whisking, until the mixture thickens, becomes shiny, and lightens in color, 5 to 8 minutes. Just before it comes to a boil, when one or two tiny bubbles begin to form around the perimeter, remove from the heat and stir in the lavender flowers.

Pour the custard into the tart shell, cover with plastic wrap, and refrigerate 3 hours or overnight. The custard will become creamy and compact.

When ready to finish the tart, preheat the broiler. In an electric mixer fitted with a whisk or in a medium-size bowl, beat the egg whites until fluffy. Add the remaining granulated sugar and continue beating until stiff peaks form. Spread the whites over the cold tart, leaving the surface rough. Place under the broiler until the meringue has browned, about 30 seconds. Sprinkle with the confectioners' sugar and refrigerate for 30 minutes. Serve cold. Remove the ring's sides while the tart is still warm. The bottom can remain.

MAKES 6 TO 8 SERVINGS

Apricot Tart

Tarte aux Abricots

Small, tart apricots are better in this simple tart than those that are large or overripe. Caramelize them first, or they will release too much juice as they bake. This tart is simple to make, but it is dynamite!

16 small, not too ripe apricots, pitted and halved
2 tablespoons unsalted butter, softened
6 to 7 tablespoons granulated sugar
2 tablespoons sour cream or plain yogurt
Grated zest of ½ lemon
1 large egg, lightly beaten
½ recipe pâte brisée (recipe follows), fitted into a 9-inch tart mold with removable bottom and baked until walnut brown and crisp in a 375°F oven
2 to 3 tablespoons pignoli (pine nuts)
1 tablespoon firmly packed light brown sugar
2 tablespoons apricot jam
1 tablespoon water

Preheat the broiler. Arrange the apricot halves skin side up on a lightly buttered baking sheet, brush them with the butter, and sprinkle with 3 to 4 tablespoons of the sugar. Broil until brown around the edges, about 3 minutes, turn over, and brown on the other side, about 3 minutes.

Preheat the oven to 375°F. In small bowl, combine the sour cream, the remaining granulated sugar, the lemon zest, and the egg. Pour the filling into the prepared tart shell and spread evenly.

Beginning at the outer rim, arrange the apricots over the sour cream mixture skin side down in concentric circles, overlapping slightly. Sprinkle with the pignoli and brown sugar (pass the sugar through a strainer if lumpy). Bake until golden, about 10 minutes.

Meanwhile, in a small saucepan over medium-high heat, heat the apricot jam and water together, stirring, until melted. Brush the glaze over the finished tart. Serve cold. Remove the ring's sides while the tart is still warm. The bottom can remain.

MAKES ONE 9-INCH TART; 6 SERVINGS

Pie Crust

Pâte Brisée

Here is a basic pie shell you can use for any sweet or savory tart.

2 cups all-purpose flour, sifted, plus extra for mixing and rolling
½ cup (1 stick) cold unsalted butter, cut into ¼-inch dice
Pinch salt
2 teaspoons sugar (optional)
1 large egg lightly beaten with 6 tablespoons cold water

On a smooth surface or in a large bowl, combine the flour, butter, and salt with your fingers and mix to the consistency of cornmeal. Form a depression in the center of the mixture and add the egg and water. Mix with your fingers until it forms a mass, adding a bit more flour if it is too wet. Divide in half, wrap in plastic, and place in the freezer for 1 hour.

When you are ready to bake, preheat the oven to 400°F. On a floured surface, roll each half into a thin circle slightly larger than a 9-inch tart pan and fit into the pan, pressing it down to fit snugly. Crimp the edges with a fork or your fingers and prick the bottom in several places with a fork. (You may use half the dough and reserve the rest in the freezer, or roll out the rest for a top crust, to be baked when the tart is filled.)

To prebake the crust, cover the dough with a lightly buttered sheet of aluminum foil pressed down onto the dough and filled with rice or pie weights. Bake 10 minutes, then remove the foil and bake until golden and crisp, 10 minutes more.

MAKES TWO 9-INCH TART SHELLS (OR 1 SHELL AND 1 TOP CRUST)

Upside-Down Apple Tart with Rosemary

Tarte Tatin aux Romarin

Rosemary, which my mother often combined with apples, offers a Provençal flavor and aroma to this classic tart. Inverting is easy if you bake the tart in a lightly buttered Teflon pan. Place a baking pan under the pie pan as it bakes to catch the overflow of juices.

2 tablespoons corn or peanut oil
8 large Rome Beauty or Golden Delicious apples, peeled, cored, halved,
    and sliced 1 inch thick
1½ cups sugar
2 tablespoons unsalted butter
1 tablespoon minced fresh rosemary
1 tablespoon orange flower water (available in specialty food stores)
1 sheet frozen puff pastry, thawed, rolled thin, and cut into a round
    slightly larger than the pan

Preheat the oven to 375°F.

In a large skillet over medium-high heat, heat the oil until very hot but not smoking, then add the apples, sugar, and butter. Stir or flip the pan until all the apples are covered with sugar and cook until brown, syrupy, and caramelized, 10 to 15 minutes. Remove from the heat and sprinkle with the rosemary and orange flower water.

Lightly butter an 8½- or 9-inch nonstick frying pan. Arrange an outer ring of apple slices standing upright against the sides of the tin (cut side facing in) to give the tart height. Then fill in the center carefully with a layer of apples lying cut side up. Add a second layer on top of the first, bringing the filling up to the height of the outer circle of standing slices, mashing down slightly.

Place the circle of pastry over the apples and press down slightly all around and firmly around the rim. Cut a small hole in the middle. Place the pan on a baking sheet and bake until crisp and brown, 40 to 60 minutes. Remove from the oven and immediately invert onto a serving platter. Serve warm (can be refrigerated and rewarmed).

MAKES 6 SERVINGS

Little Almond Hearts

Petites Coeurs de Provence

Two frequent ingredients in our desserts in the south of France are pignoli and orange flower water. These heart-shaped tarts include both, as well as another common ingredient, pulverized blanched almonds. The cakes are very light because they contain no flour and they are elegant, delicious, and subtly flavored. They are best served warm.

If you prefer to make a single large tart, bake the batter in a 6- to 8-cup pan.

½ cup pignoli (pine nuts)
1 tablespoon unsalted butter, softened
1 cup plus 2 tablespoons sugar
2 cups pulverized blanched almonds
1 tablespoon pure almond extract
Grated zest of ½ orange
3 slices white bread, crusts removed and processed into fine crumbs
1 teaspoon orange flower water (available in specialty food stores)
3 large egg yolks
2 large eggs
¼ cup corn or peanut oil
5 large egg whites

Preheat the oven to 400°F. Place the pignoli in a single layer on a baking pan and toast in the oven until brown, about 15 minutes; set aside. Brush six to eight small heart-shaped baking molds (they are available attached in a tin of six, similar to a muffin tin) with the softened butter, sprinkle with 2 tablespoons of the sugar and half of the toasted pignoli, and set aside.

In a large bowl, combine the almonds and extract. Add the orange zest, crumbs, and orange flower water and mix. Add ¾ cup of the sugar, the egg yolks, whole eggs, and oil and mix well.

Beat the egg whites in the bowl of an electric mixer with the whisk attachment or in a large bowl with a hand-held mixer. When the whites begin to form stiff peaks, slowly sprinkle the remaining ¼ cup sugar over them and continue beating until stiff.

Add the remaining toasted nuts to the batter and mix. Stir one quarter of the beaten egg whites into the batter, then fold in the remaining beaten whites. Pour the batter into the molds, filling them to the top. Bake until lightly browned and firm, 20 to 25 minutes. Unmold warm, serve warm or cold.

MAKES 6 TO 8 SERVINGS

Almond Candy Bread

Pain aux Amandes

Even though this dessert is made with bread, it is sweet and crunchy and is more like a confection than a cake. Serve small squares as an accompaniment to fruit.

2 cups thinly sliced blanched almonds
6 slices white bread, crusts removed and torn into rough chunks
1 cup sugar
⅛ teaspoon baking powder
1 tablespoon pure almond extract
3 large eggs
1 cup regular or low-fat milk

Preheat the oven to 375°F. Lightly butter and sugar a 4-cup (8½-inch) porcelain gratin dish.

Place the almonds, bread, sugar, baking powder, almond extract, and eggs in a food processor and process until combined or beat well with a hand-held electric or manual mixer. Add the milk in a slow stream as the mixture is processed. Pour the mixture into the gratin dish, cover with lightly buttered or oiled aluminum foil, and bake 20 minutes. Remove the foil and bake until firm around the edges, soft in the middle, and lightly colored (it should not be brown), another 20 minutes. Refrigerate and serve cold. Unmold warm; cool on a rack and serve cold.

MAKES 8 TO 10 SERVINGS

Apple Fritters

Beignets de Pommes

Mother used the apples from our trees to make this simple dessert. We sat around the kitchen table and ate the fritters as soon as she scooped them from the oil and rolled them in sugar.

2 tablespoons rum
½ cup plus 2 tablespoons sugar
1 teaspoon grated lemon zest
2 large Rome Beauty or Golden Delicious apples, peeled, cored, and sliced
    crosswise into ½-inch rings
¾ cup beer
1 cup all-purpose flour
Pinch salt
1 large egg, lightly beaten
3 large egg whites
4 cups corn or peanut oil

In a large bowl, combine the rum, 2 tablespoons of the sugar, and the lemon zest. Add the apple slices and allow them to marinate 1 hour at room temperature.

In another large bowl, combine the beer, flour, salt, 2 tablespoons of the sugar, and the egg and whisk well.

In the bowl of an electric mixer or in a medium-size bowl with a hand-held mixer, beat the egg whites until fluffy. Add 2 tablespoons of the sugar and continue beating until stiff peaks form. Mix one quarter of the egg whites into the beer batter, then fold in the remainder.

In a large saucepan over medium-high heat, heat the oil to 375°F, or until a piece of apple sizzles when immersed. Pour the remaining sugar in a thin layer onto a flat plate or platter.

Remove the apples from the marinade and shake off the excess. Dip each apple slice into the batter, covering it thoroughly, then fry it in the oil until golden, about 1 minute on each side. Drain on paper towels and roll in the sugar. Serve warm or cold.

Makes 4 servings

Little Bow-Tie Fried Pastries

Les Petits Noeuds Frits

These are wonderful little cookies for tea, and can be served warm or cold. Both the dough and the preparation are very simple. Test the heat of the oil with a bit of dough and keep an eye on it as you cook subsequent batches. It should be hot enough for the dough to cook immediately without absorbing oil, but not so hot that the cookies turn dark brown.

2 cups plus 1 to 2 tablespoons all-purpose flour
Pinch salt
7 tablespoons sugar
3 tablespoons unsalted butter, softened
2 tablespoons orange flower water (available in specialty food stores)
1 tablespoon grated orange zest
2 large eggs, lightly beaten
1 tablespoon extra virgin olive oil
2 cups corn or peanut oil

In a large bowl, mix 2 cups of the flour, the salt, and 3 tablespoons of the sugar together using your fingers or a fork. Add the butter, orange flower water, zest, eggs, and olive oil and mix lightly with a fork into a somewhat stiff dough.

Form the dough into a ball, sprinkle with the remaining flour, and wrap in plastic wrap. Refrigerate at least 1 hour or overnight.

When you are ready to fry the pastries, break off one-eighth of the dough, roll it about ⅛ inch thick, and cut into ½-inch-wide strips. Tie each strip into a loose knot and set aside. Repeat with the remaining dough.

Meanwhile, in a large saucepan over medium-high heat, heat the oil to 375°F, or until a piece of dough sizzles when immersed. Pour the remaining sugar in a thin layer onto a dinner plate or small tray.

Drop the bow-ties into the oil and fry until golden, about 30 seconds on each side. Remove with a skimmer, drain on paper towels, and roll in the sugar. Serve warm or cold.

MAKES ABOUT 80 BOW-TIES

Orange Cookies

Biscuits à l'Orange

These simple delicate cookies are perfect served with a bowl of ripe fruit or berries.

½ cup (1 stick) unsalted butter, softened
½ cup sugar
2 large eggs
½ cup all-purpose flour
Juice of 1 orange
1 tablespoon grated orange zest

Preheat the oven to 300°F.
In a mixing bowl, with a wooden spoon, cream the butter and sugar together.

Add the eggs and mix well. Add the flour and mix well. Add the orange juice and zest and mix well.

Drop the batter by scant tablespoonsful onto a lightly buttered cookie sheet, leaving at least 1 inch between the cookies. Bake until golden and firm, 10 to 15 minutes. Cool on the cookie sheet.

MAKES ABOUT 50 COOKIES

Provençal Cookies

Navettes

These boat-shaped confections are the premier cookies of Provence and are famous in the south of France. When I was a little boy, my grandmother made them for special occasions and stored them in decorative cookie tins. There is a big factory in Marseille that specializes in navettes, but they are very easy to make at home.

2 cups all-purpose flour, plus about ½ cup for flouring work surface and
   hands
1 cup sugar
¼ cup (½ stick) cold unsalted butter, cut into small chunks
Grated zest of 1 lemon
⅓ cup orange flower water (available in specialty food stores)
2 tablespoons extra virgin olive oil
1 large egg, lightly beaten
1 large egg yolk
1 tablespoon water

Pour 2 cups of the flour and the sugar onto a work surface. Add the butter and combine it with your fingers, softening it and working it into the flour and sugar until the mixture has the consistency of coarse meal. Add the zest and combine.

Make a well in the center of the mixture and add the orange flower water, olive oil, and beaten egg. Mix well with floured fingers into a soft, somewhat dry dough, adding extra flour as needed. Roll the dough mass around the work surface to incorporate all the flour and bits of dough. Form into a ball, cover loosely with plastic wrap, and let rest in a cool place or the refrigerator 2 hours. The finished dough should be soft but firm and not springy.

Cut the dough into thirds. On a floured surface, roll out each portion about ¼ inch thick and cut into 4- by ½-inch ribbons. Shape the ribbons into tapered boat shapes by rounding and somewhat raising the middle portions and pinching the ends into points. Arrange on buttered baking sheets. Cut a lengthwise slash down the middle of each.

Combine the egg yolk and water and brush the cookies with the wash. Bake until golden brown, firm, and somewhat dry, about 20 minutes.

MAKES ABOUT 24 COOKIES

<h1 align="center">Sweet Crêpes</h1>

Crêpes Sucrées

These crepes are easiest to cook and flip on a seasoned or nonstick pan, and you have the option of cooking with very little butter. They are the basis for many imaginative desserts: fill them with caramelized apples or bananas, fresh berries, ice cream, or applesauce.

¼ cup (½ stick) unsalted butter, melted, plus a little extra for brushing the
    pan, if needed
3 large eggs
Pinch salt
4½ tablespoons all-purpose flour
Grated zest of ½ lemon
¼ cup sugar
½ tablespoon pure vanilla extract
2 tablespoons applejack or other apple-flavored liqueur
2 cups regular or low-fat milk
½ teaspoon orange flower water (available in specialty food stores)

Place all the ingredients except the milk and orange flower water in a food processor or blender and process until combined. With the motor running, slowly pour in the milk and process until absorbed.

Pour the mixture through a sieve, pressing on the solids, into a bowl. Add the orange flower water, mix well, and set aside to rest, covered, at room temperature for 30 minutes.

Heat a seasoned or nonstick crêpe pan over medium heat, or brush a regular pan with melted butter and place over medium-high heat. Pour ¼ cup of the batter into the pan and swirl until it sets; pour off any extra. Cook until brown on the bottom, about 1 minute, then turn and cook until the other side is brown. To keep the crêpes warm, stack them and cover the stack with a sheet of aluminum foil. They may be frozen for up to 3 weeks.

MAKES ABOUT 15 CRÊPES

Buckwheat Crêpes

Crêpes au Blé Noir

These savory pancakes are a little thicker than the sweet crêpes made with white flour, and they won't get as brown, because they contain no sugar. Serve them instead of eggs with bacon, ham, or seafood, or place them in the center of the table as a substitute for bread.

3 large eggs
¼ cup (½ stick) unsalted butter, melted, plus a little extra for brushing the pan, if needed
4½ tablespoons buckwheat or whole-wheat flour
1 teaspoon salt
3 drops Tabasco sauce
2 cups water

Combine the eggs, butter, flour, salt, and Tabasco in a food processor or blender and process until combined. With the motor running, slowly pour in the water and process until absorbed. Pour the mixture through a sieve, pressing on the solids, into a bowl and set aside to rest, covered, at room temperature for 30 minutes.

Heat a seasoned or nonstick crêpe pan over medium heat, or brush a regular pan with melted butter and place over medium-high heat. Pour ¼ cup of the batter into the pan and swirl until it sets; pour off any extra. Cook until firm on the bottom, about 3 minutes, then turn and cook until the other side is firm. To keep the crêpes warm, stack them and cover the stack with a sheet of aluminum foil. They may be frozen for up to 3 weeks.

MAKES ABOUT 15 CRÊPES

Light Custard Sauce

Crème Anglaise

This classic sauce can enhance many simple desserts.

    4 cups plus 2 tablespoons whole milk
    1 vanilla bean, split lengthwise
    8 large egg yolks
    ¾ cup sugar

In a medium-size saucepan over medium heat, heat 4 cups of the milk and the vanilla bean until boiling. Reduce the heat to low and remove the vanilla bean.

In the bowl of an electric mixer or in a large bowl using a hand-held mixer, beat the eggs and sugar together until pale yellow. Slowly beat in the milk.

Return the mixture to the saucepan (wash the pan well first) over medium heat and cook, stirring with a wooden spoon, until thickened. Do not allow the sauce to boil. It is ready when it coats the back of a wooden spoon and holds the line your finger pulls along the spoon.

Strain through a fine sieve into a bowl, mix in the remaining milk, and refrigerate for up to 2 days.

MAKES ABOUT 6 CUPS

Fast and Easy Strawberry Sauce

Coulis de Fraises Rapide et Facile

When you are pressed for time, this sweet sauce takes only seconds to make. Of course it isn't Provençal, but it is good.

  1 pint ripe strawberries, washed and hulled
  ¾ cup sugar
  2 tablespoons fresh lemon juice
  3 to 4 tablespoons water

Combine all the ingredients in a food processor and puree. Use immediately.

MAKES ABOUT 2 CUPS

Strawberry Dessert Sauce

Coulis aux Fraises

Make this sauce when you have bright, juicy berries and keep it in your refrigerator, or freeze it for up to 1 month. You can also make it with raspberries.

  1 pint ripe strawberries, washed, hulled, and quartered lengthwise
  ¼ cup water
  Juice of 1 medium-size orange
  3 tablespoons sugar

Combine all the ingredients in a medium-size saucepan, place over medium heat, and bring to a boil. Cook at a slow boil (reducing the heat if necessary) until the sauce is glossy, but the berries still retain their shape, 15 to 20 minutes. Refrigerate covered up to 1 week or freeze.

MAKES ABOUT 2 CUPS

Provençal Flat Bread

Fougasse

This chewy, pepper- and rosemary-flavored bread with a crisp crust is a specialty of bakers in Provence. It is easy to bake at home and lends itself to your own imaginative garnishes, like garlic, onions, pine nuts, olives, or sun-dried tomatoes. Pile them on to your taste, or enjoy the flat loaf unadorned.

2 tablespoons plus ½ teaspoon active dry yeast
¼ cup sugar
2 cups lukewarm water, about 90°F
¼ cup extra virgin olive oil
5¾ cups all-purpose flour
5 tablespoons freshly grated Parmesan cheese
2½ teaspoons chopped fresh rosemary leaves
½ teaspoon freshly ground black pepper
2½ teaspoons salt

In a small bowl, combine the yeast, sugar, and warm water, mix gently with your fingers, and set aside in a warm place until foaming, about 10 minutes (it does not have to bubble wildly). Add the olive oil and place in the bowl of an electric mixer fitted with a whisk or paddle attachment or in a large mixing bowl. Mix on low to medium speed 10 seconds.

Combine the flour, Parmesan cheese, rosemary, pepper, and salt, and add slowly, mixing until the dough is smooth and stiff.

Turn the dough out onto a floured surface and knead 3 to 5 minutes with floured hands, until firm and elastic. Place in an oiled bowl, cover with a clean cloth, and set in a warm place to rise until doubled in volume, about 45 minutes. Remove the dough from the bowl, knead 1 minute, and roll or stretch it into a rectangle about 12 by 18 inches. Place on a greased baking sheet and allow to rise 10 minutes. Preheat the oven to 375°F.

Score the top in several places with a sharp knife. Arrange garnish on top if using, and sprinkle with olive oil. Bake until the crust is golden brown, 30 to 40 minutes.

MAKES 12 SERVINGS

Country Bread

Pain Maison

❧❧❧

This is a yeasty, flavorful loaf that will fill your kitchen with wonderful aromas as it rises and bakes. It is perfectly simple, containing only a little wheat germ in addition to its basic ingredients. For breads that are a bit more elaborate, see the variations that follow.

I give directions for mixing and kneading this bread by hand; if you prefer to use an electric mixer, simply follow the directions given in the recipe for olive and rosemary bread that follows. The machine does the job quickly and thoroughly, but you sacrifice the pleasure of mixing ingredients with your hands and feeling the consistency and smoothness of the dough as you go along. When you use your hands, you also get to know the optimum temperature for the yeast and the best finished texture for the dough.

This bread rises quickly and has a fine, light texture, thanks to the boost given it by a pinch of baking powder. The first rise is about 20 minutes and the second 10 to 15 minutes. You can delay either rise by putting the dough in the refrigerator.

1 tablespoon sugar
2½ teaspoons active dry yeast
½ cup lukewarm water, about 90°F (more if needed)

3 tablespoons unsalted butter, softened, plus extra for brushing the loaves and pans

4 cups all-purpose flour, plus more as needed

Pinch baking powder

4½ teaspoons wheat germ

Pinch salt

Egg wash made with 1 large egg yolk lightly beaten with 1 tablespoon water

In a small bowl, combine the sugar, yeast, and warm water. Mix well to dissolve the yeast. Set aside in a warm place until the mixture starts to bubble and foam, about 10 minutes.

In a small pan over medium-high heat, melt the butter. In a large bowl, combine the flour, baking powder, wheat germ, and salt. Add the melted butter and mix well with a large wooden spoon, rubber spatula, or your hands. Break up the lumps until it is the consistency of meal. Make a well in the center and add the yeast mixture, combining with your fingers to form a soft, wet dough. Mix and knead in the bowl, adding more water little by little if needed, until well mixed.

Turn onto a floured surface and knead until the dough is smooth and elastic and you don't feel any crumbs of flour in it, about 3 minutes. Place in a large bowl, brush with melted butter, and put in a warm spot to rise until doubled, about 20 minutes, uncovered. It will rise slightly faster if covered tightly with plastic wrap.

Preheat the oven to 400°F. Lightly butter three loaf pans (3½ by 6 inches and 3 inches deep). When the dough has doubled, divide it into three equal parts and form each into a ball. Hold one ball of dough in both hands with your thumbs on top. Use your thumbs to pull and stretch the dough from the top to the undersurface, give the ball of dough a quarter turn, and pull and stretch the dough again. Repeat until you have shaped a high loaf. Place the loaf in a pan and repeat with the remaining dough. Place the loaves in a warm place to rise until doubled, about 10 minutes.

Brush the loaves with the egg wash and bake until brown and firm, 40 to 45 minutes. Turn out of the pans and cool at room temperature.

MAKES 3 LOAVES

GRUYÈRE AND NUTMEG BREAD (*PAIN AU GRUYÈRE ET NOIX DE MUSCADE*): When combining the flour, baking powder, wheat germ, and salt, also add ½ cup grated gruyère and ½ teaspoon freshly grated nutmeg (too much nutmeg can ruin the taste).

GOAT CHEESE AND SAGE BREAD (*PAIN DE CHÈVRE ET SAUGE*): When combining the flour, baking powder, wheat germ, and salt, also add ½ cup crumbled goat cheese and 1 tablespoon minced fresh sage.

Olive and Rosemary Bread

Pain aux Olives et Romarin

This bread and its variation contain olive oil rather than butter. They are hearty breads, with fresh, herbal flavor. Make them in a strong mixer fitted with a paddle or bread hook (the hook is faster). Don't use a food processor, which chops the dough rather than kneading it.

Flour sprinkled over the outside perimeter of the dough near the end of the mixing will help it come free of the mixer and will give it a nice, smooth surface that won't stick to your hands when you take it out of the bowl.

You can brush the dough with butter as it rises; butter won't interfere with olive oil flavor, which is stronger.

   1 tablespoon sugar
   2½ teaspoons active dry yeast
   ½ cup lukewarm water, about 90°F (more if needed)
   3 tablespoons extra virgin olive oil
   4 cups all-purpose flour, plus more as needed
   Pinch baking powder
   4½ teaspoons wheat germ
   Pinch salt
   1 cup chopped pitted black olives
   1 generous tablespoon minced fresh rosemary
   Softened unsalted butter or olive oil for brushing the loaves and pans
   Egg wash made with 1 large yolk lightly beaten with 1 tablespoon water

In small mixing bowl, combine the sugar, yeast, warm water, and olive oil. Mix well with your fingers to dissolve the yeast. Set aside in a warm place until the mixture starts to bubble and foam, about 10 minutes.

In the bowl of an electric mixer fitted with a dough hook or paddle, combine the flour, baking powder, wheat germ, salt, olives, and rosemary. Mix on low to medium speed, gradually adding the yeast mixture. Add enough warm water just to help the dough come together and form a mass on the beater. Continue mixing until the dough is smooth and has a slightly sticky look. Then sprinkle in flour by the pinch along the side of the dough mass as it spins, to free it from the beater. The dough should come off the beater easily.

Place the dough on a work surface, sprinkle with a little flour, and form into a large ball. Place it in a large bowl, brush it with the butter or olive oil, and put in a warm spot to rise until doubled, about 20 minutes, uncovered. It will rise slightly faster if covered tightly with plastic wrap.

Preheat the oven to 400°F. When the dough has doubled, divide it into three equal parts and form each into a ball. Hold one ball of dough in both hands with your thumbs on top. Use your thumbs to pull and stretch the dough from the top to the undersurface, turning the dough as you shape it into a high loaf. Place the loaf in a buttered pan and repeat with the remaining dough. Place the loaves in a warm place to rise until doubled, about 10 minutes.

Brush the loaf tops with the egg wash and bake until brown and firm, 40 to 45 minutes. Turn out of the pans and cool at room temperature.

MAKES 3 LOAVES

SUN-DRIED TOMATO BREAD (*PAIN DE TOMATE DESHYDRATÉ*): Soak 1¾ cups sun-dried tomatoes in olive oil to cover overnight. The next day, reserve 3 tablespoons of the olive oil and add to the yeast instead of plain olive oil. Remove and chop the tomatoes (there should be 1 cup chopped) and substitute for the olives.

Provençal Garlic Bread

Pain Provençal à l'Ail

Garlic bread was made this way on our farm. The bread is coated generously with fresh herbs and garlic and quickly fried, emerging full of herbal flavor. It takes only a minute to cook and it is beautiful.

2 cloves garlic, smashed and minced
1 tablespoon minced fresh thyme
1 tablespoon minced fresh parsley
Four 1-inch-thick slices country bread, cut in half
Extra virgin olive oil for drizzling
⅔ cup corn or peanut oil

Combine the garlic and minced herbs. Drizzle the bread with olive oil on one side and pile with the garlic and herb mixture, pressing down slightly.

In a small skillet over medium-high heat, heat the corn oil and add the bread, plain side down. Cook 30 seconds, then turn and cook herb side down. Remove from the oil and pour the oil through a strainer to retrieve any loose herbs. Return the herbs to the bread and serve. (Keep the fragrant oil to cook something else.)

MAKES 4 SERVINGS

Index